Why Has China Grown So Fast for So Long?

Why Has China Grown So Fast for So Long?

KHALID MALIK

OXFORD
UNIVERSITY PRESS

OXFORD

UNIVERSITY PRESS

Oxford University Press is a department of the University of Oxford.
It furthers the University's objective of excellence in research, scholarship,
and education by publishing worldwide. Oxford is a registered trademark of
Oxford University Press in the UK and in certain other countries

Published in India by
Oxford University Press
YMCA Library Building, 1 Jai Singh Road, New Delhi 110 001, India

ISBN-13: 978-0-19-807883-8
ISBN-10: 0-19-807883-8

Typeset in Bembo Std 11.5/14
by alphæta Solutions, Puducherry, India 605 009
Printed in India at Akash Press, New Delhi 110 020

Contents

Tables, Figures, and Boxes

TABLES

FIGURES

BOXES

Introduction

China has been growing rapidly over the last 30 years. This fact alone makes China and its accomplishments a compelling story. Add the fact that it is home to 1.3 billion people, about 20 per cent of the world's population, and is poised to become in the next 20 years or so the largest economy in the world. That this rapid shift in the ranking of economies and global reach has taken place in our own lifetimes makes the story quite dramatic. As we come to grips with the changing landscape of the world, it becomes even more necessary to have a firm understanding of the forces that have driven this rapid progress. China's extraordinary culture, its long, uninterrupted history as a nation, and its recent economic and social accomplishments are all now of great interest but most of all they are a testament to the Chinese nation and spirit.

My own journey in the understanding of China started in large part when I arrived in Beijing in August 2003 to take up my assignment as the United Nations (UN) Resident Coordinator for China and the United Nations Development Program (UNDP) Resident Representative. Like others, I had followed China over many years, and prior to taking up my assignment had invested time and effort in reading up about China and talking to experts, including putting on an economist's lens (used to be one!) in trying to understand the phenomenon that China represents. Since I was at that time based in New York, I took advantage of being close to universities and research institutes, and had long conversations with well-known 'China hands'. So I felt well prepared in taking up the assignment. Yet, once in China, it became fairly clear that it was difficult to square ground realities with those being presented as received wisdom. It was in some ways a humbling experience. It was also intriguing to note that very smart people, with long experience of China, had sharply conflicting views, especially on how to interpret its recent modernity and progress. It brought to mind Thomas Kuhn's work *The Structure of Scientific Revolutions* (1962), which seeks to explain how and why well-meaning, talented people starting from different paradigms can disagree with each other and come to starkly different positions.

On settling down in Beijing, I made my round of calls on Chinese leaders, ambassadors, and eminent personalities. Along the way, I received some interesting advice. A friend made a thought-provoking comment, that if you wish to write a book about China, do it in the first three months: the ideas are clear, you know what to say, and it is possible to build a coherent narrative. Juxtaposed with this was the comment by an ambassador-friend who had some 30 years of living and dealing with China. His position was that the longer he spent in China, the less he felt he knew for certain. After so many years, he felt that he was finally at a point where he had begun to understand the basics about China.

This book comes in the seventh year of my direct association with China. In 2006 and 2007 I started giving lectures on the themes taken up in this book in China and abroad. But perhaps the stiffest test I underwent was in 2007 when I gave a version of my lecture at Cambridge University to a group of Chinese leaders who were participating in an Advanced Leadership Initiative supported by UNDP. Thankfully there was some acknowledgement that maybe I was on the right track by narrating a storyline that they could recognize and that my take on the essential forces driving economic and social progress in China was not totally off the wall.

We look at situations through our own lenses. This book represents a development economist's attempt to understand China, but grounded in the reality of living and working in China. I have had the great privilege of close interaction with the Chinese leadership, institutions, and society, and of course with international organizations and the development community more generally. The analytical concepts and thinking involved in the analysis derives from some of my earlier work on development (Malik 2002) which, combined with development experience in many parts of the world, have led me to the essential conclusion that development is fundamentally about transformation, developing broad-based capacities, changing people's attitudes, creating new and effective institutions, and how the people and their leaders take charge of their own development. It is about making mistakes, and crucially, learning from them. As Joseph Stiglitz eloquently put it in his 1998 Prebisch Lecture, 'successful development transformation must come from within the country itself, [which] must have institutions and leadership to catalyze, absorb, and manage the process of change and change to society.'

This book focuses on broad developmental change and on identifying the key social and economic forces that can help explain China's stellar success. Perhaps it might be useful in stating upfront what the book is not about. It does not analyse China's political system or work out the likely implications of the rise of China for the global order, or indeed the many other aspects of contemporary China that are of much interest these days. These topics are worthy of detailed and careful reflection, but are beyond the purview of this book.

For analysts China presents a conundrum. It is clear that there has been rapid progress, and the landscape of the world is indeed rapidly changing. Yet for decades, many, especially Western economists, journalists, and pundits, have questioned this phenomenon. They have had some difficulty in accepting many of the growth claims made by the Chinese government. There has been concern about cooked data, a worry about asset bubbles about to burst (next year it's all going to fall apart!), and so on. Yet the Chinese economy has kept growing at a blistering pace, 9–10 per cent annually, and more at times, over a span of almost three decades.

There is now much global interest in unlocking the reasons for China's stellar performance. In particular, without going into the debate about the competing visions of the Washington Consensus versus the Beijing Consensus, the heterodox nature of China's policies has prompted developing country policymakers and development practitioners to question some of the policy advice they have been receiving from developed countries and international organizations. This interest was much in evidence at a recent Conference in Addis Ababa with African ministers and senior officials asking specific and detailed questions about the different aspects of Chinese growth, a conference co-hosted by UNDP and the International Poverty Reduction Centre in China (based in Beijing).

While I have alluded to the basic rationale for this book, I need to say something about how it is structured. The first two chapters lay out the reform context and the development results attained by China. The third examines the limitations of traditional explanations. Chapter 4 essentially outlines and develops the 'development as transformation' thesis and then in Chapter 5 that approach is applied to the change in China, mostly over the last 30 years of reform. The last chapter is about China's future.

Before outlining the reasons as to why China has consistently made such stellar progress, it is necessary to assess why traditional explanations of China's success by economists are either incomplete or misleading. Chapter 3 is a critical foray into the thicket of conventional analyses of China's progress. This is where the puzzle starts. If one looks at the stories by financial journalists, even those with long experience of China, year after year the message has been strikingly the same: next year the country is going to collapse. The property sector, for instance, is severely overvalued and the economy is a bubble waiting to be pricked. In late 2007 and 2008 when the global financial crisis hit countries around the world, there were stark predictions that Chinese Gross Domestic Product (GDP) growth rates would drop dramatically and the economy was destined to go into a tailspin. The World Bank in fact dropped its projections for GDP growth to 6.5 per cent for 2008. In the end, China met its 8 per cent GDP growth target. A similar negative vein is seen in more academic writings about the economy. Most economists, when assessing the determinants of growth, typically look at the contribution of the principal factors of production—capital, labour, and at times technology. These calculations have not been able to explain fully the growth rates experienced by China over the years, either in terms of their direct contribution to growth or in relation to the efficiency gains that might be expected in the reallocation of these factors to sectors where the return is higher. There is a relatively large residual between these explanations and actual growth rates. This residual, presented as 'total factor productivity' (TFP), refers to the synergy that occurs when many factors come together. Still, in the end, TFP is more about accounting than serving as an explanation.

This book seeks to address some essential questions: Why has China grown so rapidly over such a long time, and what are the country's prospects in the future? Will it keep growing? Will it in the next few decades actually overtake the US as the largest economy in the world, as some observers have been forecasting, or will it implode as the many contradictions in the economy and society grind it to a halt? Can China manage to deal with its many challenges: from meeting the continuing aspirations of its people for ever higher living standards and more life choices; to overseeing the largest planned movement of people in the history of mankind in the next 20–30 years, some 350 million of them, from the rural to urban areas; to reducing inequalities; and cleaning up the environment. These are questions on the minds of the Chinese themselves and the many China watchers.

I take a positive view of China's future if nothing for the simple reason that the systems in place are robust and the strong leadership displayed in the past is likely to continue into the future. China has probably one of the most organized 'succession planning' systems around for a developing country, not just for its top leadership but also up and down the bureaucracy and for the leadership of the 33 provinces (and special regional entities such as Hong Kong and Macao). The legitimacy of the ruling Communist Party is inextricably linked to sustaining this rapid economic and social progress, and ensuring that the benefits of development are spread as widely as possible. Indeed, the Chinese development vision of *Xiaokang*[1] is very much about creating a harmonious, all-round, well-adjusted society with the target for this to be achieved by 2020. The challenge remains, will the target be met?

On data, it should be noted that the book, like much of the analytical work on China, is based on data derived from official sources. As already mentioned there is controversy about these sources, in part due to the somewhat different methodologies employed by China in doing the calculations. Some economists have tried to adjust this data, but the results have been mixed in terms of comparability and predictive power. These adjustments have tended to go in either direction, in some cases reducing the GDP growth rates, in others like the World Bank revision in 2008, producing higher growth estimates. Yet, it is also clear, and most analysts do now concur on this, that China is not only growing rapidly, but also rapidly transforming itself in almost every aspect of life, from lifting over 500 million people out of poverty, to the creation of modern cities, to First World quality infrastructure that rivals the US, and Chinese tourists everywhere.

---

[1] A Confucian term which refers to 'an all-round, well-adjusted society'.

The transformation thesis draws upon the post-war development experience of different countries and examines how such experience can illuminate the relationships between the essential drivers of development: ownership, capacities, and policies. Ownership can be seen as a base for everything else, it is a critical starting point, as there are few examples in history where societies have been able to make much development progress without playing a leading role themselves in determining their destinies. It is of course quite possible and at times politically fairly easy to 'own' bad policies. The Chinese story is about strong ownership of home-grown reforms which were probably good enough for Chinese society and the conditions in which they were being introduced.

The Chinese story is fundamentally about capacities: the sharply improved capabilities of people themselves through expanded health and education investments, a process which started in Mao's period, the development orientation of the ruling elites, and the strength of the government and its institutions. This meant that once reforms and policies were agreed upon, they could actually be carried out; and, strong and enduring social cohesion, a reflection of course of its culture but also specific actions that were taken over the years. This social strength is also referred to in the book as social capital which covers norms and values that taken together act as the 'glue' that holds society together and influences both development opportunity and outcomes. On policies, the 'development as transformation' framework makes a particular point that context matters, a lot. It can determine whether policies work in the manner intended and tries to explain why similar policies can have such different outcomes, and in particular, why the wholesale application of the set of policies described as the Washington Consensus has had such uneven and indifferent success.

As Chapter 5 highlights, a key feature of Chinese progress has been its comprehensiveness and the essential role played by a strong, capable state. China is a country transformed. And it continues so. In human terms, its citizens are better educated, have higher incomes, and greater choices about their lives than they have ever had. China is now among the most globally integrated economies in the world. Few countries have gained as much from globalization.

Yet, parsing China's progress in any linear fashion or only in economic numbers may not render full justice to the Chinese phenomenon. Why and how these reforms came about is a large part of the story. For instance, most economists take a before and after comparison of Mao's period with Deng's reforms that got started in 1978 and 1979. Many of Deng's reform ideas had strong antecedents in Mao's period. Some analysts have gone further to argue that without the Mao-led wrenching changes in leveling Chinese society, strengthening the apparatus of government, improving health and education of the people, and reorganizing the rural economy particularly in the 1960s, it would have been difficult for Deng's reforms to have succeeded. The ground was fertile for the introduction of Deng's reforms and for private initiative and markets to play a greater role in the economy.

This 'transformation' perspective is as much about economic numbers as it is about attitudes and expectations about the future. Deng captured it best when he stated in an interview to an American journalist that the 10-year-long Cultural Revolution, partly because of its disastrous impact, actually created the conditions for a sharp break from the past. The Chinese people, including the ruling elites, had suffered enough and were in a sense profoundly ready for a new, very different beginning.

The final chapter is about China's future and the policy and structural challenges that the country is likely to face in the coming years and decades. GDP growth projections are reviewed, the consensus being that by 2030 or thereabouts China is very likely to become the largest economy in the world. In a sense, China is in the process of recovering the relative ground it lost since the eighteenth century when it was estimated to account for one-third of the world's output. What the book does not discuss much is what this relative rise means for the world economy and whether such a feat is likely to take place on account of the many global geopolitical factors that are likely to be significant in the future. We leave that analysis to the political scientists and pundits who have many views and probably better insights on the topic. In the end, this book, true to its title, is about 'Why Has China Grown So Fast for So Long'.

This book could not have been completed without the support of many friends who took the time to discuss some of the ideas contained or review earlier drafts. I am particularly grateful to Sartaj Aziz, Pedro Conceicao, A.K. Shiva Kumar, Khalil Hamdani, Sakiko Fukuda-Parr, Tegegnework Gettu, Leo Horn-Phathanothai, Sir James Mirrlees, and Subinay Nandy. I owe a deep debt of gratitude to my research associates who put in long hours checking manuscripts, cross-referencing data, and looking for errors. I am particularly grateful to Peter Zetterstrom who spent much of 2007 and 2008 working with me reviewing the development literature and critically examining the ideas involved in this 'development as transformation framework'. Both Henrik Larkander and Yu Lei were worthy successors as they took up the research support mantle when Peter got married and left for Sierra Leone in late 2008. Most of all I am grateful for the wonderfully patient support I received from my family, especially my wife Carter, to whom this book is dedicated. Needless to say the faults of the book lie squarely with the author.

REFERENCES

Kuhn, Thomas. 1962. *The Structure of Scientific Revolutions*. Chicago: Chicago University Press.

Malik, K. 2002. 'Towards a Normative Framework: Technical Cooperation, Capacities and Development', in Sakiko Fukuda-Parr, Carlos Lopes, and Khalid Malik (eds), *Capacity for Development*, pp. 24–42. London: Earthscan Publications Ltd.

Stiglitz, Joseph. 1998. 'Towards a New Paradigm for Development: Strategies, Policies, and Processes', Prebisch Lecture at the United Nations Conference on Trade and Development (UNCTAD), Geneva, 19 October.

1

China's Progress

In 2008 China marked the 30th anniversary of its reform and opening up. By any standard, China has done remarkably well. The 30-year reform period presents a remarkable study of progress of the largest developing country in the world. Not only has growth been rapid—some 9 per cent per annum in GDP per capita since 1979–80—but it has also been accompanied by dramatic improvements in the lives of people. The Chinese people are wealthier, better educated, and healthier than they ever have been.

It has been argued that China has tried to fit 100 years of change into a few decades. And it is equally valid to contend that not all pieces necessarily fit comfortably. With success, new challenges have emerged. Inequality has gone up sharply over the last years—among people generally, between rural and urban areas, and between men and women. Measured by the Gini coefficient, inequality reached a level of 0.45 in 2001, among the highest in the Asian region (UNDP 2008a). When comparing average rural with urban incomes, China is now among the most unequal societies globally (UNDP 2005). Rapid growth has also put severe strains on air and water quality and on China's limited land resources. Challenges of environmental sustainability can no longer be ignored. Indeed it is becoming increasingly apparent that the old model of polluting first and cleaning up later is 'neither cost effective nor sustainable'.

China's broad-based growth is captured well by changes in the Human Development Index (HDI), a composite of three factors—income, health, and education—which went up from 0.56 in 1980 to 0.78 in 2006 (UNDP 2008b). China is now both a middle-income and a middle-human-development country. Another measure of this progress is by taking a relative perspective. One, by examining HDI levels of countries close to China in the year 1980, which approximates as the start of the reform period. By 2005, HDI levels of the 10 countries close to China rose by 22 per cent, whereas China's went up by 39 per cent. Two, by comparing annual GDP per capita growth rates with other countries. Chinese growth rates compare favourably with the ASEAN-4 (Association of Southeast Asian Nations) countries: Malaysia, Indonesia, Philippines, and Thailand (Figure 1.1).[1] More broadly, as Figure 1.2 highlights, China has consistently outperformed the rest of the world.

This spectacular growth was accompanied by some exceptional social outcomes. Official poverty fell from 15 per cent in 1984 to 2 per cent in 2007 (ADB 2008)(see Figure 1.3). Regardless of the measure used, China has recorded the most dramatic income poverty reduction in known history. A recent World Bank study (Chen and Ravallion 2008), using the revised minimum standards of $1.25 dollar a day, estimated that over 600 million people had been lifted out of poverty since 1981. China's progress has meant that the world's progress in meeting

---

[1] With the exception of 1989–90, China's GDP growth has consistently outperformed the ASEAN-4 countries. Since the Asian financial crisis in 1998 only Malaysia has once achieved a GDP growth (8.9 per cent in 2000) surpassing China's lowest growth rate (7.1 per cent in 1999) for the period (IMF, World Economic Outlook Database, 2007).

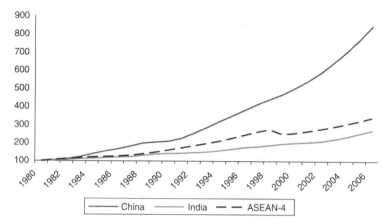

Figure 1.1 China Outperforms the Emerging Tigers
Source: IMF, World Economic Outlook Database, September 2006.
Note: Annual growth in real GDP per capita.
China vs India and ASEAN-4 (1980 = 100).

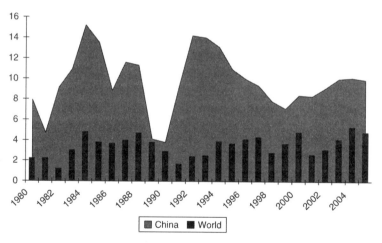

Figure 1.2 China Outperforms the World
Source: IMF, World Economic Outlook Database, October 2007.
Note: Annual growth in real GDP per capita.
China vs world, 1980–2005 (%).

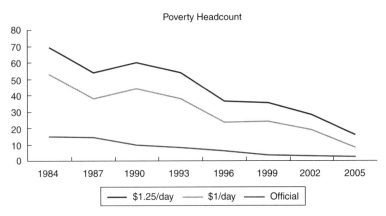

Figure 1.3 China's Success in Poverty Reduction
Source: World Bank (2008).

the primary Millennium Development Goals (MDG) target of poverty reduction is on track. If we exclude China from the calculations, global poverty actually increased by 29 million in 2008 (UNDP 2008b).

Health and education indicators recorded equally strong progress, though this is particularly true for the first decades of the reform period. Under-five child mortality and maternal mortality rates dropped to 18 per 1,000 live births in 2007 and life expectancy reached 72 by 2005 (Figure 1.4). And, remarkably for a developing country, by 2002, an astonishing 98 per cent of the population had access to electricity. In line with official interest in opening up internal markets, an extensive road network now exists, which by 2008 had exceeded that of USA.

Over the almost 30-year period, as Figure 1.1 indicates, growth has not always been linear. There appears some evidence of macroeconomic cycles, but these have been mild by international standards. Apart from two relatively short periods, 1981–3 and 1989–93, growth in per capita income has been consistently high. Both periods coincided with bursts of internal disorder. For the first period, there was extensive internal debate on whether China should take a capitalist path or maintain its drive to create

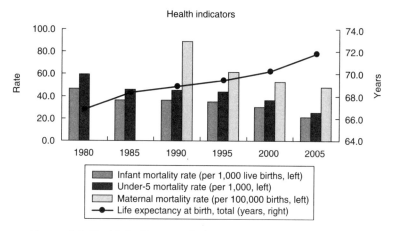

Figure 1.4 Health Indicators of China in the Last Three Decades
Source: World Bank (2008).

a socialist economy and society. Deng Xiaoping resolved the debate by taking the middle way, and officially adopted the term 'socialist market economy'. The second period was linked to the 4 June 1989 Tiananmen event which had a significant impact on economic and trade relations with other countries. Both represented non-economic events that had a large, though relatively brief, real sector impact.

Given enough time, inevitably, growth rates for fast-moving countries tend to come down as the country prospers. But will it for China? The official *Xiaokang*[2] target is to treble 2000 income level by 2020, which requires annual growth rates of 7–8 per cent over the next 11 years, by which time China would have reached 'a moderately all-round, well-off society'. By comparison, Japanese GDP growth declined from over 10 per cent during the 1960–70 decade to 5 per cent in the subsequent decade and less than 2 per cent 1990 onwards (Goldman Sachs 2003).

In historical terms, China is regaining its place among the community of nations. Angus Maddison (2007), the economic

[2] A Confucian term which refers to 'an all-round, well-adjusted society'.

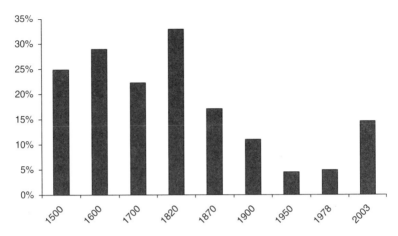

Figure 1.5 China's Share of World GDP, Selected Years (1500–2003)
Source: Maddison (2007).

historian, estimated relative shares of GDP over the 1500–2003 period based on purchasing power parities (see Figure 1.5). In 1820 China accounted for one-third of the world's output. This share of global output plummeted to less than 5 per cent in the 1950s and 1960s. China is now somewhere around 15 per cent. In 2010, China became the second largest economy in the world. Projections by Goldman Sachs (2003) predict that China would exceed, again in US dollar terms, the US economy by 2041. Indeed, their projection of China overtaking Germany in 2010, actually took place in 2007.

OVERALL VISION AND STRUCTURAL CHANGE

Over the years, there have been ongoing adjustments to the overriding developmental vision initiated by Deng's reforms, though high levels of growth consistently remained a high priority.

Under President Jiang Zemin (1993–2003), the emphasis was the maintenance of high growth at all costs. Till 2005, the guiding slogan was that 'agriculture should support industry and rural areas should support cities'. Performances of provincial authorities were assessed in terms of how well their provinces did on GDP growth. Internal debates on the quality of growth and concerns about the environment led to a recalibration in approach. To quote from the *China Daily* (9 October 2005):

> The CPC Central Committee (meeting) held on September 29 (2005) stressed the need in the next five years to persist in putting people first, change the concept of development, create a new development mode, improve the quality of development, carry out the 'five balances' (balancing urban and rural development, development among regions, economic and social development, development of man and nature, and domestic development and opening to the outside world), and earnestly shift socio-economic development onto the track of all-round coordinated and sustainable development.

At the 2005 National People's Congress, Premier Wen Jiabao announced a shift of strategy to now 'have industry support agriculture and urban areas to support rural areas'. Terms like scientific development and the five balances highlight the need for a more sustained approach to development and the pressing imperative to reduce inequality.

One major aspect of China's modernization refers to rural–urban migration and urbanization. Both were carefully managed in that still less than 50 per cent of the Chinese people live in cities, a figure lower than other developing countries at comparable income levels. In the next 20 years, the country plans to have half of the population live in cities, which translates into a shift of an additional 300 million people from rural areas. This is probably the largest planned population transfer in history.

There are other, equally noteworthy features of China's performance. The relative shares of industry and agriculture in overall output have in a sense reversed over the reform period. The share of industry in GDP grew from 20 per cent in 1952, 41 per cent in 1990, 46 per cent in 2000, to 49 per cent in 2006 (ADB 2007). Agriculture went down from 27 per cent in 1990 to 15 per cent in 2000 and 12 per cent in 2006.

PRIVATE SECTOR

An important feature of Chinese growth has been the gradual expansion of the role of the private sector. At the start of the reform period, over 80 per cent of the economy was in one way or the other state-led or state managed. By 2005 (UNDP 2005), the percentages had reversed. About two-thirds of the economy is now private-sector driven (Figure 1.6). The state used to dominate savings and investment, but now, most savings are generated by individuals and enterprises, and investment is financed by retained profits and banks. Even more dramatic has been the declining role of state-owned enterprises, and their growing embrace of markets and profit behaviour.

This growing role of the private sector has been termed by some as 'growing out of the plan' (Naughton 1995). The role of the private sector has been particularly significant in the growth of the coastal regions of China. Learning from this success, the government set explicit targets in expanding the role of the private sector as it introduced new development initiatives to accelerate growth in regions lagging behind nationally, such as the western (*Xibukaifa Jihua*) and northeast (*Dongbei Zhengxing Jihua*) regions. The *Dongbei* revitalization programme, started in 2005, focusing on the three northeast provinces of Liaoning,

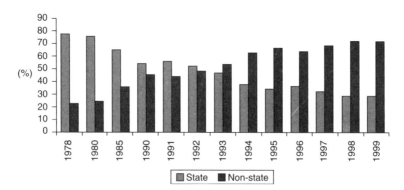

Figure 1.6 Gross Industrial Output, by Ownership
Source: National Bureau of Statistics of China (1999, 2000).

Heilongjian, and Jilin, seeks to both increase the contribution of the non-state sector and have the state-managed factories reinvent themselves as new corporate entities.

PRODUCTIVITY

But was Chinese growth efficient? Few can argue that productivity gains were close to zero for the 1949–79 pre-reform period, but accounted for 3–4 per cent growth per annum in the reform period. Output per worker grew by 3–6 per cent in the early reform period, and by as much as 8 per cent during the later stages up until today. By the early 1990s, productivity's share of output growth exceeded 50 per cent, while the share contributed by capital formation fell below 33 per cent. Such explosive growth in productivity is remarkable—the US productivity growth rate averaged 0.4 per cent during the 1960–89 period (Khan and Hu 1997).

A later chapter will go into more detail on the different sources of productivity growth. But it can be highlighted here that in the early reform years these productivity gains were particularly significant in agriculture. Prior to the 1978 reforms, nearly four in five Chinese worked in agriculture; by 1994, only one in two did. Reforms expanded property rights in the countryside and touched off a race to form small non-agricultural businesses in rural areas.

TRADE

From a mere 10 per cent of national income in 1978, and 16 per cent in 1982, China has emerged as one of the largest trading powers in the world, reaching 55 per cent in 2002, and 64 per cent in 2005 (UNDP 2006; Naughton 2007). Actual volumes were an astounding 2.2 trillion US dollars and a trade balance of $262 billion by 2007.

Chinese exports grew by an average of 13 per cent annually between 1980 and 1993 (MacMillan 1994), and has continued to grow at high rates since then—in the 1990s, China's trade growth was three times faster than global trade (WTO 2003). China moved over the reform period from a highly regulated, state-planned trade environment in the pre-1978 era (Lardy 2003) to a WTO member state in 2001 and in the process went from being ranked 32nd in the world in exports in 1978 (Lardy 1992) to becoming one of the world's largest exporters by 2008, second only to Germany.[3] In 2009, first estimates indicate that it has now overtaken Germany as well.

The other noteworthy aspect of China's exports is the breadth of its competitive strength. While dominant in the export of labour-intensive goods such as textiles, apparel, footwear, and toys, China is now globally competitive in electronics, and is a leading supplier of high-tech goods to the US (Lardy 2003). Kynge (2006) underlines the depth of expertise: 'Seventy percent of the world's photocopiers, 70 per cent of its computer motherboards, 55 per cent of its DVD players, 30 per cent of personal computers, 25 per cent of its TV sets and 20 per cent of its car audios—to name but a handful—are made in largely brand less factories.'

POPULATION

No compilation of Chinese growth results is complete without a review of its population policy, a policy heroic in many ways, yet also one which has attracted considerable criticism and controversy from international observers. Reversing Mao's policies of encouraging population growth in the 1950s, and building on earlier family planning programmes of the 1970s, Deng Xiaoping and the Chinese leadership took a strategic decision in 1980 to introduce a 'one-child policy' in order to slow down population growth (CPC 1980). They thought the decision was a selfless one, requiring sacrifices from the Chinese people in having only

---

[3] In 2007, China stood for 8.7 per cent of world exports and Germany for 9.5 (WTO 2008). If adjusted for extra-EU(27) trade, China (11.8 per cent) is still second to the EU (27) (16.4 per cent).

one child, but with benefits for both the country itself and also for the world.[4]

Demographic trends have led to a young population with low dependency rates, which is in principle conducive for growth, also referred to in the literature as a 'demographic dividend' (see Figure 1.7 for population growth trends). Two fundamental forces drive these demographics—a falling fertility rate, which dropped dramatically from 6.1 in 1949 to 1.8 in 2002 (below the 2.1 replacement rate) and rising longevity with life expectancy going from 35 in 1949 to 72 in 2005 (ADB 2007; Riley 2004). Yet the current demographic distribution in China also presents considerable challenges for the future. The UN projects that the proportion of elderly (those over 60 years) will increase to 28 per cent by 2040. With a growing number of older persons, and the financial and other implications this has for social security and welfare provision, China is beginning to experience the challenges of an advanced country while still a low-income country. Worryingly, the imbalance between boys and girls has accelerated. By 2005, the sex ratio at birth was 121 boys to girls, among the most skewed in the world, a result of the implications stemming from the one-child policy, liberalization, and the age-old boy preference.

China is the most populous country in the world, though it is worth noting that in relative terms the Chinese share of the global population went down from 30 per cent in the 1950s to 20 per cent in 2007 (Naughton 2007). By 2008, the Chinese population reached 1.3 billion. Without entering into a debate about the methods adopted, estimates are that without these population controls there would have been an additional 300 million Chinese by 2008, and per capita incomes

[4] On 25 September 1980, the Central Committee of the Communist Party of China issued an open letter to all the members of the Communist Party of China and of the Communist Youth League of China on the issue of population growth control in China. In the open letter, CC/CPC advocated/called for one child per couple. It should be noted that the family planning policy provides some flexibility for rural and ethnic minority couples. China's total fertility rate (TFR) is estimated at around 1.7–1.8 for recent years.

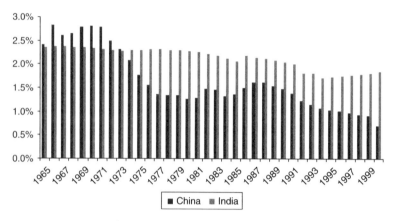

Figure 1.7 Population Growth—China and India (1965–99)
Source: Heston et al. (2009).

consequently would have been lower. As some observers have commented 'most countries get rich before they get old, but China has gotten old before it got rich'.

REFERENCES

Asian Development Bank (ADB). 2007. *Key Indicators 2007. Inequality in Asia*, Vol. 38. Philippines: ADB.

———. 2008. *Key Indicators 2008. For Asia-Pacific, Comparing Poverty across Countries: The Role of Purchasing Power Parities*. Philippines: ADB.

Chen, S.H. and M. Ravallion. 2008. 'The Developing World is Poorer than We Thought, but No Less Successful in the Fight against Poverty', Policy Research Working Paper Series 4703, World Bank.

Communist Party of China (CPC). 1980. 'On the Control of Population Growth Caused by China's Communist Youth League's Open Letter to All', Communist Youth League, 25 September.

Heston, Alan, Robert Summers, and Bettina Aten. 2009. 'Penn World Table Version 6.3', Center for International Comparisons of Production, Income and Prices at the University of Pennsylvania, August.

Khan, M.S. and Z.L. Hu. 1997. 'Why is China Growing So Fast?', International Monetary Fund, Economic Issue 8, Washington DC.

Kynge, J. 2006. *China Shakes the World: A Titan's Rise and Troubled Future— and the Challenge for America*. Boston, Massachusetts: Houghton Mifflin Company.

Lardy, N.R. 1992. *Foreign Trade and Economic Reform in China, 1978–1990.* Cambridge, UK: Cambridge University Press.

———. 2003. 'Trade Liberalization and Its Role in Chinese Economic Growth', International Monetary Fund and National Council of Applied Economic Research Conference 'A Tale of Two Giants: India's and China's Experience with Reform and Growth', New Delhi, 14–16 November.

MacMillan, J. 1994. 'China's Nonconformist Reforms', in Edward P. Lazear (ed.), *Economic Transition in Eastern Europe and Russia: Realities of Reform.* Stanford: Hoover Institution Press.

Maddison, A. 2007. *Chinese Economic Performance in the Long Run, 960–2030 AD*, Second Edition Revised and Updated. Paris: Development Centre Studies, OECD.

National Bureau of Statistics of China. 1999. *China Statistical Yearbook 1999.* Beijing: China Statistics Press.

———. 2000. *China Statistical Yearbook 2000.* Beijing: China Statistics Press.

Naughton, B. 1995. *Growing Out of the Plan—Chinese Economic Reform 1978–1993.* Cambridge, UK: Cambridge University Press.

———. 2007. *The Chinese Economy—Transitions and Growth.* Cambridge Massachusetts: The MIT Press.

Riley, N.E. 2004. 'China's Population: New Trends and Challenges', A Publication of the Population Reference Bureau (PRB), Washington DC, 59(2).

United Nations Development Program (UNDP). 2005. *Human Development Report 2005: International Cooperation at a Crossroads—Aid Trade and Security in an Unequal World.* New York: UNDP.

———. 2006. *Asia-Pacific Human Development Report 2006: Trade on Human Terms—Transforming Trade for Human Development in Asia and the Pacific.* New Delhi: Macmillan India Ltd.

———. 2008a. *Human Development Report 2007/2008: Fighting Climate Change—Human Solidarity in a Divided World.* Houndmills, Basingstoke: Palgrave Macmillan.

———. 2008b. *Human Development Report China 2007/08: Access for All—Basic Public Services for 1.3 Billion People.* Beijing: China Translation and Publishing Corporation.

World Bank. 2008. *World Development Indicators.* Available at http://go.worldbank.org/U0FSM7AQ40, accessed on 18 April 2010.

World Trade Organization (WTO). 2003. *International Trade Statistics 2003.* Geneva: WTO.

———. 2008. *International Trade Statistics 2008.* Geneva: WTO.

2

A Short History of Chinese Reforms

The ups and downs of Chinese debates on strategic direction and policy is a fascinating subject as it traces the struggle that continues to this day between different factions of the ruling elite, pitting reformers who fought for closer integration with the rest of the world—World Trade Organization (WTO) accession in 2002 being one big step forward—promoting a freer market economy, and those concerned about growing inequality and corruption, and yet others who fought to restore party disciple and wished for a return to revolutionary ideals.

In order to assess the determinants of Chinese progress over the three decades of reform, it might be helpful here to first summarize some of the key reforms and policies introduced since 1979. Economists generally divide the story of Chinese reforms into two major periods—initial reforms (1978–92) and deepened reforms (since 1993)—separated by a period of turbulence following economic overheating and the events at Tiananmen. At the same time, a proviso is necessary. It needs to be acknowledged that in several important areas Deng's reforms deepened those initiated under Mao. There was greater continuity between them than is generally accepted.

INITIAL REFORMS: 1978–92

The first phase of reform had, as its backdrop, the chaotic years of the Cultural Revolution, which laid waste to large parts of society and severely diminished the productive capacity of the country. In particular, productivity in the large agricultural sector was low and unable to keep pace with global developments. By some estimates, agricultural productivity had even decreased. This is where reforms first started, with de-collectivization of agricultural production, introduction of limited land rights, and allowing for retention of profits through the Household Responsibility System.

The Third Plenum of the 11th Chinese Communist Party Congress meeting in December 1978, by most accounts, formally kick-started the reform period. Earlier debates between Hua Guofeng, Mao's chosen successor, and Deng Xiaoping were finally settled in favour of the latter with the Plenum ratifying the shift from concerns about class struggle to the imperatives of economic development and modernization. The economic failures stemming from the Cultural Revolution acted as the catalyst for generating a deep seated commitment to reform and pushing forward economic and social progress. This view is best captured in Deng Xiaoping's own words: 'We have a consensus on the policy of reform and opening up. This should be attributed to the 10 year Cultural Revolution, the lessons from this disaster are too profound' (25 May 1988, cited in Qian 1999). 'Without the lessons from the Cultural Revolution, there would be no new policies (since 1979) … The Cultural Revolution has become our wealth' (5 September 1988, ibid.).

These reforms proved immensely powerful, and agricultural production shot up. The rapid increase in productivity both provided savings and released surplus labour into the rural non-agricultural sector. More importantly, it helped create a market for its products (Sachs and Woo 1994). The growth of light and consumer goods industries, led in the main by Township and Village Enterprises (TVEs), was equally explosive—to the surprise of many—including Deng Xiaoping himself (Deng 1994 [1987]). In comparison the reform of state-owned enterprises (SOEs) was disappointing.

Economic overheating towards the end of the 1980s coincided with the turbulence surrounding the events at Tiananmen. Reforms were put on hold as conservative factions grew in strength. An austerity programme was introduced in 1989 and 1990 to cool down the overheated economy (Qian 1999). Attempts to reverse some of the reforms, including the 'recollectivization' of agriculture, resulted in political deadlock at the national level. The combination of key local and provincial leaders who pressed on with reform and Deng Xiaoping's famous southern tour in early 1992 tipped the balance in favour of those who wished to continue, and the second phase of reform was gradually launched.

1993 ONWARDS

The second phase of reforms is different from the first in several important respects. One was the acknowledgement that reform needed to be managed in a comprehensive and coherent manner, to eliminate the great complexity and many contradictions apparent in the first period. Another was that the goal was clearly set at creating a market economy, albeit with Chinese and socialist characteristics. This goal included the setting up of market-supporting institutions incorporating international best practices and a commitment to privatize and restructure SOEs.

In November 1993, reforms became state policy with the landmark *Decision on the Issues Concerning the Establishment of a Socialist Market Economy Structure* adopted by the Party Congress. Foreign Exchange reform, monetary reform, and reform of tax and fiscal systems all followed. More emphasis was placed on establishing market-supporting institutions, and a rule-based playing field. With more genuine privatization the importance of collective ownership waned. The November 1993 decision was in many ways historic, since it represented a step-change in the course of Chinese reforms. For the first time, the state committed itself to the abolishment of the planning system altogether, with a clear goal of establishing a modern market system (Qian and Wu 2000).

Results were dramatic. Rural enterprises which had suffered under austerity measures and uncertainty quickly picked up pace—employment increased by 10 per cent in 1992 and 17 per cent in 1993. Industrial production grew even faster than before and foreign direct investment (FDI) jumped from $4.4 billion in 1990 to $11 billion in 1992, and $28 billion in 1993. By 2008, FDI exceeded $90 billion.[1]

The slowdown of China's economic growth in 1998 and 1999 was partly due to the Asian financial crisis, but also because of a slowdown of reform in some key areas. It became necessary to revitalize the economy. Prospects of WTO membership (which it joined in November 2001) also intensified the need for further reform, especially with a view of preparing the domestic economy for foreign competition. There was also a growing realization that institutions in turn needed to be upgraded and new ones created to respond to the new 'demands' for oversight and regulation being placed on the state. Strengthening the rule of law, developing small and medium-sized enterprises, diversification of the ownership of major state development banks, further SOE reform, all posed new demands for institutional innovation (Qian and Wu 2000).

HIGHLIGHTS OF KEY REFORMS

Setting the Vision

Chinese history is replete with visionary statements that signal a shift in thinking and direction. At different stages of the

---

[1] See Chiang 2009.

Box 2.1 Key Steps in China's Reform

Initial reforms

1977	• Hua Guofeng starts 'Open Door' policy, later incorporated in Deng's *Four Modernizations*
1978	• December: National People's Congress (NPC) 11th Central Committee 3rd Plenum establishes the party's commitment to economic modernization, shifts Party focus from 'class struggle' to 'economic development'
	• October: Zhao Ziyang pilots autonomy and profit retention in six enterprises in Sichuan
	• Deng Xiaoping introduces *The Four Modernizations* of step-wise economic reforms
1979	• Introduction of agricultural *Household Responsibility System* and 'specialized households'
	• July: Guangdong and Fujian allowed to reform 'one step ahead' by adopting 'special policies' and implementing 'flexible measures'
	• July: Central government propagates the Sichuanese SOE experiments nationwide
	• July: Regulation to develop People's Communes and Production Brigades (TVE precursors)
	• SEZs established in Shenzhen, Zhuhai and Shantou in Guangdong, and Xiamen in Fujian
1980	• Fiscal contracting system starts
1981	• *Economic Responsibility System* for SOEs formally introduced
1982	• *Contract Responsibility System* for agriculture adopted by the entire country,
	• The commune structure dismantled
1983	• PBC established as Central Bank and commercial operations delegated to the four state banks
1984	• May: Market track for industrial goods officially permitted, within 20 per cent band of plan price
	• May: *Ten Articles* on expanding SOE autonomy issued by State Council

- October: 12th Party Congress 3rd Plenum adopts decision on urban reform, incl. significant shift from 'plan as principal, market as supplement' to 'planned commodity economy'
- Educational requirements, age/tenure limitations, and compensations package for the bureaucracy
- Another 14 coastal cities added to Shenzhen as open to overseas investment[2]
- 98 per cent of agricultural households covered by Responsibility System
- Virtually all agricultural collectives dissolved
- Private enterprises with more than eight employees legalized

1985
- February: Market track band restriction removed and the dual track formally in place
- The first wave of *xiahai* ('jumping into private business')

1987
- *Contract Responsibility System* for SOEs reaches 80 per cent adoption by end of year

1988
- Enterprise Law passed, based on the *Ten Articles*
- Hainan becomes a separate province and is declared an additional SEZ

1989
- June 4: Tian'anmen Square incident
- Austerity programme initiated to cool the overheating economy

1990
- Austerity programme continues
- Guangdong takes lead in price liberalization, other provinces follow suit

1992
- January—February: Deng Xiaoping's Southern tour mobilized support for further, more radical reform
- July: *Regulations on Transforming the Management Mechanism* grants SOE managers '14 rights of control' over foreign trade, investment, labour, wages etc.

(Continued)

[2] Dalian, Qinhuangdao, Tianjin, Yantai, Qingdao, Lianyungang, Nantong, Shanghai, Ningbo, Wenzhou, Fuzhou, Guangzhou, Zhanjian, and Beihai.

Box 2.1 (Continued)

- September: 14th Party Congress endorsed 'socialist market economy' as the goal of reform[3]
- Reform surges to a new high nationwide; general consensus around marketization
- Most border and Yangtze cities extended special privileges, and Shanghai further still
- Inland cities establish their own 'development zones', often without approval

Second phase of reforms

1993	• JZM leads Party's Economics and Finance Leading Group and economists in drafting a grand strategy for transition to a market system[4]
	• *Contract Responsibility System* for SOEs ends
	• Dual prices phased out for almost all industrial products
	• *Civil Service Code* adopted
	• November: CCP 14th Congress 3rd Plenum endorses the landmark *Decision On Issues Concerning The Establishment Of A Socialist Market Economic Structure*—a coherent strategy to establish a rule-based system, market supporting institutions, and private ownership rights
	• SOEs privatization initiated
1994	• January: Major tax and fiscal reforms introduced in line with international best practice
	• January: Plan track for foreign exchange abolished
1995	• *Budget Law* comes into effect, restricting central and local government finance options
	• Independent auditing system introduced
	• *Central Bank Law* passed substantially reducing local governments' monetary policy influence

[3] Qian and Wu (2000) note that this differs fundamentally from the 'market socialism' in Eastern Europe: the latter implies a stipulated market supporting a socialist structure of ownership, while in the former 'socialist' is a mere adjective to the goal of market economy.

[4] Research teams included taxation, fiscal system, enterprises, and foreign trade.

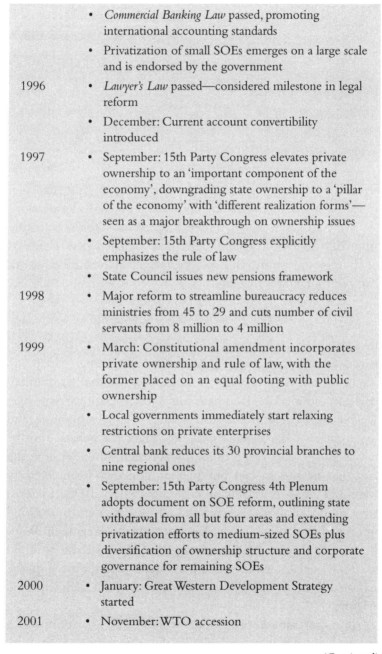

	• *Commercial Banking Law* passed, promoting international accounting standards
	• Privatization of small SOEs emerges on a large scale and is endorsed by the government
1996	• *Lawyer's Law* passed—considered milestone in legal reform
	• December: Current account convertibility introduced
1997	• September: 15th Party Congress elevates private ownership to an 'important component of the economy', downgrading state ownership to a 'pillar of the economy' with 'different realization forms'— seen as a major breakthrough on ownership issues
	• September: 15th Party Congress explicitly emphasizes the rule of law
	• State Council issues new pensions framework
1998	• Major reform to streamline bureaucracy reduces ministries from 45 to 29 and cuts number of civil servants from 8 million to 4 million
1999	• March: Constitutional amendment incorporates private ownership and rule of law, with the former placed on an equal footing with public ownership
	• Local governments immediately start relaxing restrictions on private enterprises
	• Central bank reduces its 30 provincial branches to nine regional ones
	• September: 15th Party Congress 4th Plenum adopts document on SOE reform, outlining state withdrawal from all but four areas and extending privatization efforts to medium-sized SOEs plus diversification of ownership structure and corporate governance for remaining SOEs
2000	• January: Great Western Development Strategy started
2001	• November: WTO accession

(Continued)

Box 2.1 (Continued)

2004	• China signs a trade agreement with 10 Southeast Asian countries; the accord could eventually unite 25 per cent of the world's population in a free-trade zone.
2006	• Abolition of agricultural income taxes
2007	• Law introduced to protect property rights
2008	• A $586bn stimulus package announced

reforms, new slogans were rolled out as a way of capturing such shifts. For the reform period, phrases like Four Modernizations (1978), Xiaokang (2000), Three Represents (2002), Scientific Approach to Development (2003), all signaled new elements or strategic directions, all however within the broad framework laid out by Deng Xiaoping.

The Four Modernizations and Xiaokang

In December 1978, the Third Plenum of the 11th National Party Congress Central Committee put Deng Xiaoping's stamp on reform and China's future. The Central Committee decision outlined the landmark four modernizations, *Si ge Xian Daihua*: of agriculture, industry, science and technology, and the military. Class struggle was no longer the central issue as it was under Mao. Deng himself was careful to underscore the fact that he was in fact building on concepts formulated by Mao and Zhou Enlai. For instance, in January 1975, the term four modernizations was first raised by Zhou Enlai, drawing upon earlier statements by Mao, in his final Government Work Report to the 4th NPC, stressing that the goal was to build a strong socialist country with modern agriculture, industry, national defence, and science and technology, in a short period of time.

An important aspect of modernization was education, where it was now necessary to rebuild the educational institutions destroyed under Mao.

Deng Xiaoping was clear about the implications of this historic shift. In an interview to a US journalist in November 1979, he stated (Deng 1984),

> modernization does represent a great new revolution. The aim of our revolution is to liberate and expand the productive forces. Without expanding the productive forces, making our country prosperous and powerful, and improving the living standards of the people, our revolution is just empty talk. We oppose the old society and the old system because they oppressed the people and fettered the productive forces. We are clear about this problem now. The Gang of Four said it was better to be poor under socialism than to be rich under capitalism. This is absurd. (Excerpt from a talk with Frank B. Gibney and others, 26 November 1979)

Deng was also clear that for China to achieve its goals, it needed international cooperation. He put particular emphasis on making full use of advanced technologies and scientific achievements from around the world, and in securing international funding so that China could accelerate the four modernizations.

Deng rejected the argument that market economies can exist only under capitalism. He laid out the vision for China not only as one of pursuing a market economy, but also, crucially, as a socialist market economy that 'mainly regulates interrelations between State-owned enterprises, between collectively owned enterprises and even between foreign capitalist enterprises' (ibid.).

In December 1979, Deng Xiaoping, when meeting with the Japanese Prime Minister mentioned the term '*Xiaokang*', which he explained was the goal of China's modernization. In September 1997, in his address to the 15th Congress of the Communist Party of China (CPC), Jiang Zemin, the party secretary, put forward the creation of a *Xiaokang* Society as the primary mission of the Communist Party. In November 2002, at the 16th Congress of the CPC, he formally reiterated the national task to 'build an all around *Xiaokang* society by 2020', by which time the expectation was that China would quadruple its GDP with 2000 as the base. *Xiaokang* is a Confucian term which outlines a 'basically well off society' whereby people are able to live relatively comfortably. It explicitly refers to the idea that economic growth needs to be balanced with social equity and environmental protection. It was the first time that the Communist Party used a classical Chinese concept to legitimize its vision for the future of China.

The Scientific Concept of Development

In 2003, a new vision referred to as the 'scientific concept of development' was outlined by President Hu Jintao. This vision was a response to the concerns for social stability stemming from growing inequality and environmental degradation. Later that year President Hu elaborated his vision further by calling for all-round, balanced, and sustainable development. This vision was reiterated in 1997 in his report to the 17th National Congress of the CPC.

This represented an attempt by the Chinese leadership to rethink China's economic and social model for the future. The vision emphasizes the slogan of 'putting people first', that people are the ultimate purpose of development, and calls for a balance between economic and social development as part of the drive to build a harmonious society. Similar to the concept of human development promoted by the United Nations, it covers four key characteristics (UNDP 2008):

People-oriented Development The fruits of progress must be reflected in the improvement in the lives of people and be equitably shared with all members of society.

Comprehensive Development Progress is necessary in all areas of national life—economic, social, cultural, and political.

Coordinated Development The benefits of development need to be equitably shared among the different regions, between rural and urban areas, and different social groups. This required as well rationalizing the relationships between central and local governments, balancing individual and collective interests, and balancing national interests and global needs.

Sustainable Development   The nation has to embrace a resource-saving and environmentally-friendly society. The speed, structure, and quality of development has to enable people to live and work in a sound, ecological environment and co-exist in harmony with nature, so that prospects of future generations are not compromised by the current generation.

Household Responsibility System

In 1978, some 20 peasants in Anhui province put their fingerprints on land 'contracts' dividing communal land among the 20 households they represented. They took over all rights over production decisions, except the right to dispose of land. At the same time, to not risk conflict, they re-committed themselves to fulfilling the centrally mandated grain targets. The parlous state of agriculture and their near destitution prompted these farmers to take on this radical initiative, a reform which was to have large national consequences. The practice spread rapidly, and was supported by Wan Li, the reform minded provincial governor in Anhui, despite not having any formal endorsement from Beijing.

   Agricultural output shot up. By late 1980, the Centre was forced to take notice by the sheer success of the reforms. Even then, the Party only allowed the household responsibility system in poor areas. The Party took on more active and broader support of the reform by early 1982. By the end of 1982, some 80 per cent of agricultural households had adopted this reform, and by 1984 almost all had done so.

   Once decollectivization proved successful, central officials took up the cause of extending it vigorously nationwide. Reformist leaders like Hu Yaobang and Zhao Ziyang toured slow-moving provinces, and criticized their provincial leaders. Those who did not support the reform were removed from office. The centralized political system of China proved valuable here. It enabled the grassroots initiative once proven to be rolled out in a few years to the entire country (Cai and Treisman 2006).

These agricultural reforms were recognized as the first successful reform in China. In the words of one senior official,

> why did reforms make its first breakthrough in the rural areas? This is by no means an accident and has historical reasons. This is because peasants suffered the most under the old rigid system and thus had the strongest desire for reform. At the same time, rural areas were the weak sector in the old system (ie lack of lack of strong vested interests), and became the breakthrough point of reform. (Qian 1999)

Opening Up and Special Economic Zones (SEZs)

The early years of China were characterized by a fairly closed economic model, even if the 1950s were relatively open to imports from the soviet bloc. For the 1970s and 1980s, China's trade/GDP ratios rarely exceeded 10 per cent. In the early 1990s, China took decisive steps in opening up and integrating with the world economy. The 30-year reform period has been characterized by successive waves of liberalization and trade promotion. Since 2002, with WTO accession, trade volumes surged even more. Innovations in the 1990s like the SEZs in the coastal areas served as important vehicles for initial investments and knowledge transfer from Hong Kong and Taiwan. Indeed, WTO requirements coincided with the interests of the reformers, who were able to use the aim of WTO membership to push through the reforms.

By the late 1990s, China accelerated its efforts to liberalize the country's trading and FDI regimes. Even before the WTO accession in 2002, China had one of the developing world's most open trade systems. China's embrace of openness and globalization, in addition to the direct return from export income, also encouraged greater competition in the domestic economy, and enhanced consumer welfare within the country (Branstetter and Lardy 2006).

The SEZs in particular, were an attempt at introducing market economies in specific geographical areas. They were first established in 1979 in four cities in Guangdong and Fujian Provinces (Shenzhen, Zhuhai, Shantou, which is adjacent to Hong Kong, and Xiamen). These were later extended to many other types of zones, totaling around 3,000 by 1993.

The SEZs' introduction coincided with the beginnings of reform of state-owned enterprises, which had started in 1978, with change in the incentive systems and greater autonomy. These changes were introduced on an experimental basis initially, in the provinces of Sichuan and Hubei. These incentives were essentially about the retention of profits by the firms. Zhao Ziyang played a leading role here, with his leadership as provincial party chief of Sichuan. He secured the support of the centre for the Exclusive Economic Zone (EEZ) experiment. Close scrutiny by central authorities helped, with the emphasis being on lessons learned. Whereas in Sichuan the focus was on greater autonomy, in Hubei the experiment was about 'tax for profit', with remittances of profits replaced by taxes and required payments for fixed capital (Naughton 1985).

SEZs enjoyed various privileges, from open trade, retention of foreign exchange earnings, and tax advantage, to the right to authorize small foreign investments (Cai and Treisman 2006). Importantly, the EEZs 'enjoyed a special institutional and policy environment and gained more authority over their economic development. For instance, they were granted the authority to approve foreign investment projects up to $30 million' (Qian 1999).

The SEZ experiment soon received visible and strong support from Deng Xiaoping. While there was, understandably, some ideological opposition, the fact that these experiments were taking place in some of the least industrialized areas of China such as Fujian, reduced considerably, major potential resistance from entrenched interests. Once the SEZ experiment got underway, and showed some results, local leaders lobbied the Centre for similar privileges and flexibilities.

Dual-track Approach to Market Liberalization

The success of the rural reforms influenced the conduct for reforms in the wider economy as well. Success of rural reforms was mostly a win–win proposition, largely because a dual-track system had been adopted. To protect overall food security, the state set production targets for key crops, which the governmental system procured (Naughton 2007). Under the reform, farmers were allowed to keep whatever they produced above the targets. These surpluses were traded in the markets, which allowed markets to grow and mature. By 1993, to use Naughton's phrase, 'the market sphere had expanded sufficiently that the economy had grown out of the plan'.

The Chinese term *shuannuizhi* refers to 'coexistence of a traditional plan and a market channel' (ibid.). These two parts often operated in the same enterprise or industry. Anything above the mandated targets could be sold directly in the emerging markets. This system imposed increasing market discipline on firms, including SOEs. Lau, Qian and Roland (2000) take a view that this approach, in fact, under the conditions prevailing in China at that point, represented 'efficient Pareto-improving reform'. Under the system, economic agents—farmers, factory managers, and others— were contracted to provide specific quantities at fixed prices to the state and industrial producers. Once these obligations are met, they could move on to a market track. This dual-track approach represented a major step forward in liberalizing markets in China and for a growing part of the economy accepting the discipline of the market. Such reforms are not without precedent even in the advanced economies. For instance, even in advanced countries there exist two-tier wage systems, with lower wages for newly recruited employees in some industries such as the US airlines system. Similar examples abound for many pension schemes.

In agricultural reform, the dual track approach was introduced simultaneously with the household responsibility system. In urban state-owned enterprises, a 'contract responsibility system' was introduced to expand autonomy and grant profit retention to enterprises. Both reforms introduced profit-driven incentives, though this was less so in the case of industrial enterprises (ibid. 2000).

The result in agriculture was dramatic. Between 1978 and 1985, the share of transactions at plan prices in agricultural goods fell from 94 per cent to 37 per cent. In industry, the dual track approach was less successful. Crude oil was a test case. Dual pricing was introduced in 1981. Government allowed the export of crude oil at market prices for amounts above the centrally mandated quota. In 1984, the market track was extended to all industrial goods but with a crucial restriction of the market price not exceeding a 20 per cent premium. The comparable share of transactions fell from 100 per cent to 64 per cent over a similar period and to 45 per cent in 1990 (Xu 1997).

Labour market liberalization on the other hand took longer. Until the 1980s, employers were allocated specific numbers of workers at specific wages. The market track only applied to new and additional employment. The success of agriculture and the emergence of 'surplus labour', combined with China's high savings rate, allowed for a rapid increase in the non-state sector, which in turn meant new jobs. Between 1978 and 1994, employment in the non-state sector increased by 318 per cent (with an increase of 171 per cent in urban areas and 426 per cent in rural areas). By comparison, employment in the state sector increased by only 50 per cent over a similar period (Lau et al. 2000).

By the 1990s, the plan tracks had mostly phased out. By 1996, the plan track represented a modest 16.6 per cent in agricultural goods, 14.7 per cent in industrial producer goods, and only 7.2 per cent in total retail sales of consumer goods (*China Daily* 22 August 1997).

Fiscal Decentralization

Fiscal relations between the central and local governments in China have changed substantially over the past 30 years. There were broadly two phases, the first burst of decentralization starting in 1978–9, and recentralization since the mid–1990s. Prior to the reform period, the fiscal system in China was highly centralized.

The system of financial relations between the centre and the provinces, labeled as *tongshou tongzhi* (unified revenue and budget appropriation) reflected the centralized nature of production in China. Provinces did not prepare separate budgets. It was the centre which consolidated all revenues into one overall budget. This budgeting process also covered state-owned enterprises.

Pre-1980, there were some emerging forces. The rapid growth of non-state enterprises, the loss-making of SOEs, and the growing autonomy of local entities, all combined to strengthen the case for changes in the revenue collection and expenditure systems.

Like other reforms, fiscal decentralization also started as a pilot, this time in Jiangsu. By 1980, the central government set up new revenue sharing arrangements guided by a principle of assigning revenues and expenditures at different levels of government. This gave local governments a large share of marginal profit or income tax revenues. Fiscal contracts were established by the centre with provincial governments over the division of tax revenues. By 1989, more than two-thirds of the provinces had the right to keep all marginal revenues. This larger retention of taxes helped fuel other positive aspects of development. For instance, by creating incentives, provincial governments encouraged the growth of non-state enterprises as one way of increasing their tax base. Cai and Treisman (2006) cite the study of 29 provinces by Jin et al. (2005) during 1982–92 which found that 'higher marginal rates were associated with faster employment and growth in non-state enterprises and faster reform of state-owned enterprises'.

This push to decentralize fiscal powers had other, less positive consequences as well. It led to declining overall revenues and a sharp drop in the share of revenues for the centre which in turn created pressure for further reforms to respond to these challenges. The centre's share of revenues declined from 39 per cent in 1985 to 22 per cent in 1993. The 1994 reforms were critical, and were specifically aimed at reversing these declines and enhancing the centre's capacity to conduct macroeconomic policy and set up a more equitable equalization formula.

There is an ongoing challenge here, as the central government increases its focus on the overall redistributive effects of the system to ensure that greater fiscal attention goes to poorer regions and poor and vulnerable groups generally. These reforms, in particular, were seeking to address the imbalance between expenditure responsibilities at the sub-national level, including unfunded mandates and the inability of lower level governments to raise their own revenues at the margin.

Role of the State in the Provision of Social Services

China has undergone profound economic restructuring and social transformation since the founding the People's Republic in 1949. Basic public services are vital conditions for the development of people's capacity to live a full life.

Apart from the central level of government based in Beijing, there are four other layers of government. They cover the 31 province-level entities representing the second tier, of which there are 22 provinces, five autonomous regions, and four municipalities (Beijing, Shanghai, Tianjin, and Chongqing). The third tier consists of 331 prefectures. The fourth tier refers to counties and cities, and the fifth to villages and townships.

The revamping of the old public service system was linked to the reform of the basic entities around which people organized their lives. The disbanding of the people communes and the de-collectivization of agriculture, which took place in the early years of reform, led in a short time to the collapse of public service institutions based on the collectives. Basic healthcare and education became more difficult and expensive for much of the rural population. In urban areas, public provisioning dragged on until the deepening of the state-owned enterprise reform in the 1990s. One key feature of this was the shedding by SOEs of their expensive social obligations in favour of more commercial, market driven arrangements. 'The dismantling of the cradle-to-grave health, education and social insurance services was one of the first outcomes of SOE reform and fiscal decentralization' (UNDP 2008).

Fiscal decentralization created a large challenge. Upper levels of the administration—provincial and prefecture governments—are generally in a better fiscal situation than lower levels such as counties and townships. But the lower levels are responsible for the provision of most social services. Their lack of fiscal resources led to severe gaps in the delivery of social services at the local level and policies that made public service providers such as schools and clinics responsible for much of their financing through the collection of fees. It shifted and ultimately reduced government responsibility for public service provision. There were other implications as well. While preparing their budgets, local governments were constantly presented with choices between building infrastructure—which potentially increased local profitability and attracted additional capital—and supporting the provision of social services or bailing out loss-making enterprises. Social commitments inevitably got reduced.

Mechanisms for social insurance coincided with a surge in personal income that led to stronger household demand for public services. Nolan (2004: 32) captures it well: 'The outcome of the increasing use of the market to provide educational services has been "growing disparities in per-capita (education) expenditure across regions, both inter-provincial and intra-provincial" ... there appears to be "significant gaps between the stated national goals and the actual provision of education and health services in poor regions".'

The same applies to health. As documented in the first chapter, China's progress in health outcomes has been impressive. The reforms led to a substantial improvement in people's incomes, which in turn facilitated greater household expenditures on better nutrition and health. This coincided with a general relative withdrawal of state responsibility in the social sectors. UNDP (2008) estimates that the share of rural households' income allocated to medical expenses rose from less than 1.5 per cent in 1988 to 4.9 per cent in 1995, to 6.5 per cent in 2005.

Since 2006, the Chinese government has set a policy of 'gradually equalizing basic public services', the issue of effective fiscal equalization has remained a policy concern for the Chinese leaders. Growing income disparities among people and between the regions has made this a priority concern. By 2003, the National Health Survey found illness had become the leading cause of rural poverty accounting for one-third of rural poverty incidence. By comparison, a previous survey in 1998 found illness was only the third most important cause.

Rural–urban income and development gaps are rooted, in part, in the uneven provision of social services.

Public Sector Reform and the Civil Service

Despite many early reforms, till the 1990s, the basic government bureaucratic structure in China remained intact. In early 1998, a major reform to streamline government took place. 'Large industrial ministries such as the textile and machinery industries were abolished and replaced by much smaller bureaus,… the number of ministries in the central government was trimmed from 45 to 29 … (and) the number of civil servants was cut by half from 8 million to 4 million' (Qian 1999). More broadly, in 2005, an estimated 62 million people (or 5 per cent of the population) were hired by the public sector and 'ate the rice of imperial court' (*chi huangliang*). This represents a sharp drop from the number of 109 million in 1993 (almost 10 per cent of the population) when public sector reform started.

The shrinking of the public sector was the result of enterprise and structural reforms in late 1980, mostly the direct outcome of the contraction of the state-owned enterprise sector (*guoyouqiye*). Employees in government (*jiguan*) and public service units (*shiyedanwei*) have remained relatively steady in number. In 2006, a broader definition of what constitutes government was adopted, which included manual workers and personnel in the different bodies of the governance system such as people's congresses, people's political consultative conferences, courts, etc. Under this definition, China had 6.5 million civil servants in 2004 (compared to around 5.3 million under the earlier definition) (Chou 2007), with over 90 per cent working in the local governments. Public service units refer to health and education sectors, as well as a wide array of market regulatory bodies such as banking, insurance, and securities.[5]

The shrinking of the public sector was the result of enterprise and structural reforms in late 1980, mostly the direct outcome of the contraction of the state-owned enterprise sector (*guoyouqiye*). Employees in government (*jiguan*) and public service units (*shiyedanwei*) have remained relatively steady in number.

China was keenly aware that a strong capacity to innovate and implement government policies and reforms was at the heart of moving the country forward. Leaders invested considerable effort in shaping the civil service to respond to emerging reform challenges. Success of the economy as well, produced additional pressures for the government. The reform of state-owned enterprises, and private sector development since the mid-1980s created many opportunities for civil servants to pursue alternative careers. It created pressure to further reform the civil service. Civil

---

[5] Not all employees in the government are civil servants. Figure 2.1 includes non-civil servants such as employees in political parties (mainly CCP), democratic parties, mass organizations, and religious organizations. Before 2006, the number of civil servants remained at around 5.3 million. The number was not based on the old definition of civil servants, referring to all employees, except manual workers working in people's governments at various levels. (Source: National Bureau of Statistics, *China Statistical Yearbook*, various years. Beijing: China Statistics Press.)

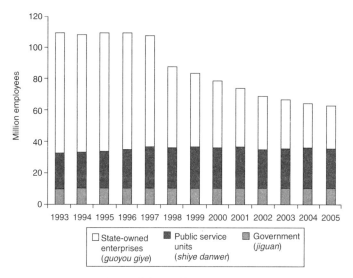

Figure 2.1 Size of the Public Sector (1998–2005)
Source: Chou (2007).

service reform touched the transition from cadre management to civil service system, staffing, wages, and staff development.

A few points can be highlighted: One, like other reform efforts there was considerable experimentation, and results were at times mixed. The thrust of reforms, however, remained with reducing the size of the civil services and professionalizing it. For instance, in the late 1990s, specific targets were set by Zhu Ronghzi to reduce the civil service, from 47 per cent in provincial level government staff to 50 per cent elsewhere in the country. In the end, actual figures of provincial level staff varied from only 4.7 per cent in Shanghai to 33.7 per cent in Hunan (Chou 2007).

Open recruitment was introduced. Life employment—once a norm in China's cadre policy—was phased out. Other measures included bringing in younger and better educated technocrats to gradually replace revolutionary cadres who owed their positions to their political credentials. Experimentation was the norm, particularly at the provincial and lower levels of government. For instance, to alleviate the brain drain of professionals, Jilin province pioneered a flexible wage system at the end of 2003.

Civil servants hired under this system could earn salaries two to fifteen times higher than the ones on the national pay scale. Wuxi city of Jiangsu province and Zhuhai city of Guangdong province rapidly followed suit.

With economic reforms, national commitment to local GDP growth was embedded in performance appraisal systems. It is rare to visit provinces and not to have provincial leaders list the GDP growth numbers of their respective provinces. In recent years, however, with the growing emphasis on sustainability and reducing inequalities, other social and environmental indicators also became important. Local leaders tended to push for high GDP growth and generally ignore such important issues as environmental protection and the provision of social services. It was reported that in 2004, pollution caused losses of 512 billion yuan (or about 3 per cent of the GDP) whereas estimated cost of pollution treatment amounted to 287 billion yuan (or about 1.8 per cent of the GDP) (Chou 2007).

Chinese enterprises have had close links with the government. Business enterprises were owned and managed by different branches of the government, including the military, the police, and the judiciary. Recognizing some of the intrinsic conflicts of interest, by 1998, the government severed all the ties between these government agencies and their business enterprises.

Township and Village Enterprises

Rural enterprises have a long history in China. Traditionally, farming in China was supplemented in a variety of ways by incomes from handicrafts, small rural industries processing agricultural produce, and servicing rural development generally. The new command economy introduced in the 1950s disrupted long standing market networks connecting agricultural suppliers with needs of the rural economy. 'Grain, cotton, silk, peanuts and soybeans— the staple supplies of nonagricultural businesses—were taken by the state immediately after the harvest. In fact, during the 1950s the countryside became de-industrialized' (Naughton 2007).

The Great Leap Forward and the communes introduced were disasters which took some years for rural areas to recover from. In 1970, a new wave of reforms tried to kick-start once again, rural industrialization under the rubric of 'commune and brigade enterprises'. This rural industrialization went beyond the processing of agricultural produce, and highlighted 'five small industries' that included iron and steel, cement, chemical fertilizer, hydroelectric power, and farm implements. These industries were generally capital intensive and the expected economies of scale did not materialize, and they equally did not absorb much labour.

This is was the context in which TVEs got started in 1979. The new policy was 'whenever it is economically rational for agricultural products to be processed in rural areas, rural enterprises should gradually take over the processing work' (Naughton 2007). TVEs were collectively owned but were given considerable freedom to function as market-driven entities. In next almost two decades, from 1978 to the mid-1990s, TVEs became a vibrant part of the national economy. TVE employment grew from 28 million in 1978 to a peak of 35 million in 1996. Its share of GDP went from 6 per cent in 1978 to 26 per cent in 1996. TVEs aggressively competed with SOEs, resulting in changes in the incentives systems for SOEs so that they could respond to this competitive pressure. TVEs did not follow any specific prescribed organizational form, they responded to locational needs and interests. The farmers in Wenzhou, in Zhejiang province, drew upon longstanding entrepreneurial traditions to exploit the market opportunities for simple consumer items such as buttons and ribbons that SOEs had either ignored or were not adequately servicing. Households became specialized in the production of specific items, and in a sense scaled it up. In this way production chains emerged for different commodities. In contrast, TVEs in the Pearl River Delta prospered as a result of investment from close-by Hong Kong. Business and local governments joined hands to start factories which grew quickly as export-oriented manufactures (Smart and Hsu 2004).

Privatization and Restructuring of SOEs

The Chinese use of the term 'non-public ownership' is indicative of the uneasiness that terms like privatization evoke.

China did not privatize any SOEs prior to 1992. China's industry was at this point dominated by small and medium-sized enterprises, most of which were supervised by local governments. Privatization of SOEs started in 1995 with experiments at the local level in a few provinces such as Shandong, Guangdong, and Sichuan. The emphasis in particular was on small SOEs as the state continued to hold on to larger units. This approach is well captured in the Chinese slogan, *zhuada fangxiao*, 'grasping the large and letting go the small'.

At this stage, the Chinese economy was mostly about small and medium SOEs. They represented 95 per cent of the total number, 57 per cent of employment, and 43 per cent of the state industrial output. By the end of 1996,

> up to 70 per cent has been privatized in the pioneering provinces and more than half were privatized in many other provinces. In addition, ten million workers from SOEs and urban collectives were laid off … and an additional 11.5 million workers were laid off in 1997. Though presented as a large problem by the media, the layoff itself was a big achievement for reform: never before had state employees been laid off and state enterprises closed down. (Qian 1999)

The intention to restructure the SOE sector took on greater significance with China's entry into WTO in 2002. Traditionally, losses in the SOEs were covered by loans from the state banking system. This is being substantially reduced as authorities streamline and modernize the financial sector. Increasingly, SOEs are being forced to adapt to market conditions. First of all, China has to substantially reduce state level subsidies to the SOE sector according to the Agreement on Subsidies and Countervailing Measures (SCM). China also agreed to gradually open up its financial service sector, which will foster competition among banks. As a result, subsidies to the SOE sector from state-owned banks through preferential loans will be reduced greatly (Bajona and Chu 2009).

To help SOEs meet the challenge of increasing international competition, the Chinese Government has adopted a variety of reform measures, such as reforming the ownership structure of SOEs and instituting standardized corporate governance to increase their productivity and efficiency. It upgraded an earlier Asset Management Agency to a full ministerial level body, State-owned Assets Supervision and Administration Commission of the State Council (SASAC), in 2003 to regulate and oversee the management of these state assets. The number of central level (as opposed to provincial level) SOEs has been reduced from 196 in 2003 to 159 in 2006 (Shi 2007).

Financial System Reform

Like other areas of the economy, China initiated gradual financial reforms in 1979, though it has tended to lag behind other changes in the economy. Even if many changes have been brought in areas such as banking, insurance, and stock markets, the state continues to play an important part in China's financial system. Poor lending policies have in the past led to a massive buildup of non-performing loans. Authorities have responded to these challenges in several ways, and by 2009 much of these debts had been cleaned up.[6] The reforms got an added stimulus with the Asian financial crisis as leaders became aware of the implications that financial crises could have for the real economy. Government control over financial institutions has gradually relaxed. Modernization of the financial system remains an unfinished task.

The largest domestic financial institutions are owned by the state. In 1979, the government removed the monopolistic position of the People's Bank of China (PBC) by creating four specialized banks: The Agricultural Bank of China for

---

[6] According to China Banking Regulatory Commission, non-performing loans of commercial banks has been reduced from 7.09 per cent of total loans as of end-2009 to 1.58 per cent as of end-2009.

rural financing, the People's Construction Bank for investment financing, the Bank of China for international financial transactions, and the Industrial and Commercial Bank for working capital financing. Afterwards, in 1983, a two-tiered banking structure emerged with PBC as China's central bank, divesting it of all commercial activities in 1993 and allowing for competition among the commercial banks. Government controls over financial institutions were relaxed, with PBC increasingly playing a more indirect role in influencing events through setting capital reserve requirements, etc.

Financial reforms from 1994 were centred on separating commercial lending from policy lending by transforming the four specialized banks and the urban credit cooperatives into commercial banks (Shirai 2002). Three state-owned policy banks were created: the Agricultural Development Bank of China, China Development Bank, and the Export-Import Bank. As their capacity got built up, they gradually took over the policy lending function from the commercial banks. This process was taken a step further when foreign banks were allowed to function in the first instance in the economic zones, and then later were gradually allowed to expand their business (foreign exchange) throughout China.

In 1995, a new commercial bank law was enacted, which gave the central bank the legal foundation to operate in a market environment under the leadership of the State Council. By 2001, WTO accession opened up the sector to foreign ownership. Since late 2005, 'foreign banks have been subject to national treatment concerning RMB business' (Hofman and Wu 2009). In keeping with the approach of testing out new ideas in specific locations, all geographical and customer restrictions for RMB business were lifted in four major cities: Shanghai, Shenzhen, Tianjin, and Dalian.

In contrast, capital markets have been much slower in developing. In 1981, the authorities permitted the issuance of bonds—including enterprise bonds and enterprise shares—under close supervision so as to avoid any conflict with priorities set in their credit plan (Mehran and Marc 1996). Stock markets were started by the end of 1980s. The bond market, initiated in 1998 and 1990 in selected cities, has grown dramatically in recent years. With bond issuance now at 34 per cent of GDP, China ranks third in Asia, after Japan and South Korea (Maswana 2008). The general thrust of these reforms, however, has been on consolidating the financial sector and preparing it for further and more fundamental reforms. While financial sector development has generally facilitated China's progress by providing vehicles for converting growing savings into investment, reducing transactions cost, and promoting institutional diversity, studies show that the non-state sector appears to have financed itself mainly from retained earnings or principal–owner savings, as well as foreign direct investments rather than from bank credit or the capital markets (Aziz 2002). Financial intermediation in China is largely bank-based and dominated by the four state commercial banks. Bond and equity markets are still at an early stage of development. Nonetheless, the growth of non-state banks and non-bank financial institutions has helped extend financial services to the areas where state banks were previously not so active (Cheng and Degryse 2009).

REFERENCES

Aziz, J. and D. Christoph. 2002. 'Growth–Financial Intermediation Nexus in China', IMF Working Paper, Asia and Pacific Department, WP/02/194.

Bajona, C. and T. Chu; 2009. 'Reforming State Owned Enterprises in China: Effects of WTO Accession', *Review of Economic Dynamics*, 13(4): 800–23.

Branstetter, L. and N. Lardy. 2006. 'China's Embrace of Globalization', Working Paper 12373, National Bureau of Economic Research.

Cai, H. and D. Treisman. 2006. 'Did Government Decentralization Cause China's Economic Miracle?', *World Politics*, 58(4): 505–35.

CBRC. (2007). Report on the Opening Up of the Chinese Banking Sector, China Banking Regulatory Commission (CBRC), January.

Cheng, X. and H. Degryse. 2007. 'The Impact of Banks and Non-bank Financial Institutions on Local Economic Growth in China', *Journal of Financial Services Research*, 37(2–3): 179–99.

Chiang, L. 2009. 'China 2008 FDI Rises 23.6 pct to $92.4 Billion', *Reuters*, 14 January 2009.

Chou, Kwok Ping. 2007. 'China's Civil Service Reform: Success and Pitfalls', EAI Background Brief No. 338.

Deng, X. 1984. 'We Can Develop a Market Economy under Socialism', in *Selected Works of Deng Xiaoping (1975–1982)*, First edn. Beijing: Foreign Languages Press.

———. 1994[1987]. 'We Shall Speed Up Reform', 12 June 1987, *Selected Works of Deng Xiaoping 1982–1992*. Beijing: Foreign Languages Press.

Hofman, B. and J. Wu. 2009. 'Explaining China's Development and Reforms', Commission on Growth and Development. Washington DC: World Bank.

Jin, H., Y. Qian, and Barry R. Weingast. 2005. 'Regional Decentralization and Fiscal Incentives: Federalism, Chinese Style', *Journal of Public Economics*, 89(9–10): 1719–42.

Lau, L.J., Y. Qian, and G. Roland. 2000. 'Reform without Losers: An Interpretation of China's Dual-track Approach to Transition', *Journal of Political Economy*, 108(1): 120–43.

Laurenceson, J. and J.C.H. Cai. 2003. *Financial Reform and Economic Development in China*, Advances in Chinese Economic Studies Series. UK: Edward Egler Publishing Limited.

Maswana, J.C. 2008. *China's Financial Development and Economic Growth: Exploring the Contradictions*, EuroJournals Publishing, Inc. 2008, Issue 19.

Mehran, H. and Q. Marc. 1996. *Financial Reforms in China, Finance and Development*. Washington DC: International Monetary Fund (IMF).

Meyer, R.L. and N. Geetha. 2000. 'Rural Financial Markets in Asia: Policies Paradigms, and Performance', Study of Rural Asia: Volume 3, Asian Development Bank, International Research Journal of Finance and Economics.

Naughton, B. 1985. 'False Starts and Second Wind: Financial Reforms in China's Industrial System', in Elizabeth J. Perry and Christine Wong (eds), *The Political Economy of Reform in Post-Mao China*. Cambridge: Council on East Asian Studies, Harvard University.

———. 2007. *The Chinese Economy: Transition and Growth*. The MIT Press.

Nolan, Peter. 2004. *China at the Crossroads*. Cambridge, UK: Policy Press.

Qian, Y. 1999. 'The Process of China's Market Transition (1978–98): The Evolutionary, Historical, and Comparative Perspectives', Stanford University, Department of Economics, Working Papers, J.RePE c:wop:stanec:99012.

Qian, Y. and J. Wu. 2000. 'China's Transition to a Market Economy: How Far across the River', Center for Research on Economic Development and Policy Reform, Stanford University.

Sachs, J.D. and W.T. Woo. 1994. 'Structural Factors in the Economic Reforms of China, Eastern Europe, and the Former Soviet Union', *Economic Policy*, 9(18): 102–45.

Shi, C. 2007. 'Recent Ownership Reform and Control of Central State-owned Enterprises in China: Taking One Step at a Time', *University of New South Wales Law Journal*, 30(3): 855–66.

Shirai, S. 2002. 'Banking Sector Reform in the People's Republic of China—Progress and Constraints', Chapter III, in *Rejuvenating Bank Finance for Development in Asia and the Pacific*. United Nations and Asian Development Bank.

Smart, A. and Hsu, J. 2004. 'The Chinese Diaspora, Foreign Investment and Economic Development in China', *The Review of International Affairs*, 3(4): 544–66.

United Nations Development Program (UNDP). 2008. *Human Development Report China 2007–08: Access for All—Basic Public Services for 1.3 Billion People*. Beijing: China Translation and Publishing Corporation.

Xu, L.C. 1997. 'The Productivity Effects Of Decentralized Reforms—An Analysis of the Chinese Industrial Reforms', World Bank Policy Research Working Paper 1723.

3

Why Standard Explanations are Insufficient

striking feature of China's reforms has been their 'non-conformist' nature. The Washington consensus has long represented a core global policy perspective that countries cannot develop without well-established laws of commerce, private ownership, and functioning markets. And that for markets to work efficiently, prices need to reflect scarcity values so that they can effectively allocate goods and services. Yet, in recent years, this core set of assumptions on how societies develop has been increasingly challenged, especially when confronted with the actual development experience of nations as diverse as China and the ASEAN countries. In some ways, this debate seems to have come a full circle, when one of the high priests of the consensus, Jim Wolfensohn, President of the World Bank, declared in 2004 at the Global Poverty Reduction Conference held in Shanghai that 'the Consensus is dead, so let's not talk about it'.

Both China and Eastern European countries went through a similar two-stage process of reform in their move from a centrally planned system to a market-driven economy. Hungary, Poland, and the Soviet Union started their reforms early, but their efforts on reform prior to 1990 are generally regarded as not having been very successful. This Eastern European experience led Kornai, in 1992, to conclude that 'in spite of generating a whole series of favourable changes, reform (in socialist countries), is doomed to fail' (Qian 1999). This failure helped create the conditions for the political changes that re-ignited the efforts to transit to a market system. Some observers have concluded that the 'big bang' transformation in these countries after 1990 was a response by leaders and the ruling elites to the early, less successful attempts to restructure society and the economic system.

In contrast, China went through its own failed comprehensive attempts to transform society: the equally disastrous Great Leap Forward and the 10-year Cultural Revolution from 1966 to 1976. Reforms after 1979 were a response to these early failed experiments. Starting from 1978–9, the reforms introduced a step-by-step approach to the economy and social engineering. The difference between the Eastern European experience and China's is that China's first stage was a big success, with the second stage of reforms building on the achievements of the first.

There has been a long and at times heated debate among economists and journalists in explaining the Chinese growth phenomenon. Recent books by James Kynge (2007) and Ted Fishman (2005), both journalists and business writers, give a sense of how China's growing prowess both fascinates and worries Western observers. Some admire China's success, others essentially conclude that the growth is a bubble waiting to be pricked, and yet others take the view that China's experience is no different from other fast-growing countries in East Asia like South Korea and Japan.

While they are differences of view and nuance, most of the explanations are derived from the basic tenets of neoclassical economics. In taking the view that Chinese growth is no different from the growth paths of other fast-growing countries, some economists conclude that gradually growth rates in China will settle down to single-digit figures. Can China continue to grow as it has done over the last 30 years? *The Financial Times* (*FT*) Economics correspondent Martin Wolf (2005) concluded that the only exceptional feature about China is its scale. Otherwise it was at an early stage of the paths followed by Japan, Taipei, and South Korea. Indeed China could have grown even faster had its growth been more efficient. In comparing incremental capital output ratios (ICORs), a measure of overall investment efficiency, Japan's ICOR during the 1960s and 1970s was close to three and South Korea and Taipei between two and three, whereas China's ICOR is at five.

Other leading China watchers such as Sachs and Woo posit that the basic two-sector growth model can capture the essential forces at play in Chinese growth, as surplus labour from agriculture was redirected to higher productivity manufacturing (see Sachs et al. 1994; Woo 1999). The large pool of labour in the Chinese rural areas kept wages low and return to investment high. But many countries have had similar conditions and the question remains as to why other countries did not grow equally fast.

An alternative perspective which is developed in this book is to take a broader historic and political economy perspective, in line with the work of economists like Stiglitz (1999, 2001), looking at the interplay of reforms and China's overall guiding vision, and examining the role of markets as opposed to ownership and the complex relationship between institutions, the state, and people. But all that in an analytical framework that seeks to identify the forces essential to the transformation of an economy and society.

GROWTH AND THE FACTORS OF PRODUCTION

As conventional growth theory credits a limited number of factors which drive the process of growth and economic development, it might be helpful to go through its main arguments, and identify aspects of the China story which might benefit from a broader framework of analysis.

At the heart of traditional economics lies the production function. Output is a function of combining the factors of production—capital and labour. By adding labour or capital, companies, industries, and sectors can produce more and thereby achieve higher growth rates.

The function, and the explanation, becomes more sophisticated as we add new factors of production such as technology or when quality dimensions are taken into account to reflect skill levels of workers. Joining skilled workers with better techniques and technologies are likely to yield a higher level of output. Over the years, ideas of technological progress and the concept of human capital have emerged as important factors in explaining why some countries have done better than others. Trained, skilled labour clearly influences the prospects of a nation; indeed much of the success of the East Asian model has been attributed to this factor of production. Radelet et al. (1998), for example, present evidence that shows the importance of quality institutions, schooling, and overall stock of human capital (literacy rates in East and Southeast Asia were 73 per cent in 1970), and how that human capital together with outward-oriented trade policies positioned the region very favourably to kick-start a trend of high growth rates.

This section presents an overview of the role that different factors of production are believed to have contributed to economic growth in China, followed by a discussion of their limitations in fully explaining such a sustained, rapid expansion. In order fill the gaps, a number of conflicting views and alternative drivers are introduced, paving the way for a broader framework.

Factor Accumulation

In the case of China, there is much agreement that accumulation of capital and expansion of the labour force have played a significant role in the overall growth that has taken place. Both the capital

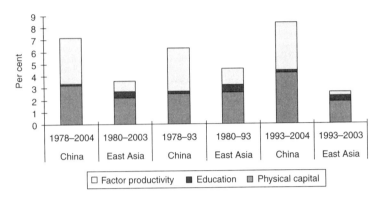

Figure 3.1 Capital and Labour Shares for China and East Asia
Source: Bosworth and Collins (2006).

stock and the labour force have grown considerably throughout the past decades, expanding the economy in the process.

Several studies show that following reforms, total labour force grew between 2 per cent and 3 per cent per year. However, estimates as to their contribution to GDP vary (Figure 3.1) from 2.5 and 2 percentage points in the studies by Dekle and Vandenbroucke (2006) and Bosworth and Collins (2006), respectively, for the periods 1978–2003 and 1978–2004, and the less than half a percentage point for 1978–98 in Ao and Fulgitini (2005) or under one point according to Zheng et al. (2006). Breaking down the period into pre-1993 and post-1993, both Bosworth and Collins and Zheng et al. conclude that the effect of labour force growth in the former was twice that of the latter.[1]

As for capital, China, like most developing countries, was capital constrained at the outset of reforms—savings averaging only 2 per cent of household income prior to the start of reforms, in contrast to 35–40 per cent in later years (Naughton 1994a). A combination of high household savings rates and (later) large inflows of foreign direct investment (FDI) has provided room for substantial capital accumulation since reforms began. Using 1993 as the cut-off point, the annual increase in the capital stock has

---

[1] Bosworth and Collins find a 2.5 per cent versus a 1.2 per cent contribution to growth; Zheng et al. find 1.25 per cent versus 0.55 per cent.

been put at around 9 per cent for the first period and as high as 12 per cent for the latter.[2]

While there is a general consensus that this very rapid accumulation of capital was significant for Chinese growth, there is considerable difference as to the *size* of its contribution. Estimates vary from the 2.5 percentage points (1978–93) or 3.2 points (1978–98) found by Bosworth and Collins (2006) and Ao and Fulgitini (2005), respectively, to the 4.3 and 4.8 points presented by Zheng et al. (2006) and Woo (2001), respectively, for the period 1978–93. And there is equally a large difference when comparing different time periods. As the studies show, there is a much larger impact for the post-1993 period (4.2 versus 2.5 points in Bosworth and Collins and 6.0 versus 4.3 in Zheng et al.).

These differences illustrate an important point of contention. Some economists argue that accumulation of factors—capital in particular—and their improved allocation in the economy explain nearly all of Chinese growth.[3] Others see these as factors among many, emphasizing the importance of other dimensions and more complex dynamics driving growth—including what *generates* factor accumulation, which is sometimes taken exogenously.

An analysis of the role of foreign capital flows can be contextually helpful here. At the outset, it is worth pointing out, that FDI inflows in fact grew large only mid-1990s onwards (Figure 3.2), when high growth had already been under way for over a decade.

Factor Reallocation

In addition to accumulating production factors—whether in terms of quantity or quality—the economy can grow by rendering their allocation more efficient. By employing their use

---

[2] See, for instance, Zheng et al. (2006), Ao and Fulgitini (2005), or Woo (2001).
[3] See Young (2000), Woo (1998), and Sachs and Woo (1997).

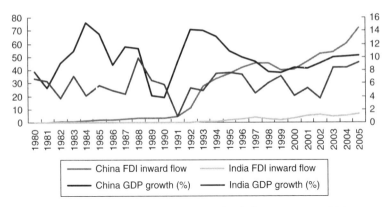

Figure 3.2 FDI Flows for China and India (billion current USD)
Source: UNCTAD (2004), IMF (2009).
Note: There is some dispute on the underlying data, which may change estimates
for both the rate of increase in the capital stock and its impact on GDP (Holz
2006a). The trends remain the same.

where they exhibit the greatest marginal return, the economy
can maximize output per unit of input. In economies where the
allocation is sub-optimal, there are thus efficiency gains to be
made simply by shifting factors from one use—often sector—to
another.

At the start of reforms, China's labour force was working in a
collectivized and highly inefficient agricultural sector.[4] Changing
those basic production conditions through de-collectivization
and household contracting (*household responsibility system*) freed
large amounts of labour for other, more productive purposes
and sectors. The very high share of the population engaged in
agriculture—75 per cent—magnified the productivity enhancing
effect, a point which has sometimes been used to argue that
similar reforms would not have yielded the same results in Russia,
Poland, or other transition economies in Eastern Europe, where

---

[4] However, despite the lack of state investment in agriculture, agricultural
output increased substantially during the First Five Year Plan (1953–7), averaging
increases of about 4 per cent a year (Worden et al. 1987).

labour-force participation in the agricultural sector was considerably lower.[5]

Similarly, economic planning had created a distorted setting where the relatively scarce capital available was steered towards heavy industry, often taking little account of factor endowments and associated competitive strengths (Lin et al. 2004). This policy both reduced the marginal return to capital and starved other sectors of the economy. When relaxation of this policy was combined with the financial surpluses generated by early reforms, freer and more abundant capital was able to underpin the expansion of other parts of the economy, including more labour-intensive forms of industry using the manpower freed up by agricultural reforms.

There is general agreement that the reallocation of labour and capital made possible by reforms opened for the expansion of previously virtually non-existent sectors of the economy—notably light industry and services—and that the higher returns in these sectors resulting from their relative scarcity was one important factor behind growth in the first phase of the reform.

This led to a large positive shift in labour productivity—a doubling between 1980 and 2000 (Figure 3.3). This productivity increase enabled growing grain production and a continuing reallocation of labour from agriculture to industry and services (Figure 3.4). This reallocation was particularly important in the first phase of the reform process. Bloom et al. (2006) find that sectoral shifts contributed 2.3 per cent increase to growth in 1970–80 and 1.3 per cent in 1980–2000, whereas Woo (1998) estimated a somewhat lower figure of 1.1 per cent for 1978–93.

Concerning capital, there is some evidence that pre-reform China suffered from over investment in heavy industry. Starting in 1978, the government embarked on a shift in its investment strategy. By 1981, the government halved its investment in new plants and service-producing facilities, while increasing its focus

---

[5] 14 per cent (Sachs et al. 1994) and 26 per cent in Russia and Poland (Dries and Swinnen 2002), respectively.

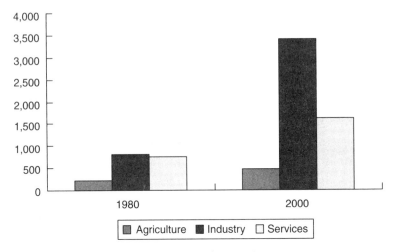

Figure 3.3 Productivity: GDP per Worker per Sector
Source: Database of National Bureau of Statistics (NBS) of China. Available at http://219.235.129.58/welcome.do.

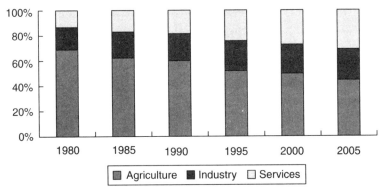

Figure 3.4 Labour Allocation per Sector
Source: Bloom et al. (2006).

on upgrading existing facilities, and investing in light and consumer industries. As labour was reallocated from agriculture to other sectors, there was a concomitant shift in investment to more productive industries (Naughton 1995).

Despite this relative consensus, there is some disagreement regarding the level of remaining efficiency of factor allocation in the economy and its ramifications for past and future growth. Most notably, market-allocated land rose only from 15 per cent in 2002 to 30 per cent in 2003, while government departments and the state-owned enterprise (SOE) sector accounted for 65 per cent of allocated credit in 2002 (Ministry of Land and Resources, PRC 2007).

Many critical observers have argued that the abundance of capital and continuous control of credit flows has led to over-supply and allocative inefficiency, weakening past growth and eroding the productivity of capital towards unprecedented levels. Coupled with a supposed high dependence of Chinese growth on capital investment, this large and increasing inefficiency will, according to this analysis, inevitably slow down future growth considerably.

Similarly, labour movements are still restricted to a large extent through the official registration or *hukou* system, although less than half of the workers migrating to the cities are estimated to do so through official channels. Whalley and Zhang (2007) test the possible effects of removing the hukou system and find such a measure would result in a one-time increase in GDP of 6.9 per cent, and some 175 million to further migrate. It is interesting to note that according to Ministry of Human Resources there were about 200 million migrants in 2008. Taking a sectoral cross-section, Bosworth and Collins (2006) estimate that whereas the primary sector accounted for 47 per cent of employment in 2004, its contribution was a mere 9 per cent to national value added. For the secondary and tertiary sectors, the numbers were 22 per cent and 21 per cent employment with a respective contribution of 58 per cent and 33 per cent to overall value added.

While the inefficiencies themselves are generally not contro-versial, their impact on the growth process is. The most obvious objection to this argument is that given the observed growth rates, the impact of these inefficiencies appears to have been of second order importance. While it could be argued, and some-times is, that the impact will become more devastating as the

Chinese economy takes on more conventional characteristics, current growth rates appear not to give evidence of such an impact.[6]

A second line of reasoning is that to the extent that allocation is still imperfect, there is commensurate potential for further efficiency gains—and thus further growth—in the future. Studies again confirm this. Zhang and Tan (2007) point to potential gains of 8.8 per cent in GDP with a 10 per cent shift of the rural agricultural labour force. And a 10 per cent shift of capital from cities to the rural areas could yield 3.9 per cent growth in GDP.

Productivity Gains

In the neoclassical model, growth in the long run is not determined by the accumulation of factors, since these are expected to converge to a steady-state equilibrium level where capital and output per unit of labour are maximized, given the savings rate. Instead, long-term growth must come from improvements in the effectiveness with which the factors are utilized, a concept referred to as total factor productivity (TFP).[7]

TFP is used in growth accounting exercises to denote the residual effect not explained by changes in the quantity or quality of factors. It is thus inherently a concept that lends itself to a variety of definitions and interpretations. Various economists have included elements such as technology, human capital, and the sector composition of production in the estimation of TFP, while others choose to break one or several of these out and label as TFP only the remaining residual.

---

[6] There is also the perennial question of reliability of data, particularly for capital stock estimates. Economy-wide fixed asset data is not available. And the fixed asset measure itself comprises net fixed assets plus three items that do not measure contribution to production (Holz 2006b).

[7] The intellectual precursor of the application of the concept stems from Ahluwalia and Chenery's surprising results (1974) when they estimated the shares of capital and labour in national income among countries. Their findings produced relatively low estimates for their contribution, raising the obvious question as to how to explain the differences in growth among countries.

The rate and importance of TFP growth in China has been debated both across the economy at large and for its constituent sectors.[8] Several studies by economists sceptical of the uniqueness of China's reform path, such as Woo (1998) and Young (2000), argue that China's GDP growth has been overstated and conclude specifically that improvements in TFP have been considerably lower than generally assumed. Both argue that China's growth—as well as that of the earlier East Asian fast growers—has been driven largely by factor accumulation and allocation. China's performance since the start of reforms is, in the words of the latter, 'respectable, but not outstanding' with gains in TFP of 1.4 per cent per annum, mainly concentrated in the agricultural sector. Like Young, Woo (1998) argues that most of TFP growth has in fact been the result of factor reallocation—and thus transient—rather than evidence of any underlying structural improvements. He estimates 'net TFP growth' to be only between 0.7 per cent and 2.2 per cent in 1979–93, contributing around 1.2 points to growth in the same period and most of that in the first few years.[9]

Others, however, argue that TFP growth has not only been considerably faster than this, but also potentially a crucial factor behind Chinese growth. Zheng et al. (2006) estimate TFP growth 1978–93 to 4.15 per cent, moderating to 2.45 per cent in 1993–2005. Bosworth and Collins (2006) find 3.8 per cent annual TFP growth in the period 1978–2004, but with the period since 1993 the slightly better performing of the two. Ao and Fulgitini (2005) use two different methods to conclude that TFP grew at between 3.4 per cent and 3.7 per cent in 1978–98. Hu and Khan (1997) found annual TFP growth to be 3.9 per cent,

---

[8] For studies of the agricultural sector, see Nyberg and Rozelle (1999); Fan and Zhang (2002). For the state-owned sector, see Bigsten et al. (2003). For the foreign-invested sector, see Whalley and Xin (2006).

[9] Woo (1998) goes on to state that 'when illegal immigration is taken into account, the reallocation of labor from agriculture accounted for 37 per cent to 54 per cent of TFP growth in the whole period, and 45 per cent to 100 per cent of TFP growth in the second subperiod.'

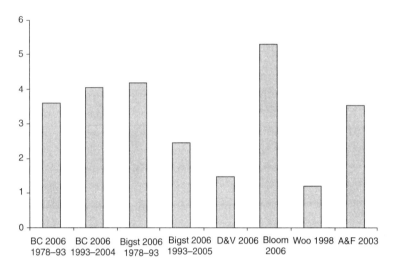

Figure 3.5 TFP Contribution to China's GDP Growth
Source: Bosworth and Collins (2006), Bigsten et al. (2006), Delke and Vandenbroucke (2006), Bloom et al. (2006), Woo (1998), and Ao and Fulginiti (2005).

explaining more than 40 per cent of China's growth for the 1979–94 period (Figure 3.5).[10]

Generally however these studies seem to concur that increases in China's TFP account for a significant part, some 30–58 per cent, of the growth for the early reform period (Xu 1997). The reasons can be summarized as follows: first, the success of rural reforms due to the household responsibility system which led to a sharp increase in agricultural productivity; second, town and village enterprises (TVEs) and related reforms encouraged indus-trial enterprises, managers, and workers to improve efficiency as they had to increasingly function in a market environment; and 'rising labour force participation, improvement in educational attainment, the transfer of labour out of agriculture and later narrowing technology gaps between China and developed econ-omies' (Zheng et al. 2006).

[10] Also see Wang and Yao (2001); Borensztein and Ostry (1996); Fleisher and Chen (1997); and Chen (1993).

TFP growth rates, however, appear to have slowed down for China's second period of reform. Time series estimates of TFP growth by Zhang (2002) indicated a downward trend from 1993 to 1998. Zheng and Hu (2006) confirmed this for 1995–2001, accounting for only 7.8 per cent of total GDP growth over the same period. This period seems to have coincided with sluggish growth in the rural areas and widespread inefficiency in industry. Growth in the capital stock appears to have been more important than TFP for this second period of reform. Capital stock, for instance, grew by an incredible 12 per cent annually (ibid.).

It is worth noting that Young's very similar results for the East Asian countries have been criticized by several studies for severely underestimating TFP growth. Klenow and Rodriguez-Clare (1997) show that when per capita output—arguably the more interesting measure—is substituted for that of total output, TFP growth accounts for a much larger share of output increases. Hsieh (1999, 2002), meanwhile, shows that substituting capital prices for disputed data for the capital stock leads to a significant increase in estimated TFP growth for nearly all of Young's cases. Naughton (1994a) argues that by ignoring weaknesses in the collection of price data, estimates for the early reform period all understate TFP growth—and that the attempt in Woo et al. (1994) to correct this problem fails to do so for the same reason.

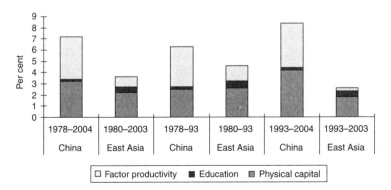

Figure 3.6 TFP Contribution in Relation to East Asia
Source: Bosworth and Collins (2006).

TFP calculations have been further refined to include concepts of technology transfer and to capture the role of external capital in that. In the case of China, FDI-induced technology transfer is credited by many observers with explaining a significant part of growth (Sachs 1997; Wu 2001; Hale and Long 2007). Yao and Wei (2006) conclude that FDI contributed up to 30 per cent of total technological progress in 1979–2003, in spite of being a mere 5 per cent of total investment.[11] Whalley and Xin (2006) estimate that foreign enterprises accounted for about 40 per cent of the GDP growth in 2003 and 2004. This added 3.4 points to overall growth. And Wang and Yao (2001) and Fleisher and Chen (1997), looking at regional variations in productivity, estimate that technological progress accounts for one-third of the total output increase since the start of reforms (Figure 3.6).

TFP: A Concept in Search of a Theory

Easterly and Levine (2002) in a large comparative exercise using both cross-sectional and longitudinal data to examine what drives growth differences across countries as well as over time conclude that 'overwhelmingly, the answer is total factor productivity, not factor accumulation'. Their empirical exercise leads them to estimate that TFP improvements on average tend to account for around 60 per cent of growth in output per worker. This in turn leads the authors to point out the lack of both empirical and theoretical work to 'provide much more shape and substance to the amorphous term "TFP"'.

An important review by Prescott (1997) of the TFP concept captures some of the dilemmas inherent in the concept when using it to explain income differences among countries. His basic conclusion is that TFP is unable to stand up to scrutiny as a theory of economic development, especially since differences in savings rates account for only a small part of international income differences.

---

[11] It is worth noting that the annual growth of technological progress was estimated to 4 per cent in the eastern provinces, but less than 2 per cent in the central and less than 0.2 per cent in the western ones.

These studies illustrate the range of results in estimating countries' productivity performances, but more profoundly the insufficiency of the TFP concept in understanding and explaining the differences in growth between countries or between periods in the same country. Rather than providing much in the way of useful answers, TFP growth estimates can perhaps be more usefully thought of as the beginning of the search for an explanation.

Empirical research globally is pointing in this direction, suggesting that production factors cannot explain growth patterns even in the short run, let alone differences in performance over the longer term. In some ways TFP remains the 'residual', the 'black box' in any explanation of the growth process. Indeed Felipe (1997), in his review of TFP growth in Asia, went further and concluded that the theoretical problems underlying TFP were so significant that the whole concept should be discarded. And that depending on the assumptions made and data sources used, the TFP results vary considerably, even for the same country and for the same period. In some ways we are back to the starting point, the need to understand the forces and policies that drive economic growth.

The Institutional Context: Private Property and Markets

The conventional economics framework is founded upon a set of institutional assumptions, including secure private property rights, rule of law, competitive markets with pricing that reflects the scarcity of goods and services, free entry of new producers, enterprise autonomy from the government, and so on. In recent years, some economists have put great emphasis on the design of these institutions and related policies, arguing that getting prices right is insufficient or even impossible until the institutional setting is right—that is, the one defined by neoclassical economic theory and Western economic practice.

In China, most of these initial or institutional conditions have not been fulfilled. While reforms have included increasing elements of developing markets, pricing and entry, improved rule of law, and a reduced share of government production in the economy, these have been introduced only in a piecemeal and gradual fashion. Following a track dramatically different from that of most other so-called transition economies—where the above reforms were generally introduced in a very rapid fashion, prompting the term *big bang*—China took one cautious step at a time, introducing partial reforms and transient institutions for experimentation or in response to practical needs.

Many economists have voiced strong criticism of the Chinese attempt at institutional unorthodoxy. Initially, it was argued that growth could never take off without the standard set of institutions. As growth has continued unabated, this argument has been refined somewhat to posit that as the Chinese economic institutions step by step have come to increasingly resemble standard neoclassical ones, they have started to deliver growth results accordingly. According to this view, experimentation was neither necessary nor beneficial since we know the right institutions, for which the 'innovations' created in the Chinese reforms are simply imperfect substitutes.

This argument is based on the assumption that there is no need for periods of institutional transition—indeed if standard market policies and institutions had been put in place right at the beginning of reforms, there would have been even more rapid growth. Economists of this inclination often argue that supporters of the gradualist approach to China's reforms have made economic virtues out of political necessities: gradualism was mainly due to lack of consensus, not out of choice, and as such was not even a conscious strategy; meanwhile, gradualism has been attempted several times in other transition countries, with failures each time (Sachs and Woo 2002; Sachs 1993).

Property Rights

One of the underlying conditions for growth in standard economic theory is the existence of well-defined private property rights, based upon which informed and rational actors—consumers and producers—make self-interested decisions on how to allocate the resources under their disposal, in accordance with their preferences.

For transition countries then, establishment of secure private property rights and privatization of publicly owned assets are among the most fundamental steps—along with macroeconomic stabilization and price liberalization—that must be taken early in the process.

Until quite recently, the Chinese economy has been a very long way from being based upon such property rights. From its starting point as a socialist economy with only public ownership, China has expanded the possibility and extent of private ownership only slowly, in an approach very different from that applied in most other transition economies. On the contentious issue of land, the government remains the only supplier, but competition can exist on the demand side when prices are set by bidding or auction, particularly for land taken for urban development. The fact that the Chinese reform process, especially in the earlier years, has assigned a relatively minor role to private property but generated such staggering growth, is directly contrary to the expectations of most orthodox economists.

Instead, the Chinese experience appears to suggest that parts of the economy under public ownership can perform very well given proper incentive structures, and that residual claimant rights and hard budget constraints can ensure a high level of economic efficiency even in the absence of formal property rights. The TVEs are the most obvious example of this, being far from private entities—essentially part of the local government, for which they became a potentially large source of revenue—but also existing outside the cushioned environment of the SOEs (Naughton 1994b). It does not, of course, necessarily imply that retaining a large SOE sector is a suitable strategy for the long run. Indeed, several authors argue that maintaining the SOEs in China has had a positive impact by stabilizing the economy, particularly the labour market, in the short and medium term (Naughton 1994a).

Market/Price Liberalization

A cornerstone of introducing markets in a socialist economy is the liberalization of prices—of goods as well as production factors—and the free access of producers and buyers alike to the market.

China did not undertake explicit pricing reform until relatively late and in a gradual fashion. After introduction of the market tracks in 1982, the last plan track—in the energy market—was removed only in 1993.[12] Many economists have criticized this in strong terms, arguing that freeing prices is fundamental to the proper functioning of the economy, that it must be done fully and immediately and that not doing so will hamper growth and most likely lead to the failure of reform efforts (Murphy et al. 1992).

Other observers have argued that China demonstrates that price reform can indeed be done gradually. By opening a market track alongside the planned one and permitting free entry by state and non-state actors alike to sell output under the market track—after quotas assigned under the plan had been fulfilled—reformers oversaw a gradual adjustment of prices. Over time, an ever larger share was produced under the market track, overall price levels converged and the planned track was eventually removed. The argument is made that since economic decisions are made at the margin, the existence of the market track can be quite sufficient to ensure efficiency—with the plan track viewed merely as a lump-sum tax (MacMillan and Naughton 1992).

The process of liberalization has, however, continued. By 2003, for instance, 87 per cent of all producer prices, 96 per cent of retail prices, and 87 per cent of all farm commodities

---

[12] To quote Naughton (2008: 118) 'the "dual-track" system was eliminated at a stroke when planned allocation of materials was abolished at the end of 1993'.

were market-determined. More than two-thirds of Chinese GDP now originates in the broadly defined private (non-state) sector, which predominates even more as a source of jobs (OECD 2009). Product and agricultural markets are now quite well-integrated, and past problems of local protectionism appear to be 'declining in importance' and capital mobility has improved over the reform period (OECD 2009). Wages for both formal and informal work are now mostly set by market forces.

Government still controls or influences the pricing of key production factors such as land and capital. Prices for key inputs such as land, electricity, and utilities, including water, are kept low through subsidies and controlled pricing. In many cases, land was provided at nominal prices. Electricity, for instance, was provided for FDIs at half the cost. Cheap finance, made possible by the growing savings rates over the reform period, underwrote the ambitions of many large companies and SOEs. Local governments, in particular, have played an active role in driving investment. Real estate investments have played and continue to play a critical role in the financing of local budgets (over which Beijing tends to have at times limited influence). Importantly, prices of labour, capital, and land all remain subject to the restrictions placed on mobility, and migration, in particular, is subject to the household registration system (hukou), which restricts rural migrants' access to education, medical, and other services in urban areas (Hope and Lau 2004).

★★★

Part of the insufficiency of the standard explanations of China's growth rests on the concepts embedded in neoclassical economic thinking. The most natural conclusion based on neoclassical explanations (or variations upon it) is that growth in China would take place only temporarily, after which numerous deficiencies would grind it to a halt. This was, indeed, the expectation of many or most observers during the early years of reform. Yet the reverse has turned out to be true. After three decades of reform, China is expanding faster than ever—achieving in 2006 its highest growth rate in 11 years, 10.7 per cent—to reach a nominal GDP level of $2.68 trillion.[13]

In addition, there is considerable disagreement as to the size of the effects in China of the standard neoclassical growth drivers. If 'advantages of backwardness' like a large rural sector, capital scarcity, and low level of technology were the decisive factors, why do we not see many more such successes? If factor reallocation gains were key, how do we explain the sustained momentum that China has displayed in its growth as well as in the reform process itself, given that such gains are by definition transitory? If factor allocation and agents' incentives remain inefficient, how can such high growth still be achieved over such a long period of time? Why were the early predictions of failure not fulfilled?

In trying to make sense of Chinese reforms, economists have come up with many different and innovative explanations. One of them is about economic coherence and the idea that Chinese reforms had an internal logic, that there was strong interaction among reforms that sustained the progress of individual reforms (Fan and Woo 2009). Reform bottlenecks occur if there is an 'incoherence' between different parts of the reforms. The authors contend that the two major bottlenecks that China now faces are financial reform and political reform. They point to the fact that non-state manufacturing industries contribute more than 70 per cent of output but use less than 30 per cent of financial resources. Using a general equilibrium model, and extending the notion of allocative efficiency to reforms, they highlight such inconsistencies, yet fail to address why 'China has grown so fast for so long'—the subject of this book.

The conclusion that appears more reasonable is that neoclassical models are simply inadequate in fully understanding the development process. Their scope is too narrow and, perhaps

---

[13] NBS as quoted in *China Daily*, 26 January 2007.

even more important, they do not raise the important questions. Production and development are not deterministically influenced by labour and human or physical capital alone, but are a result of factors more elusive and complex, with strong historical and geographical attributes. Similarly, the orthodoxy of sequencing and institutional setting posited by many economists as a basic prerequisite for growth comes strongly into question by the unrelenting expansion in China, where almost none of the regularly prescribed recipes for transition have been used.

A similar argument can be made about the coherence of reforms. Few people argue that China's leaders had a clear outline in mind for each of the many reform steps to be taken on their gradual path to reform. This does not, however, preclude either useful individual lessons or a coherent pattern from emerging out of the experimentalist approach they employed. That gradualism stemmed partly from political disagreement, as expounded by Sachs and Woo (2000) and others, is important but for other reasons than as a counterargument to what they call the Experimentalist School. Indeed, this is arguably the whole point of experimentalism: it is a method, not a textbook—thus the end results may inevitably differ considerably from any *ex ante* plans or presuppositions.

The global debate about the 'right' set of policies and the 'right' institutions, however, continues. Some economists have taken a new tack: China is seen as an outlier, as somehow its development path is unique and has few lessons for other developing countries. This book argues otherwise. All countries are unique in their sense of history and institutional context. Stiglitz (2006) captures it best in his book *Making Globalization Work* when he states 'there are no magic solutions or simple prescriptions. The history of development economics is marked by the quixotic quest to find the "answer", disappointment in the failure of one strategy leading to the hope that the next will work'. Learning from China's 30-year-long, consistently stellar performance has become increasingly attractive.

REFERENCES

Ahluwalia, M.S. and H. Chenery. 1974. 'A Model of Redistribution and Growth', in H. Chenery, M.S. Ahluwalia, C.L.G. Bell, J.H. Duloy, and R. Jolly (eds), *Redistribution with Growth: Policies to Improve Income Distribution in Developing Countries in the Context of Economic Growth*. London: Oxford University Press.

Ao, X. and L. Fulgitini. 2005. 'Productivity Growth in China—Evidence from Chinese Provinces', University of Nebraska-Lincoln, Mimeo.

Bigsten, A., J.H. Zheng, and A.G. Hu. 2006. 'Can China's Growth be Sustained? A Productivity Perspective', Working Papers in Economics 236, Göteborg University, Department of Economics.

Bigsten, A., J. Zheng, and X. Liu. 2003. 'Efficiency, Technical Progress, and Best Practice in Chinese State Enterprises (1980–1994)', *Journal of Comparative Economics*, 31(1): 134–52.

Bloom, D.E., D. Canning, L. Hu, Y. Liu, A. Mahal, and W. Yip. 2006. 'Why Has China's Economy Taken Off Faster than India's?', Paper presented at the Pan Asia 2006 Conference, Stanford Center for International Development, 3 June 2006.

Borensztein E. and J.D. Ostry. 1996. 'Accounting for China's Growth Performance', *American Economic Review*, 86(2): 224–8.

Bosworth, B. and S.M. Collins. 2006. *Accounting for Growth: Comparing China and India*. Washington DC: Brookings Institution.

Chen, P. 1993. 'China's Challenge to Economic Orthodoxy: Asian Reform as an Evolutionary, Self-organizing Process', *China Economic Review*, 4(2): 137–42.

Dekle, R. and G. Vandenbroucke. 2006. 'Wither Chinese Growth? A Sectoral Accounting Approach', Department of Economics, University of Southern California.

Dries, L. and J.F.M. Swinnen. 2002. 'Institutional Reform and Labor Reallocation during Transition: Theory Evidence from Polish Agriculture', *World Development*, 30(3): 457–74.

Easterly, W. and R. Levine. 2002. 'It's Not Factor Accumulation: Stylized Facts and Growth Models', Working Papers Central Bank of Chile 164, Central Bank of Chile.

Fan G. and W.T. Woo. 2009. 'The Parallel Partial Progression (PPP) Approach to Institutional Transformation in Transition Economies, Optimize Economic Coherence, Not Policy Sequence', *Modern China*, 35(4): 352–69.

Fan S. and X. Zhang. 2002. 'Production and Productivity Growth in Chinese Agriculture: New National and Regional Measures', *Economic Development and Cultural Change*, 50(4): 819–38.

Felipe, J. 1997. 'Total Factor Productivity Growth in East Asia: A Critical Survey', EDRC Report Series No. 65, Asian Development Bank.

Fishman, T. 2005. *China, Inc. How the Rise of the Next Superpower Challenges America and the World*. New York: Scribner.

Fleisher, B.M. and J. Chen, 1997. 'The Coast–Noncoast Income Gap, Productivity, and Regional Economic Policy in China', *Journal of Comparative Economics*, 25(2): 220–36.

Hale, G. and C. Long. 2007. 'Is There Evidence of FDI Spillovers on Chinese Firms' Productivity and Innovation?', Yale University Economic Growth Center Discussion Paper No. 934.

Holz, C.A. 2006a. 'New Capital Estimates for China', *China Economic Review*, 17(2): 142–85.

———. 2006b. 'Measuring Chinese Productivity Growth, 1952–2005', Mimeo, Social Science Division, Hong Kong University of Science and Technology.

Hope, N. and L.J. Lau. 2004. 'China's Transition to the Market: Status and Challenges', Stanford Center for International Development, Working Paper 210.

Hsieh, C.T. 1999. 'Productivity Growth and Factor Prices in East Asia', *American Economic Review*, 89(2): 133–8.

———. 2002. 'What Explains the Industrial Revolution in East Asia? Evidence from the Factor Markets', *American Economic Review*, 92(3): 502–26.

Hu, Z.L. and Mohsin S. Khan. 1997. 'Why is China Growing So Fast?', *Economic Issues 8*, International Monetary Fund.

International Monetary Fund (IMF). 2009. *World Economic Outlook Database*, April 2009.

Klenow, P.J. and A. Rodriguez-Clare. 1997. 'Economic Growth: A Review Essay, *Journal of Monetary Economics*, 40(3): 597–617.

Kynge, J. 2007. *China Shakes the World: A Titan's Rise and Troubled Future—and the Challenge for America*. Boston: Houghton Mifflin Company.

Lin, J.L. 2004. 'Lessons of China's Transition from a Planned Economy to a Market Economy', Development Economics Working Papers 446, East Asian Bureau of Economic Research.

Lin, J.Y., G. Wang, and Y. Zhao. 2004. 'Regional Inequality and Labor Transfers in China', *Economic Development and Cultural Change*, 52(3): 587–603.

MacMillan, J. and B. Naughton. 1992. 'How to Reform a Planned Economy: Lessons from China', *Oxford Review of Economic Policy*, 8(1): 130–43.

Ministry of Land and Resources of the PRC (2007). *Annual Statistics Bulletin*. Available at http://www.mlr.gov.cn/zwgk/tjxx/200912/t20091215_699754.htm.

Murphy, K.M., A. Schleifer, and R.W.Vishny. 1992. 'The Transition to a Market Economy: Pitfalls of Partial Reform', *The Quarterly Journal of Economics*, 107(3): 889–906.

National Bureau of Statistics of China. 2008. *China Statistical Yearbook 2008*. Beijing: China Statistical Press.

Naughton, B. 1994a. 'What is Distinctive about China's Economic Transition—State Enterprise Reform and Overall System Transformation', *Journal of Comparative Economics*, 18: 470–90.

———. 1994b. 'Chinese Institutional Innovation and Privatization from Below', *The American Economic Review*, 84(2): 266–70.

———. 1995. *Growing out of the Plan—Chinese Economic Reform 1978–1993*. Cambridge, UK: Cambridge University Press.

———. 2008. 'A Political Economy of China's Economic Transition', in L. Brandt and T.G. Rawski (eds), *China's Great Economic Transformation*, pp. 91–135. Cambridge, UK: Cambridge University Press.

Nyberg, A. and S. Rozelle. 1999. *Accelerating China's Rural Transformation*. Washington DC: The World Bank.

Organisation for Economic Co-operation and Development (OECD). 2009. *China: Defining the Boundary between the Market and the State*. Paris: OECD Publishing.

Prescott, E.C. 1997. 'Needed: A Theory of Total Factor Productivity', Research Department Staff Report 242, Federal Reserve Bank of Minneapolis.

Qian, Y., 1999. 'The Institutional Foundations of China's Market Transition', *Annual Bank Conference on Development Economics*, pp. 28–30.

Radelet, S., J. Sachs, and J.W. Lee. 1998. 'The Determinants and Prospects of Economic Growth in Asia', *International Economic Journal*, 15(3): 1–29.

Sachs, J. 1993. 'Can Communist Economies Transform Incrementally: The Experience of China—Comment', *NBER Macroeconomics Annual*, 8: 137–47.

———. 1997. 'Nature, Nurture and Growth', *The Economist*, 343(8021): 19.

Sachs, J.D. and W.T. Woo (eds). 1997. 'Chinese Economic Growth: Explanations and the Tasks Ahead', *China's Economic Future: Challenges to U.S. Policy*, pp. 70–85. Washington DC: Government Printing Office.

———. 2000. 'Understanding China's Economic Performance', *Journal of Economic Policy Reform*, 4(1): 1–50.

———. 2002. 'China's Economic Growth after WTO Membership', *Journal of Chinese Economic and Business Studies*, 1(1): 1–31.

Sachs, J., W.T. Woo, S. Fischer, and G. Hughes. 1994. 'Structural Factors in Economic Reforms in China, Eastern Europe and the Former Soviet Union', *Economic Policy*, 9(18): 101–45.

Stiglitz, J. 1999. 'Whither Reform? Ten Years after the Transition', in *World Bank Annual Bank Conference on Development Economics*. Washington DC: The World Bank.

————. 2001. An Agenda for Development for the Twenty-first Century', in *The Global Third Way Debate*, pp. 340–57. Cambridge: Polity Press.

————. 2006. *Making Globalization Work*. New York: W.W. Norton & Company.

United Nations Conference on Trade and Development (UNCTAD). 2004. 'South–South Investment Flows—A Potential for Developing Country Governments to Tap for Supply Capacity Building', Background Paper No. 3, Doha High-level Forum on Trade and Investment, 5–6 December 2004, Doha, Qatar.

————. 2010. Foreign Direct Investment Statistics from UNCTADstat. Available at http://unctadstat.unctad.org.

Wang, Y. and Y.D. Yao. 2001. 'Sources of China's Economic Growth, 1952–1999: Incorporating Human Capital Accumulation', World Bank Policy Research Working Paper No. 2650, World Bank.

Whalley, J. and X. Xin. 2006. 'China's FDI and Non-FDI Economies and the Sustainability of Future High Chinese Growth', NBER Working Paper 12249, National Bureau of Economic Research.

Whalley, J. and S. Zhang. 2007. 'A Numerical Simulation Analysis of (Hukou) Labour Mobility Restrictions in China', *Journal of Development Economics*, 83(2): 392–410.

Wolf, M. 2005. 'China has Further to Grow to Catch Up with the World', *Financial Times*, 12 April.

Woo, W.T. 1998. 'Chinese Economic Growth: Sources and Prospects', in M. Fouquin and F. Lemoine (eds), *The Chinese Economy*. London: Economica.

————. 1999. 'The Real Reasons for China's Growth', *The China Journal*, 41: 115–37.

————. 2001. 'Recent Claims of China's Economic Exceptionalism: Reflections Inspired by WTO Accession', Working Papers 01–3, Department of Economics, University of California at Davis.

Woo, W.T., H. Wen, Y.B. Jin, and G. Fan. 1994. 'How Successful has Chinese Enterprise Reform Been?', *Journal of Comparative Economics*, 18(3): 410–37.

Worden, Robert L., Andrea Matles Savada, and Ronald E. Dolan (eds). 1987. *China: A Country Study*. Washington DC: GPO for the Library of Congress.

Wu, X.D. 2001. 'Impact of FDI on Relative Return to Skill', *Economics of Transition*, 9(3): 695–715.

Xu, L.C. 1997. 'How China's Government and State Enterprises Partitioned Property and Control Rights', World Bank Policy Research Working Paper Series.

Yao, S.J. and K.L. Wei. 2006. 'Economic Growth in the Presence of FDI: The Perspective of Newly Industrialising Economies', *Journal of Comparative Economics*, 35(1): 211–34.

Young, A. 2000. 'The Razor's Edge—Distortions and Incremental Reform in the People's Republic of China', *The Quarterly Journal of Economics*, November, 115(4): 1091–135.

Zhang, X.B. and K.Y. Tan. 2007. 'Incremental Reform and Distortions in China's Product and Factor Markets', MPRA Paper 6804, University Library of Munich, Germany.

Zhang, Z. 2002. 'Productivity and Economic Growth: An Empirical Assessment of the Contribution of FDI to the Chinese Economy', *Journal of Economic Development*, 27(2): 81–94.

Zheng, J.H., A. Bigsten, and A.G. Hu. 2006. 'Can China's Growth be Sustained? A Productivity Perspective', Working Papers in Economics 236, Department of Economics, Göteborg University.

Zheng, J. and A. Hu. 2006. 'An Empirical Analysis of Provincial Productivity in China (1979–2001)', *Journal of Chinese Economic and Business Studies*, 4(3): 221–39.

4

Towards a Transformative Framework

In the previous chapter, I have tried to make the case that traditional explanations of China's rapid progress are either incomplete or misleading. This chapter seeks to dig deeper into what constitutes the concept of 'development as transformation', and to lay out a framework which can be helpful in understanding China's performance.

With rapid change and transformation, the basic production conditions are themselves in play. Indeed, this is the very nature of development. It is difficult to think of fixed production functions, or assume that relationships between factors of production are stable and unchanging. This chapter then is about the evolving nature of production itself. It refers as much to the function itself [the f in the $y=f(k,l)$], as to the elements (or factors) inside the production function. At different points of history, the nature, and shape of the production function are likely to be quite different.

Development and change are almost interchangeable concepts. Development is far from the search for equilibrium that underlines economic theory as taught in most universities. Stiglitz (1996) likens this search for equilibrium to a misleading metaphor that provides little help in comprehending the wrenching change going on in developing countries. In some ways it requires a conscious effort to 'unlearn' some of the basic assumptions and concepts acquired from a study of conventional economics, which draws upon, to a large extent, the precepts of neoclassical thinking.

To understand development as transformation, the analysis has to be necessarily extended to include what may be called complex and 'soft' factors such as leadership and vision, norms and values, rules and institutions, trust and cohesion, all that influence the organization of society, and their interplay with specific policies and reforms. And, crucially, how the processes of transformation can come together under the right conditions to generate and sustain development. And once transformation becomes the focus, a long-term perspective to development becomes necessary.

Despite its well documented limitations, neoclassical thinking has had a dominant influence on development economics and regrettably on development policies. It has led to an unfortunate simplification of the complex processes at work as countries grow and develop. Further, they have contributed to a premise that development is intrinsically a technical problem requiring technical solutions—such as increasing the capital stock, better resource allocation, and preventing market failure (Stiglitz 1998).

It was not always so. From Adam Smith down, classical economists were deeply concerned with understanding the forces at play in defining economic and social progress of nations. Other more radical thinkers sought to build on Marxian thought by linking roles of capital and labour to historical processes of change and modes of production. Their analytical framework inevitably led them to focus on the relationships between society and production systems.

Equally contemporary economists are now re-examining some of their basic assumptions. Faced with the success of the development trajectories of countries like China, South Korea, and others, and a growing consensus that many of the standard policy prescriptions were just not working, there is now growing interest in pursuing broader analyses of development differences. Joseph Stiglitz, the 2001 Nobel Laureate, has been particularly vocal about promoting the notion of 'development as transformation' and in his rejection of the policies of the Washington Consensus. Despite this, the stylized growth models by Solow, and by Harrod–Domar, remain influential, perhaps even dominant in the current literature on development analysis.

During the 1950s and 1960s, in the immediate post-colonial period, as newly independent countries began their development journey, there was a sense that most countries would follow a similar pattern, the less developed being at an earlier stage of growth, with a gradual convergence of their living standards to those obtaining in the developed economies. Rostow (1960), a leading exponent of this perspective, nonetheless had an important insight that the relationship between different forces of change may well vary at different development stages. Other thinkers like Gunnar Myrdal and Arthur Lewis took on a broader, more political economy approach to the analysis of differences of growth among developing countries, even if translating such analysis into development policy remained challenging. Lewis (1955), for instance, acknowledged that 'the difficulty that education raises is that it is both a consumer and an investment service'.

Contemporary economists like Rodrik (2003) do not consider any contradiction in taking on a broader perspective to development and neoclassical analysis. The latter in Rodrik's view is sufficiently flexible to incorporate broader considerations like institutions and context specific conditions in the analysis of growth differences among countries. A distinction is drawn between neoclassical tools and their more 'vulgar' application in specific policies, and most notably as part of the Bretton Woods supported adjustment programmes of the 1980s and 1990s. In his view, core economic principles such as property rights and contract enforcement, may not map into unique policy packages. Different approaches may work in different contexts,

China being a good example of that. Still, good institutions are those which deliver these core economic principles effectively. In particular, he and others have advanced the useful idea that growth promoting policies tend to be context specific, adding a cautionary note that development lessons may not travel well or easily between countries or situations.

Justin Lin and Celestin Monga (2010) take a step forward in extending neoclassical analysis by presenting a framework to complement previous approaches in the search of sustainable growth strategies. This framework accepts that an economy's structure of factor endowments evolves over one stage of development to another. It presents the idea of infrastructure (both soft institutions and hard roads) as an additional factor of production, and accepts the important role of industrial policy and the state in promoting development. With markets as the basic mechanism for effective resource allocation, Justin terms this approach as 'New Structural Economics'.

Still others have attempted to look deeper into the significance of non-economic forces in development such as geography and climate. Hausmann (2001) argues for instance that development outcomes are significantly shaped by geography, as most poor countries happen to be either landlocked or located in the tropics, or both, a conclusion that does not fully explain historic shifts in the development ranking of countries. Some have singled out air conditioning as one factor in enabling countries along the equator to develop over the recent decades (Sachs 1997).

The question remains as to what works and what does not, as policymakers struggle with new policies and new ideas to promote development. Perhaps there is not an either or perspective here. What these studies increasingly have in common is their willingness to move away from simple explanations of growth differences. They reinforce the importance of understanding the context and initial conditions of growth, the role of institutions, and the need to understand better the broader societal forces that policies and development strategies have to be mindful of in order to influence development outcomes.

THE 'DRIVERS' OF TRANSFORMATION

Successful development transformation must come from within the country itself, (which) must have institutions and leadership to catalyse, absorb and manage the process of change, and the changed society.
                                   —Joseph Stiglitz, 1998 Prebisch Lecture

In this chapter, drawing upon some earlier work (Malik 2002), it is argued that there are three essential forces that taken together shape transformation and development: Ownership, Capacities, and Policies.

National Ownership (and Leadership)

There is a growing body of work highlighting the importance of ownership for development results (UNDP 2003). While ownership is intrinsically an elusive concept, some key dimensions can be highlighted. This book defines ownership as the independence and self-sufficiency of actors to make plans and decisions as well as the buy-in at lower levels of plans and decisions taken at higher levels.

Leadership, a related concept, is fundamentally an exercise of will by specific actor(s) and the ability to bring along others towards a specific objective. Visionary leadership in the development context is about the ability of an individual or a group to understand the imperatives of a nation and its future and forge a constituency in favour of change and progress.

In the development field, one clear dimension of ownership is that of a country's independence from undue outside influence in the processes of policymaking and implementation.

Examples of weak ownership that come to mind include developing nations especially those in Africa in the 1980s subjected to the aid conditionalities of structural adjustment programmes mandated by international financial institutions (IFIs) based on Western experience, priorities, and interpretations. The blame for the failure of these programmes has often been placed on the lack of regard for or understanding of the local context that characterized the policy recommendations given by the outside advisors upon which loans were conditional. Local governments who were more aware of the local situation, however, were in a weak bargaining position and had much to lose from not receiving the promised funds. Mkandiwire (Malik 2002) highlights with an anonymous quote some of the contextual differences when local elites are confronted with such challenges, 'when donors take the driver's seat, Africans move to the back seat. When donors try to do the same in Vietnam, Vietnamese get out of the car.' More generally, as Stiglitz notes in his Prebisch Lecture (1998) 'this much seems clear: effective change cannot be imposed from the outside. Rather than encouraging recipients to develop their analytical capacities, the process of imposing conditionalities undermines both the incentives to acquire those capacities and recipients' confidence in their ability to use them'.

Another dimension is internal to the country itself and refers to the subsidiarity of decision-making and the level of buy-in at lower government levels of plans and policies handed down from higher levels. A third dimension has to do with the participation, agreement, and buy-in of individuals in the development process and related government policy initiatives.[1]

National ownership does not require full consensus within a country. It means that the government can mobilize and sustain sufficient political support to adopt and implement the desired programmes and policies even in the presence of some opposition. For example, major policy changes require strong political support at the national level. A relatively small-scale programme may require only local-level community support. In deciding upon

---

[1] A different dimension refers to what can be described by ownership at the community or recipient level. This is the context of 'development in action'. It focuses on the role of the people, especially the poor in the concept and process of ownership. This context has become even more prominent of late with results-based development work and the concept of democratic ownership and accountable governance. There is considerable scope for further normative work in defining useful ways of how ownership can be built, as well as identifying entry points for effective citizen intervention and areas for donor response.

and designing support for programmes and policies, external partners need to assess the extent of ownership at the appropriate level.

Development is a complex and multifaceted process that operates and can be understood in different contexts and dimensions in each country. At the macro level, the exercise of independent political will, leadership, and capacity as prerequisites of national ownership are better understood in the context of the evolution of a country's political governance and international relations, its post-colonial circumstances, and the geopolitical influences that shape how a government relates to its foreign development partners (Thalayasingam 2007).

Market liberalization and aid have tended to go together. Aid has often been perceived by recipient countries as being closely connected to the foreign policy interests of donor countries. As such relations between donor and partner country have had profound implications for the content of policies of aid-dependent developing countries (ibid.).

Promoting ownership is therefore linked to the imperative of preserving policy space. The experience in Sri Lanka in the 1970s is interesting as it tried to balance development partners from the two competing Cold War blocs. Thalayasingam (2007) concludes that the emergence of new bilateral donors, such as China and India as well as large private foundations like the Gates Foundation, may well allow for greater policy flexibility in the future.

Johnson and Wasty (1993) identify four sets of ownership indicators: the locus of initiative; the level of intellectual conviction among key policymakers in the partner country; the expression of will by top leadership; and efforts towards consensus building among various constituencies (Johnson and Wasty 1993). Examining the relationship between ownership and results of 99 structural adjustment loans in 42 countries, Johnson and Wasty find that there exists a positive correlation between partner country ownership and the results of the development activities funded. In 73 per cent of the cases examined, borrower ownership was strongly predictive of the programme success (ibid.). Interestingly enough, four factors were highlighted as having limited or no significance: the nature of the political regime; the intensity of external or exogenous shocks; initial conditions or structural weaknesses in the economy; and the frequency and amount of government–bank interaction.

In another study by the World Bank, Baser and Morgan (1996) examine the effects of ownership and partner country commitment on the outcome of 20 technical assistance loans. These authors also determine that there is a strongly positive link between project performance and partner country ownership and cite borrower commitment to the design and plan of implementation as the critical determinant of good performance. The converse was also deemed to be true: that the absence of borrower commitment essentially guaranteed the loan's ineffectiveness. Most of the loans that were not regarded as satisfactory were supply driven by the Bank and lacked borrower initiative, whereas demand driven loans have proved to be sustainable or have helped develop national capacities (World Bank 1995, 1996, 1997).

Leadership (and Elites)

That leadership matters may appear an obvious statement but economists have not spent much time looking at it, let alone integrating it into an overall framework of developmental analysis. As Rodrik (2007a) put it 'economists don't even have the language to talk about how or why leadership matters in economics—even though I guess that deep down most of them think it is very important'.[2]

Young (1991) describes leadership as a deliberative process of setting agendas, finding innovative solutions to problems, and driving ideas 'that shape the intellectual capital available to those

---

[2] 'Leadership in Economics', from Dani Rodrik's weblog. Available at http://rodrik.typepad.com.

engaged in institutional bargaining'. Effective leaders shape societal preferences and influence 'negotiation procedures' among groups in ways that bring people closer to leaders' own preferred position (Tallberg 2006). There is a moral dimension involved as well. The Chinese perspective on leadership is profoundly influenced by Confucianism. Leadership in the Chinese view is not about manipulating others to achieve something, but rather is about developing others for the common good. It emphasizes the notion of self-cultivation and concern for human relationships. Confucian texts go into some detail on the essential qualities of a leader like impartiality, truthfulness, and concern for others (See 2008).

Economists take the concept a step forward by accepting that leadership represents 'symbolic' capital, including charisma that reflect respect, social prestige, and moral authority. This symbolic capital is closely connected to the concept of 'social capital', specifically in relation to issues of trust and social networks. Leaders do not function in a vacuum. Their ability to influence is dependent on a range of factors. Apart from personal aptitude in media and trans-cultural skills, for leaders to be effective, they require an ability to successfully mobilize pre-existing organizations at opportune political moments and third party support, which in turn necessitates flexibility in adapting themselves to the preferences of powerful potential supporters (Nepstad and Bob 2006).

Empirical work by Jones and Olken (2005) links shifts in growth performance in countries to changes in the national leaders. They find that exogenous leadership transitions (induced by the natural death of existing leaders) generate observable effects on policy and growth. A more theoretical paper by Majumdar and Mukand (2008) goes further and contends that individual leaders can be central to the transformation of organizations, political institutions, and many instances of social and economic reform. Importantly they conclude that 'while underlying structural conditions and institutions are important, there is an independent first-order role for individual agency in bringing about change and thus transforming the institutions'. Like the dynamic between economic groups and the state, there is a two-way interaction between leaders and followers that can endogenously give rise to visible threshold effects. Even slight differences in the leader's ability or the underlying structural conditions can dramatically improve the prospects for successful change. Thus by virtue of having followers, both 'good' and 'bad' leaders may be effective at bringing about change. It also provides an understanding as to how and why 'bad' leaders can stay on in power for long periods.

At the economy-wide level, leadership requires that the leader, or more broadly, ruling elites, seize an appropriate 'window of opportunity' to persuade firms, unions, workers, and other groups to invest in the reform. Examples of the initiation of reform include Bill Clinton who showed his leadership in persuading various interest groups in the US to sign onto North American Free Trade Agreement (NAFTA). In each of these instances, the set of firms, workers, and other groups who are well positioned for change and global integration may constitute the set of committed followers. If circumstances look propitious and support for reform is large enough, then enough fence-sitters (the 'non-followers' in Majumdar and Mukand's model) may also join the process of reform. Presented in this way, Deng Xiaoping's Southern Tour can be seen as playing a pivotal role in convincing a broad range of interests in the value of economic reform in China. Reinforcing this point, in a study of major reforms in 13 countries, Williamson (1994) found that a visionary leader played a key role in 9 of the 10 successful reforms.

Capacities

The literature on the notion of capacities and capacity development is vast. Much of it is about the needs and purposes of organizations—the ability of institutions to solve a specific development aim or supply a specific service (UNDP 1995).

It is task-driven and mission-oriented, referring to the capacity to perform certain functions. The limitations of these definitions are equally well-documented (Malik 2002). The value of 'capacities' is best ascribed in its relation to development, which in turn begs for a broader understanding of the macro relationship between capacities and development.

This book takes a view of capacity as the sustained ability of individuals, constituencies, institutions, and societies to identify their development needs, set objectives, and design and implement policies and strategies to achieve them. This relatively broad perspective raises the issue of the *acquisition* of capacities and their effective *application* to advance growth and development.

Capacity complements and interacts with the concept of ownership discussed above. A country, constituency, or individual with higher capacity have better preconditions for taking ownership of processes which concern them. Conversely, particularly valid in the aid context, the weakest ownership tends to be exhibited by poor countries that have weak systems of governance and lack the capacities to identify and address their development problems.

In China, the strong capacity of the central government as well as its implementing bureaucracy has arguably been an important factor in fostering the strong intellectual and practical self-sufficiency that the country has displayed throughout the reform period.

This concept of capacity can be broken into three essential, connected parts: *human capabilities, state and institutions,* and *social capital.*

Human Capabilities

Amartya Sen, the 1998 Nobel Prize laureate, laid the groundwork for a profound rethinking of the notion of development and progress of nations. He posited the concept of 'capabilities' that people end up having. In his view the poor are poor because their set of capabilities is small—not because of what they do not have — but because of what they cannot do. It refers to the ability of individuals to secure a healthy and productive life, of being a full active part of a community, of being able move around freely (Emmerij et al. 2005). Progress then, is about expanding the possibilities of not only what people have, but also about doing more of what they would like to do. It expanded the idea of progress far beyond the neoclassical terms of utility and income.

As Sen states (in Emmerij et al. 2005), 'ultimately the focus is on the expansion of human freedom to live the lives people have reason to value'. Sen's pioneering work on capabilities and Mahbub ul Haq's leadership at UNDP led to the launch in 1990, of the Human Development Reports. Human development was defined as the search for the expansion of choices, from incomes, to education, to being able to live in a secure neighbourhood, and so on. And the Human Development Index was introduced as a way of measuring such progress.

The measure then of progress becomes not one exclusively of raising incomes, but importantly, 'the people's capabilities to lead the lives they value. Nor should commodities be value in their own right—they should instead be seen as ways of enhancing such capabilities as health, knowledge, self-respect and the ability to participate in community life' (UNDP 1996).

The aim of human development (and development policy) becomes one of developing and using all human capabilities. 'Capabilities are not only qualities in themselves (which have the potential to be expanded and improved), but also tools to be used for the individual possessing those capabilities and the larger society' (UNDP 1990). But developing these capabilities are not enough, they have to be used as well.

Equity and freedom of choice are the underlying threads in these concepts. Both have a direct bearing on development. Addressing social and economic inequalities can be as vital for growth as level of investments. The link between human development and economic growth has by now been well established empirically, both at the specific and general levels. More years of education, improved health, and higher nutrition levels are correlated with increases in the earnings and productivity of individuals and groups (Ranis et al. 2000).

Human development then is not just the 'end product of growth but is an input as well and a key ingredient in the development process' (Boozer et al. 2003). There are threshold effects as well. For instance, the return from literacy may exhibit threshold effects that are dependent on the proportion of the population that is literate (ibid.). Studies have established clear linkages between overall human development levels and aggregate economic growth in large cross-country data sets (Stewart and Ranis use around 70 countries).[3] The reverse may not be true however. As the UNDP Human Development Reports (HDRs) have amply documented, high income levels may not automatically translate into a high level of human development. The relationship is complex and worthy of careful reflection, especially when designing policies and in setting broad strategic aims for development.

In an important paper Ranis et al. (2000) examine the cross country evidence of the two-way relationship between economic growth (EG) and human development (HD), the latter measured in this case more narrowly in terms of health and education expenditures. Their paper contends that there is a two way link between EG and HD, with public expenditures on health and education, notably female, especially important in the link from economic growth to human development, and the investment rate and income distribution significant in the HD to EG chain. They point to some of the complex sequencing implications that are involved in this two-way relationship. They found, for instance, that 'countries initially favoring economic growth (may) lapse into the vicious category, while those with good HD and poor EG sometimes move into the virtuous category'.

EG to HD: The potency of investments in health and education in their contribution to economic growth is well documented. Increasing incomes for the poor generally lead to an

---

[3] See, for instance, Ranis and Stewart (2007: 32) or Boozer et al. (2003).

increase in food expenditures and calorie consumption. There are equally important studies that point to the positive effects of family income change on schooling for children. A country's stage of development may in turn determine the return on public investments. In the early stages of development, for instance, basic education may have a larger impact on HD than tertiary education.

HD to EG: 'Higher levels of HD, in addition to being ends in themselves, affect the economy through enhancing people's capabilities and consequently their creativity and productivity' (ibid.). There is ample evidence to suggest that as people get healthier and better educated they have stronger capabilities to contribute more to economic growth. That these links are not automatic is equally well-documented. More skills investments may not lead to jobs without a growing economy and the creation of opportunities. At the micro level, investments in both health and education have systematically, across country and time periods, produced high returns. At the macro level, 'virtuous' cycles can be identified where a 'mutually reinforcing upward spiral with high levels of HD leading to high growth and high growth in turn leading to promoting HD'.

Policies have to pay special attention to ensuring strong linkages between EG and HD (and vice versa). If social expenditures are low even when there is good economic growth, the linkages between EG and HD will, in time, have a knock-down effect on growth rates. In reviewing the evidence for 13 countries and looking at the movements of these countries over three decades (1960–70, 1970–80, 1980–92), the authors find a virtuous relationship between HD and EG (and vice versa) for most of the East Asian countries, and a vicious, cyclical link for countries in Sub-Saharan Africa. That countries may move from one group to the other underscores the importance of the policy context. The positive policies highlighted by their study cover: shift in resource allocation to social services, promoting greater equity, and creating opportunities for the unemployed. A final conclusion of the study which has particular resonance for China is the need for HD to be strengthened *before* a virtuous cycle can be attained. In short, an exclusive focus on economic growth is unlikely to be sustained, and high levels of HD may be needed to kick-start growth.

States and Institutions

Role of the States and Governments   That governments are important in shaping development outcomes appears as a self-evident fact. But what role should they play?

The success of unorthodox development strategies in East Asian countries, and the active role of government in driving these strategies gave rise to debates among economists about the 'development state', which refers to an 'activist' government and a political elite that sees rapid economic development as their primary aim. Some go further and add an additional feature, a state which gives power and authority to the bureaucracy to plan and implement development policies. High rates of growth and the improvement of living standards in turn provides the state apparatus and the ruling elites their legitimacy (Abe 2006). The development state explicitly recognizes that markets by themselves are not sufficient to produce rapid economic progress. Property rights may or may not play a critical role in this thinking given for instance the disparate development paths taken by South Korea, China, and Japan. Originally outlined to describe the South Korean development experience, it evolved into a concept to capture the role of government and state elites in driving development strategies which could not be easily explained from a neoclassical perspective. There has been an unfortunate tendency by observers to lump such strategies with dictatorships, and free markets with democracy, implying that rapid progress cannot be easily achieved in democracies. There is a need to distinguish authoritarian states from development states. Not all authoritarian regimes are developmental. Equally it does not imply that states have to be authoritarian in order to be developmental. Examples like Brazil, India, and South Africa, as well as Mauritius and Botswana provide ample attestation that democratization and developmental orientation of states can occur simultaneously (Fritz and Menocal 2007).

For our purpose, we are defining developmental states as those states who explicitly accept that markets are insufficient in the drive to modernize and transform their countries, and that 'active' policies are needed to build institutions, and develop their economies and societies. Defined in this way, a strong state becomes arguably a necessary condition for development, and the analysis of state an important topic to cover when assessing development conditions or progress.

Whether governments are on balance a positive or negative force for development depends on the 'orientations' they pursue and relationships they seek to foster with society? How bureaucrats and society interact can be described as: (i) 'a grabbing hand', a model where the government is interventionist but not helpful. In this case, there are a large number if bureaucrats pursuing their own agendas, including pursuing corruptive practices; or (ii) 'a helping hand', where the government and bureaucrats are committed to promoting the positive action of society and promoting a unified development purpose. Several authors present a third category, as the 'invisible hand' model where the 'government is non-interventionist but well organised, generally not corrupt and relatively benevolent' (Frye and Shleifer 1997). Presented as 'ideal types' the authors recognize that in reality all governments are a mix of all three. The description of the last category however implicitly indicates a value-preference of the authors in favour of private enterprise and markets (Table 4.1).

As governments function in a specific societal context, the nature of their interactions with economic groups can be significant in shaping development outcomes. In assessing comparable reform packages introduced in Poland and Russia, Frye and Shleifer (1997) argue that a key reason for the markedly different development outcomes is the very different relationships

Table 4.1 Economic Role of the State

	Legal Environment	**Regulatory Framework**
Invisible hand	Government is not above law and uses power to supply minimal public goods. Courts enforce contracts.	Government follows rules. Regulation is minimal. Little corruption.
Helping hand	Government is above law, but uses power to help business. State officials enforce contracts.	Government aggressively regulates to promote some businesses. Organized corruption.
Grabbing hand	Government is above law and uses power to extract rents. The legal system does not work. Mafia replaces state as enforcer.	Predatory regulations. Disorganized corruption.

Source: Frye and Shleifer (1997).

between government and business (society) in the two countries. By reviewing evidence from Moscow and Warsaw shops on their dealings with bureaucrats involved with legal and regulatory matters, the authors consider that the 'invisible hand' model is a better fit in describing Poland (a good outcome), and the 'grabbing hand' model to Russia (a less good outcome). Polish local authorities were more helpful to entrepreneurs and business generally.

A larger, transformative role for governments however is not without precedent. In the early stages of development, governments of the more advanced economies did play key roles in laying the conditions for later economic and social progress, be it in Japan after the Meiji Restoration of 1868, or in post-war Germany. For instance, the German government played an active role in coordinating decisions about investments in heavy industry, which stands in contrast to the more spontaneous growth of industry in the United Kingdom. Kornai (1992) goes further to argue that it is only when fundamental policies were flawed or institutions ill-equipped that even a proactive role of the state produced little result, as in the communist bloc. The context and sequencing of transformative development policies become important in determining the speed and efficacy of the development path.

Narayan and Woolcock (2000) go a step further and contend that states can more directly invest in the organizational capacities of the poor and help them build bridges with other social groups, as social networks are a primary resource for the poor to manage risk and vulnerability. They add that states can help link 'structural' social capital (institutions) with 'cognitive' social capital norms (norms and values). Social policies can encourage child care systems so that women are not unduly burdened and the rise of social enterprises point out the new links that can be created between markets and people. It merits a mention that states can be predatory as well, and actively disrupt these networks in order to minimize perceived threats to power and privilege.

Institutions

I wish to assert a much more fundamental role for institutions in societies; they are the underlying determinant of the long-run performance of economies.

—North 1990

The state sets the formal rules of society including rules that govern economic activity, establishes the rule of law, and creates conditions for peace and security. Institutions are the instruments of the state in defining and conducting these rules. North (1981) provides a broader, perhaps more libertarian, definition of institutions as 'a set of rules, compliance procedures, and moral and ethical behavioural norms designed to constrain the behaviour of individuals in the interests of maximizing the wealth or utility of principals'.

With economic progress, rules get more sophisticated. As the production process gets more complex and more specialized, an 'effective' demand is in effect created for a greater formalization of political, judicial, and economic rules. Poorly functioning rules (institutions) can reduce economic activity, reduce trust in government, and create conditions that slow collective decision-making. Poorly defined rules increase 'transaction' and 'information' costs, leading to ineffective allocative signals and reducing efficiency.

Most economists are confident that acquisition of high-quality institutions is an essential part of the arsenal of measures needed to accelerate growth in developing countries. Growth can be jump-started by a variety of ways, including pumping in more investment, but sustaining it requires robust, effective institutions which can ensure that and help protect the economy from shocks.

Whereas the above is generally accepted, the proposition that property rights are an essential part of rule setting is more controversial. Property rights in conventional economics are seen as essential to long-term contracts, which in turn is considered an essential building block for capital markets and economic growth. Yet, much of the empirical research on national institutions has tended to focus on property rights and the rule of law.

But what comes first: 'good' institutions or 'good' growth? While comparing, for instance, the development trajectories of North Korea and South Korea over the past 60 years, it is a fair comment that while 'South Korea obviously has better institutions as measured by constraints on the executive, these institutions are the outcome of economic growth after 1950 rather than its cause. It would be wrong to attribute South Korea's growth to these institutions rather than the choices made by its dictators' (Glaser et al. 2004).

North (1990) contends that weak institutions may have a direct effect on growth because they reduce the efficiency of investment. The quality of institutions can substantially influence the level of development, though causality may not be entirely one way, as it is possible to consider the proposition that a higher level of development can 'demand' better institutions in order for it to be sustained.

Figure 4.1 presents the impact of policies, government consumption, and the quality of its institutions on income growth over three decades across 94 developed and developing countries. Other things being equal, in countries with weak institutions and poor policies, per capita income grew only 0.4 per cent annually. In contrast, in countries with strong institutions and good policies, per capita income grew at average of 3 per cent annually.

'Better performing institutions may improve growth by increasing the volume of investment—for instance by eliminating bureaucratic red tape and rent-seeking costs—and (more weakly) by improving the efficiency of investment, say, by enforcing well-defined property rights' (Aron 2000). Empirical evidence of the link between institutions and growth is less clear cut, in part due

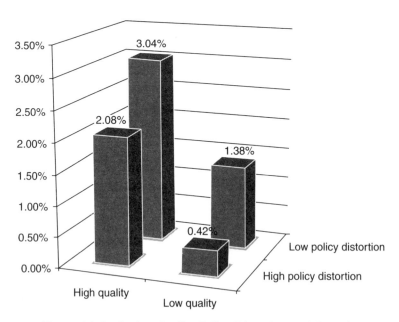

Figure 4.1 Institution Quality, Policy Distortion, and Growth
Source: Chhibber (2000).

to the inherent problems of data and the stylized nature of the models being considered. The variables about institutions that seem to have some predictive power on investment and growth are measures that capture performance or quality of institutions such respect for contracts, property rights, and civil freedom. There is some evidence that the quality of institutions has a significant indirect influence on growth, through its influence on the volume of investment, and more weakly by improving the efficiency of investment by, for example, enforcing well-defined property rights. There is evidence, though weak, for a direct link between institutions and growth (ibid.).

Rodrik (2003) also raises an important point on institutional non-convergence. The internal dynamics within different societies are likely to produce different institutional choices. This he considers is the result of different social preferences and the trade-off between equity and opportunity. North (1994) as well accepts that 'transferring the formal political and economic rules of successful Western economies to third-world or Eastern European economies is not a sufficient condition of good economic performance'. Indeed the experience of China and rapidly growing ASEAN countries seem to indicate that home-grown institutions are likely to be far more enduring.

The strong development results demonstrated by 'authoritarian states' such as South Korea, China, and Taiwan raise a difficult conundrum for contemporary economists. How to explain their success by using traditional models? Barro (1996) in fact finds that after a certain threshold, extension of political rights (one of the measures of efficiency) could slow down growth. He reached an interesting conclusion, that it may not be desirable to 'export' democratic institutions to developing countries. As always there are alternative explanations. Perhaps one explanation might be that higher standards of living foster greater demand and accountability to ensure that the benefits of growth are being equitably shared, which in turn may slow down growth as society adjusts to different expectations. Whatever the reasons, it is fair to state that in a dynamic development context, there is some value in matching the state's role to its capabilities, and that this dynamism itself requires constant adjustment of institutions so their impact on development progress can be sustained.

One can go further and argue that if development is about transformation, then the state itself has to take on an integrated and active approach to the development of institutions relevant to such transformation, including the market. Much of the economic literature on institutions however is about the relationship between institutions and markets, about how institutions enable, or regulate markets, as opposed to developing or transforming markets themselves.[4]

Social Capital

Social capital is fundamentally about relationships. Individuals gather in groups and communities, they both influence and are defined by them. Groups can serve a positive purpose or pursue those with nefarious intent. Woolcock (2000) defines it as 'norms and networks that facilitate collective action', highlighting the need to distinguish between its 'sources' and its 'consequences'. By this definition, trust would not be part of social capital, since it is an outcome, not a source of social relations that foster repeated interactions. Social capital is linked to the idea of civic virtue, which is most powerful when embedded in a dense network of reciprocal social relations. When networks of civic engagement are dense, reciprocity and trust are fostered, 'lubricating social life' (Putnam 1993).[5]

At its broadest point definitions of social capital include the government and its institutions. This book takes a more restrictive approach. There are of course, similarities, as Government

---

[4] See Pandey in Malik and Waglé (2002).

[5] The concept of social capital arose from its character of civic engagement; its first use is attributed to Lyda J. Hamilton who, as a Superintendent of schools in West Virginia in 1916, highlighted the importance of community involvement in the success of schools.

can be seen as a hierarchical non-market organization with its own internal set of rules. However, given its dominant role, its ability to influence social relations and overall development, it makes more sense to keep the social capital definitions mostly connected to notions of civil society (Collier 1998).

Is social (and organizational capacity) important or relevant to development as a concept? Woolcock (1998) illustrates its value by comparing two different experiences:

> It is only a four-hour flight between Madras and Singapore, but the difference between the conditions surrounding one's departure from the former and arrival at the latter can make the distance seem more like four centuries. The contrasts most striking to the visitor are organizational. Simple routines familiar to western travellers ... forming orderly queues to check luggage ... are all apparently alien practices in South India. Singapore on the other hand basks ... in prestigious international awards for its meticulously clean and efficient airport.

Is there an observable link between state institutions and social capital? Can public policies deepen social capital? The concept of social capital, as has been pointed out by many economists, is not only difficult to define, but also difficult to quantify and perhaps difficult to influence (Waglé 2001).

Social capital can also be viewed as 'embedded' and comprised of autonomous social relations. Polanyi (1957) and others present development as a process whereby the economy gets differentiated or moves away from ad hoc or arbitrary rules governing social relations. In the move from a pre-industrial to a modern industrial state, according to this perspective, it is worthwhile to examine the shift in the nature of the 'embeddedness' of social relations. Social ties, cultural practices, and political contexts, all have a powerful effect on shaping development opportunities and the constraints that individuals face in their efforts to advance economically.

While definitional challenges remain formidable, it is equally difficult for us to ignore its validity in the understanding of development and in the design of public policies. It points us to how and under what terms and conditions we relate to each other. Drawing upon Woolcock (2000) and Stewart (2000) several aspects can be highlighted.

First, a low stock of 'bridging' social capital among different groups reduces information flow and resource transfer. If discriminatory practices along gender, caste, and ethnic lines are allowed to persist, this makes development more difficult.

Second, as has been particularly observed in crisis situations, the absence of such capital is visible in reduced trust and confidence (and social cohesion). Edwards (2000) paraphrases Ramon Daubon in likening social capital to the Indian Ocean: 'Everyone knows where it is, no one cares where it begins or where it ends, but we know we have to cross it to get from India to Africa. Specific policies are then required then to the building back of such capital'. Repairing institutions alone without a similar effort to rebuild social capital is unlikely to be long lasting. 'Good' policies are insufficient if different groups in society are not appropriately represented in their conduct as well.

Third, institutions affect how communities draw upon social capital to manage risks and opportunities. In countries where states are weak and the norm includes rampant corruption, and rights are suppressed, institutions may not be able to fully demonstrate their effectiveness in showcasing development, through schools, roads, and hospitals.

The larger normative implications of social capital have been belittled by development practitioners for the obvious reasons that it is hard to engineer trust, tolerance, and social cohesion (Edwards 2000). The term is also considered too broad. It lends itself to being interpreted in contradictory ways to justify public policy prescriptions (Woolcock 2000). Solow (2000) as a theorist goes further and questions whether social capital can even be usefully compared to capital (which is a product of past investments) and the feasibility of actually measuring such 'capital'.

In some ways, social capital (and more broadly the notion of capacities) may be usefully viewed as influencing the nature and shape of the production function, rather than being treated on par with other factors or production like capital or labour. Dasgupta (2000) refers to it as a shift in the production function, affecting, positively or negatively, the outcome of the mixing of different factors of production. It might be possible to go a step further and argue that a positive, durable form of social capital may even determine the sustainability of the production function itself. If trust breaks down, groups may find it difficult to interact effectively in the production process, an extreme example of which is civil strife.

Without adding to the controversy, the interest here is to use terms like social capital to understand better how society organises itself, how development takes place, and what are those critical capacities essential to the transformation process.

Social capital complements traditional economic theory which starts with the individual and aggregates up to the economy. Traditional public policy prescriptions are based on how individual behave, how they save or invest. When the individual's behaviour is a function of change, that is, when 'I' becomes an endogenous variable, the analysis forces us to look at broader societal issues. In particular this requires us to examine the notion of social norms and how change influences behaviour. Individual behaviour is the product of social interactions and the point in history at which societies find themselves.

Development tends to get focused on 'hard' things, even when dealing with civil society, quantitative numbers become important such as getting a project completed, or enumerating the number of civic organizations established. That may still be useful. However, for sustained building of social capital, there is inevitably a need for understanding social relations and for 'indigenous' viewpoints for what works and what does not. Successfully transferring ideas and institutions requires the existence of local capacities to undertake the adaptation, why because as Stiglitz (2000) puts it, 'the chances of a successful transplant are much larger if the tree is simply pulled up in one place and planted in another'. 'Adaptation may take longer, but this process involved ensures that the policies that arise are "better prepared for the local soil"' (Malik 2002: 39).

> As countries transform themselves, they have to develop different capacities. But it is important to recognize that they do so not merely as an aggregate of individuals. It is a much richer and more complex concept that weaves individual strengths into a stronger and more resilient fabric. If countries and societies want to develop capacities, they must do more than expand individual human skills. They also have to create the opportunities and the incentives for people to use and expand these skills. Capacity development therefore takes place not just in individuals, but also between them, in the institutions and networks they create—through what has been termed the 'social capital' that holds societies together and sets the terms of these relationships. (Malik 2002)

Woolcock (1999) contends that development outcomes are likely to be shaped by the extent to which social dilemmas are resolved. Good outcomes occur when social relations are well defined and easy to access. Woolcock present four layers of such relations people can draw upon: (i) within their own local communities, (ii) between local communities and other social groups which have more extensive links to civil society, (iii) between civil society and macro-level institutions such as government institutions, and (iv) within the corporate sector.

What are some of the implications for public policy and civic action? The Grameen Bank experience in Bangladesh of using peer groups as an alternative source of collateral for the extension of credit to the poor, can illustrate some of the points raised here. Grameen Bank explicitly worked on deepening trust, strengthening networks, and created incentives all together to produce positive development outcomes.

Policies (and Reforms)

When you get right down to business, there aren't too many policies that we can say with certainty deeply and positively affect growth.
— Arnold C. Harberger (2003)

Policies are a set of statements of principles, values, and intent that outline expectations and provide a basis for consistent decision-making. In the context of development, it refers to an act of executive will by governments to influence specific social and economic outcomes.

As indicated elsewhere, increasingly few development economists and policymakers are now convinced that liberalization, deregulation, and privatization are on their own likely to kick-start or sustain growth and development. The rationale for arriving at this conclusion is connected with the important theoretical work on the second best by Lipsey and Lancaster in 1956.

The primary focus of their theory is on what happens when the optimum conditions are not satisfied in an economic model. Absence of some of the optimal conditions leads to a situation that the next best option secured by the presence of the remaining conditions may not be a better outcome. Lipsey and Lancaster's results underscore the need for pragmatic approaches to policymaking, since policy analysis may not provide easy answers on the 'right' policies. Rodrik (2007b) nicely outlines the dilemma this presents for the community of economists. Empirically minded economists eager to get the government's hands on the economy appreciate the logic of the 'theory of the second-best', while others in thrall of the power of markets are in the grip of a lovely but illusory ideal. By empirically minded economists he has in mind economists like himself and Joseph Stiglitz, who face squarely the many imperfections of real-world markets, in sharp contrast to the *laissez faire* crew who blithely ignore these flaws, lest they be forced to concede the need for corrective government guidance in economic affairs.

Social Policy, Budgets, and Macroeconomic Policies

Markets, prices, incentives all have a role to play in shaping development outcomes. Policies seek to influence them in one way or the other.

Overall macroeconomic stabilization and the design and content of fiscal and monetary measures have dominated the content of most development policies, particularly those negotiated with international financial institutions such as the Poverty Reduction Strategy Papers (PRSPs). Spending on social sectors is generally treated as residual expenditure, that is, what is left over after more important matters are attended to and the country balances its budget. Social welfare policy is seen mostly about managing the impact of development strategies and programmes as governments seek to move their countries forward.

If development is about transformation, the role of social policy has to be substantially re-thought. Social policy has to go beyond policies concerned with how society treats the poor and other vulnerable groups, towards the kind of society that a nation wishes to become, and how to influence social attitudes and norms that can facilitate development. Much of the work on social policy focuses on the design of social safety nets, which treat the issue as a matter of protecting the welfare of society's vulnerable groups, hence its treatment as residual nature when talking about budgets.

Looking at the role of social policy is particularly useful when examining successful transitions of former planned economies to market economies. The former planned economies have much in common with developing countries in this context—except over a shorter time frame, since they realized early on that what they had to do in the end was to transform society, and in that process to develop a new relationship between social norms, development, and the state. Fundamentally, this shift required policies and strategies to influence how people interface with their government, and whether a new political culture can be sustained with preferred attributes of greater transparency, representativeness, and accountability (Griffin and Khan 1995).

This broader, society-driven approach affects how we look at traditional policy instruments. Macroeconomic policies, for instance, are rarely society or 'poor-neutral'. Social policy has to connect with economic policy considerations, bearing in mind that the composition of national budgets is not a value neutral exercise. In particular national budgets have to be assessed in terms of their political and social context. Partly because budgetary matters are seen as technically complex, macroeconomic policies often escape close public scrutiny, despite the reality that these technical decisions have a large impact on people and the progress of nations. Policy conclusions, for instance, are likely to be very different if expenditures on health and education are seen as investments rather than a matter of social support. Mahbub ul Haq, the founder of the UNDP Human Development Reports, was fond of stating that budgets were often balanced on the 'backs of the poor'.

Trade Policies, Globalization, and Opening Up

Few countries, especially those who are small or medium in size, have managed to grow easily over long periods without opening themselves to global markets. Yet it is also not true that all countries have done well while opening their domestic markets to global trade. Like anything, when moving away from theory into reality, the key is in the terms of engagement: how the country treats capital accounts, how technology transfer processes are being managed, and what shock absorbers exist when external crises hit. There is a broader political economy context of unfair globalization here as well, where the rules of the game tend to favour advanced industrial countries. Developing countries with low wages, low human capital investments, and limited industrial infrastructure are unlikely to spontaneously move up the chain of industrial sophistication without active policies to do so.

The lessons emerging from contemporary experience are that countries have to be willing but careful in their embrace of globalization. It may require selective approaches to the speed with which specific domestic markets are opened up and whether speculative monies should be given free rein to come in or go out. The East Asian crisis of the late 1970s was a wakeup call for most governments in the region, and led to a growing interest in pragmatic, generally heterodox approaches to protect domestic development efforts from the uncertainties implied in globalization. Loss of jobs and insecurity are some aspects of the globalization challenge. Unlike developed countries, developing countries generally do not have robust mechanisms such as welfare payments and unemployment insurance to insure against such risks (Stiglitz 2006). These concerns, in turn, are further intensified with global warming, since poor countries and poor communities are likely to bear the brunt of adjustment.

Transformative policies can benefit from globalization, as the case of Bangladesh brings out vividly, whereby the need for an educated labour force led to investments in education for women in particular. Positive linkages are possible. But equally, domestic efforts to make progress can easily be set aside as global forces can profoundly influence who is likely to succeed. Policymakers have to look at this link carefully so that sufficient provision is made for such positive effects and mitigate and be prepared for the more negative aspects of globalization.

TRANSFORMATION NARRATIVES

A Macro Perspective

Traditional societies may have high levels of organizational and social capital, though this may not be in the form that facilitates change and development (Stiglitz 1998). What stock of social capital exists might be destroyed in the course of development, or as in Russia, transitions may happen without the easy emergence of a new functioning social order and capital. This perspective leads to the proposition that public policy needs to go beyond narrowly defined state capacities to consider approaches that promote broader social capabilities—institutions, incentives, and social structures that encourage productivity, thrift, and entrepreneurship—and reinforce the ability of governments to design and implement public policy.

In a traditional society, there may well be alignment between the three categories: a coherent vision of society with well-established priorities, institutions that manage the conduct of these priorities, and social capital that sustains that level of development (Figure 4.2). Development change and the imperatives of new production systems 'demand' a realignment of social systems. Once we accept that development is about transformation, then in this context, the challenge is to manage the transition from a traditional to a modern society. Policies then require a focus on not just dismantling or reforming established institutions and capacities but on the judicious management of the development process to create a social environment that sustains and enriches new social structures and alignments conducive to a modern society. In periods of rapid change, there is bound to be at times profound misalignment among the three components making transformation management a daunting task. And, in terms of development policy, it bears reiteration that, first, social policies need to be given more prominence, at a minimum they are at least as important as economic policies and, second, that development

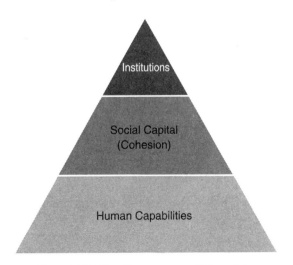

Figure 4.2 The Components of Capacities

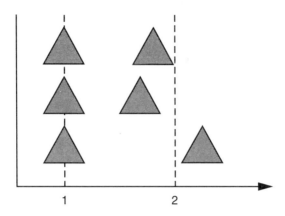

Figure 4.3 The Three Drivers

policy and development leadership have to consciously be about influencing all three elements and the need for their alignment.

A society is in balance, given its chosen mode of economic organization, when there is an overall alignment of the three elements. Change inevitably shifts the relationship between the three drivers. Managing that change is about securing an alignment of the transformation drivers at higher levels of development (Figure 4.3). To illustrate: the first alignment of the three elements can be a stylized description of pre-reform Soviet Russia, where over time centrally planned policies had provided for the basic needs of the people. In terms of social norms, Soviet citizens accepted as normal the availability of social facilities such as crèches in the work place, generous leave entitlements, and widespread access to leisure. But income levels were much lower than Western economies. Comparing this with the situation of Russia post-*perestrioka* is revealing. The disastrous results are well documented—the collapse of incomes, a huge rise in inequality, shortened life spans—some unprecedented since World War II. Dramatic new policies were introduced (with support from the international community) without fully assessing their implications for the design or creation of new institutions, and new social norms and networks that might have allowed for their success. While the failure of the 'big bang' approach is widely accepted, the fault may not have been just with the content of the new policies, but also for not having allowed for the context in which they were being introduced. One reason for this mismatch, which refers to the second driver (policies), was that the 'experts' and agencies charged with assisting the transition saw it as a conventional problem of weak markets and democratic institutions requiring standard solutions in the form of more loans and more technical cooperation (Putnam 1993; Sachs et al. 2000).

The state can and does influence social norms and practices. One example is in the instances of discriminatory and exclusionary practices linked with race, gender, ethnicity, and religion. Social exclusion can be redressed through improving the outreach of public services, for instance, by setting up schools and health facilities in rural areas. Stronger forms of such action can be through special policies such as affirmative action (*World Development Report 2000–2001*). Such policies have to become part of the standard tool box of development practitioners and economists.

Moving then from one system, or aligned level, to the other raised issues of absorption and sequencing. Much of the debate on 'absorptive' capacities is linked to the role of public policy in influencing the ability of developing countries to absorb 'new ideas, norms and techniques' (Koo and Perkins 1995). In South Korea, this led to investing in education first so that the transfer of skills and knowledge through international assistance could be better absorbed. The East Asian crisis is a different example. Here the role of governments was well established, with generally strong, well managed institutions and a mix of policies mostly regarded as growth-friendly. And perhaps even more important, these countries had succeeded to a considerable extent in transforming their societies. So what went wrong? In this case the challenge was more in terms of policies and the global context. While critical observers fault the volatility of short-term capital flows and less than useful external advice (Radelet and Sachs 1998), there was also serious questioning of key aspects of the Washington Consensus such as premature capital account convertibility and inadequate financial supervision in developed country economics, a charge which has re-emerged in a major way in the current global financial meltdown. The East Asian and current crises call for more, not less governmental action and for more and better international financial coordination and supervision, as has been now accepted by government leaders at the G-20 Summit meeting in London in March 2009.

State–Groups Interaction

An important part of the social transformation dynamic is how economic groups interact with the state. There is a dynamic aspect here as these groups both contribute to and are influenced by state policy. Economic groups function within a context of a particular history and regulatory/institutional framework. A subset of these relations refers to civil society and institutional arrangements that mediate and influence the link between states and markets. The context then can either facilitate the interaction of different economic groups, or undermine their capacity as civil society actors in the attainment of specific development outcomes. Such groups in turn can play an important role in shaping government policies and performance. Woolcock (1998) articulates it well:

> The nature of state–society relations is thus crucial to understanding the prospects of economic groups and the efficacy if their role to influence the willingness and ability of the state (and other large corporate actors) to act in a developmental manner. The development effectiveness of state-society relations therefore turns on the articulation of the interests, needs and resources of both parties.

A range of development outcomes is possible. Extreme examples are the so-called 'failed' states such as Somalia where there is little state organizational capacity and where the state, and with it basic law and order, simply ceases to exist in any meaningful form. Economic groups in turn are unable to coalesce into any semblance of a working economy. The synergy is not there. These states are close to what has been described in the literature as 'predatory states'. There is a critical role here that leadership and elites play in shaping development outcomes.

Bangladesh is also an example of weak state capacities, but where a robust civil society has facilitated better development outcomes. The country has produced exceptional leaders like Muhammad Yunus (Grameen Bank) and Fazle Abed (BRAC) who in turn, over the years, galvanized an increasingly large movement of civic leaders to re-invest in society. Bangladesh has made more progress on the attainment of Millennium Development Goals (MDGs) than any of the other South Asian countries including fast-growing India. Life expectancy went up 22 per cent in 18 years, to 66 years in 2008, and population growth declined to 1.41 per cent from 2.19 per cent in 1990. Growth rates kept steady around 6 per cent over the past decades.[6] The reasons for this are less to do with a developmental state or 'good' policy packages. Three key factors came together in a virtuous circle: gains in female literacy—mostly due to a combination of private sector needs (initially in the garments export sector) and civil society investments; an extensive micro-finance network reaching many millions of the poor; and large remittances from Bangladeshi immigrants whose cash transfers led to direct increase in their family incomes. These factors came together and contributed to stronger social capital and kick-started entrepreneurship traditions that led to higher growth rates.

Recent economic history provides many examples of how relations between economic groups and the state have had decisive influence on development outcomes. High organizational strength of the Soviet Union and Eastern Europe may have been a case of 'too much bureaucracy' and not enough of the synergy represented by a 'development state' which can join elements of support, cooperation, and accountability (Woolcock 1998).

---

[6] Data source: World Bank, World Development Indicators. Available at http://datafinder.worldbank.org/about-world-development-indicators.

Rent-seeking, inefficiency, and ineffectiveness become the characteristics of a dysfunctional development environment, and of group–state relations.

Institutions, Social Capital (Cohesion), and Growth

Easterly et al. (2006), in a joint paper, identify social cohesion (or social capital) as an important factor in explaining why even good leaders find it difficult to carry out 'good' policies. Social cohesion as a concept works better in this context since it focuses on broader social issues, whereas social capital as a term can also refer to specific, more micro level aspects, for instance, when examining social networks and community organizations. Social constraints inevitably limit the space that politicians have in enacting policy changes. The authors define social cohesion as 'the nature and extent of social and economic divisions within society'. Socially cohesive societies have fewer divisions which can be exploited by different factions or individuals, and more opportunities to harness the potential that exists in diversity.

By combining direct and indirect data of social cohesion,[7] they arrive at important conclusions that confirm the results of earlier studies, for instance, by Rodrik (2000) that cohesive societies tend to grow faster than less cohesive societies and that the latter are better in dealing with crises and exogenous shocks. Countries that are deeply divided among caste, language, and community, present large challenges for the best of leaders and policymakers. There is a virtuous aspect here. Good development outcomes are generally more likely in countries governed by effective public institutions and those institutions in turn are more likely to be found in socially more cohesive societies.

---

[7] Easterly et al. (ibid.) present evidence to show that social cohesion can influence the quality of institutions in a broad-based study drawing upon different data sets covering common measures of social exclusion such as membership rates of organizations and civic participation, trust (an aggregate of answers from surveys), and indirect measures such as the income distribution (Gini Coefficient) and ethnic heterogeneity.

Two main conclusions are, in particular, highlighted by the authors. More social cohesion leads to better institutions and better institutions lead to higher growth. States clearly can influence both social cohesion and the quality of institutions. Both are in the main endogenous variables. An important part of the state's arsenal of policies is education, which can exercise considerable influence on social cohesion. When education is well organized and the right curricula is pursued, it can contribute to fostering harmony among different groups and ethnic communities; and it can reinforce a common purpose among a nation. If public services—health, education, and social security—are provided fairly and equitably they go some distance in creating a society which feels itself more united and cohesive.

Calls to improve policies and institutions are based on an 'implicit assumption ... that realizing them is simply a matter of choice, technocratic skill, and/or sheer political will' (ibid.). Social and international power relations play a large role in determining the policy space that may in fact exist for leaders and governments in developing countries. A certain degree of social cohesion is essential to generate the confidence and commitment needed to carry out reforms. Citizens have to trust their governments. Inclusiveness of communities and institutions can act as shock absorbers in facilitating change, when reforms challenge existing power relations and class divisions. As societies transform, and being mindful of these relations, policymakers have to develop a broader reference for their policies and the intended impact of policy changes on society.

Ownership, Policies, and Globalization

There are abundant examples where weak ownership of 'good' policies has led to unhappy or poor outcomes. The onus of the failure of these policies have often been put on insufficient policy implementation capacities, which in turn has produced a plethora of well meaning advice and technical assistance to improve such capacities. Equally, strong ownership of 'bad' policies is unlikely to help much in moving economies and societies forward.

The cost of misplaced or inappropriate advice has been considerable. Countries that have followed the recipes of the IMF, from Bolivia to Mongolia, have raised basic, necessary questions: We have felt the pain of IMF-supported structural adjustment programmes, we have done everything you have told us to do; when do we start reaping the benefits. Meanwhile, countries that took on a more independent course, like China, or those that have been more selective, like Chile, have fared better (Stigltiz 2002).

There are other examples where development policy advocates have come up short in relation to actual experience. For instance, in the area of foreign investment, China has arguably been among the most successful in attracting foreign direct investment (FDI). This took place despite caution from advocates of capital market liberalization that it is difficult to attract FDI without, at the same time, opening up the country to short-term capital flows. Equally, in many developing countries, many of the poorest people remain in the rural areas, and are likely to remain there for decades to come. Neglect of agriculture and the rural sector has made progress in poverty reduction, at best, limited. So if poverty reduction is a key policy objective, then clearly, close attention to the sector is warranted. Industrial policies in particular cannot ignore agriculture and the rural sector more broadly. Both China and Taiwan's early success was built on a rural-based development strategy (ibid.).

There are no simple policy prescriptions. The hard work has to be done by national leaders, and institutions themselves. They can draw upon the lessons learnt from other development experiences, successful or otherwise, and craft home-grown solutions. Investing only in education at the expense of a growing economy is a process which is unlikely to be sustained. Markets and incentives are important if people are to realize their productive potential, but if their access and ability to participate is limited, then that as well has to become part of the challenges that policies have to address. Low productivity in agriculture combined with poor roads and infrastructure is unlikely to lift famers out of poverty. And, reducing barriers to developing country imports, endemic in global markets, has to become part of the enabling framework for developing countries to make progress. Simply opening up their economies to the outside world by itself is unlikely to help developing countries necessarily benefit from globalization. 'Even if (their) GDP increases, the growth may not be sustainable, or sustained. And even if growth is sustained, most of (their) people may find themselves worse off' (Stiglitz, 2006).

The next chapter is a study of how China achieved its remarkable progress by pursuing a broad-based 'development as transformation' strategy on its own terms, led by its leaders, a strong bureaucracy, and related institutions which have delivered on, to a large degree, the modernization vision laid out by its leaders at the beginning of its reform period.

REFERENCES

Abe, M. 2006. 'The Developmental State and Educational Advance in East Asia', *Educate*, 6(1): 6–12.

Aron, J. 2000. 'Growth and Institutions: A Review of the Evidence', *The World Bank Research Observer*, 15(1): 99–135.

Barro, R.J. 1996. 'Democracy and Growth', *Journal of Economic Growth*, 1(1): 1–27.

Baser, H. and P. Morgan. 1996. 'Review of Technical Assistance Loans in the World Bank', Washington DC, World Bank, OPD.

Boozer, M., G. Ranis, F. Stewart, and T. Suri. 2003. *Paths to Success: The Relationship between Human Development and Economic Growth*, Economic Growth Center, Yale University. Available at http://ideas. repec.org/p/egc/wpaper/874.html, accessed on 7 April 2010.

Chhibber, A. 2000. 'Social Capital, the State, and Development Outcomes, in I. Serageldin (ed.), *Social Capital: A Multifaceted Perspective*, pp. 296–310. Washington DC: World Bank.

Collier, P. 1998. *The Political Economy of Ethnicity*. Oxford: Institute of Economics and Statistics, Centre for the Study of African Economies, University of Oxford.

Commander, S., H.R. Davoodi, and U.J. Lee. 1997. *The Causes of Government and the Consequences for Growth and Well-being*, World Bank.

Available at http://ideas.repec.org/p/wbk/wbrwps/1785.html, accessed on 31 March 2010.

Dasgupta, P. 2000. 'Economic Progress and the Idea of Social Capital', in I. Serageldin (ed.), *Social Capital: A Multifaceted Perspective*. Washington DC: World Bank Publications.

Easterly, W., J. Ritzen, and M. Woolcock. 2006. 'Social Cohesion, Institutions, and Growth', *Economics and Politics*, 18(2): 103–20.

Edwards, M. 2000. 'Enthusiasts, Tacticians and Skeptics: Social Capital and the Structures of Power', presentation on 'Practical Theory, Reflective Action: Social Capital and Development Projects at the World Bank', Boulder, Department of Geography, University of Colorado.

Emmerij, L., R. Jolly, and T.G. Weiss. 2005. 'Economic and Social Thinking at the UN in Historical Perspective, *Development and Change*, 36(2): 211–35.

Fritz, V. and A.R. Menocal. 2007. 'Developmental States in the New Millennium: Concepts and Challenges for a New Aid Agenda, *Development Policy Review*, 25(5): 531–52.

Frye, T. and A. Shleifer. 1997. 'The Invisible Hand and the Grabbing Hand', *The American Economic Review*, 87(2): 354–8.

Glaeser, E.L., R. Porta, F. Lopez-de-Silanes, and A. Shleifer. 2004. 'Do Institutions Cause Growth?', *Journal of Economic Growth*, 9(3): 271–303.

Griffin, K. and A.R. Khan. 1995. 'The Transition to Market Guided Economies: Lessons for Russia and Eastern Europe from the Chinese Experience', in B. Magnus and S. Cullenberg (eds), *Whither Marxism? Global Crises in International Perspective*. New York and London: Routledge.

Harberger, A.C. 2003. 'Interview with Arnold Harberger: Sound Policies Can Free Up Natural Forces of Growth', *IMF Survey*, International Monetary Fund, Washington DC.

Hausmann, R. 2001. 'Prisoners of Geography', *Foreign Policy*, 122: 44–53.

Johnson, J.H. and S.S. Wasty. 1993. *Borrower Ownership of Adjustment Programs and the Political Economy of Reform*. Washington DC: World Bank Publications.

Jones, B.F. and B.A. Olken. 2005. *The Anatomy of Start–Stop Growth*. Cambridge, Mass.: National Bureau of Economic Research.

Koo, B.H. and D.H. Perkins. 1995. *Social Capability and Long-term Economic Growth*. Basingstoke: Macmillan.

Kornai, J. 1992. *Socialist System: Political Economy of Socialism*. Oxford: Oxford University Press.

Lewis, W.A. 1955. *The Theory of Economic Growth*. Homewood, Ill.: R.D. Irwin.

Lin, Justin Yifu and Celestin Monga. 2010. 'The Growth Report and New Structural Economics', Policy Research Working Paper Series 5336, World Bank, Washington DC.

Majumdar, S. and S. Mukand. 2008. 'The Leader as Catalyst—On Leadership and the Mechanics of Institutional Change', CESIFO Working Paper No. 2337.

Malik, Khalid. 2002. 'Towards a Normative Framework: Technical Cooperation, Capacities and Development', in Sakiko Fukuda-Parr, Carlos Lopez, and Khalid Malik (eds), *Capacity for Development: New Solution for Old Problems*, pp. 23–42. New York: Earthscan and UNDP.

Malik, K. and S. Waglé. 2002. 'Civic Engagement and Development: Introducing the Issues', in Sakiko Fukuda-Parr, Carlos Lopez, and Khalid Malik (eds), *Capacity for Development: New Solution for Old Problems*, pp. 85–99. New York: Earthscan and UNDP.

Narayan, D. and M. Woolcock. 2000. 'Social Capital: Implications for Development Theory, Research and Policy', *The World Bank Research Observer*, 15(2): 225–49.

Nepstad, S.E. and C. Bob. 2006. 'When Do Leaders Matter? Hypotheses on Leadership Dynamics in Social Movements', *Mobilization: An International Quarterly*, 11(1): 1–22.

North, D.C. 1981. *Structure and Change in Economic History*. New York: Norton.

———. 1990. *Institutions, Institutional Change, and Economic Performance*. Cambridge: Cambridge University Press.

———. 1994. 'Economic Performance through Time', *The American Economic Review*, 84(3): 359–68.

Polanyi, K. 1957. *The Great Transformation*. Boston: Beacon Press.

Putnam, R.D. 1993. 'The Prosperous Community', *The American Prospect*, 4(13): 35–42.

Radelet, S. and J. Sachs. 1998. 'The East Asian Financial Crisis: Diagnosis, Remedies, Prospects', *Brookings Paper*, 28(1): 1–74.

Ranis, G. and F. Stewart. 2007. 'Dynamic Links between the Economy and Human Development', in J. A. Ocampo, K. S. Jomo, and S. Khan (eds), *Policy Matters: Economic and Social Policies to Sustain Equitable Development*. London: Zed Books.

Ranis, G., F. Stewart, and A. Ramirez. 2000. 'Economic Growth and Human Development', *World Development*, 28(2): 197–220.

Robeyns, I. 2003. 'Sen's Capability Approach and Gender Inequality: Selecting Relevant Capabilities', *Feminist Economics*, 9(2): 61–92.

Rodrik, D. 2000. 'Institutions for High-quality Growth: What They Are and How to Acquire Them, *Studies in Comparative International Development (SCID)*, 35(3): 3–31.

———. 2003. *Growth Strategies*. National Bureau of Economic Research.

————. 2007a. *Leadership in Economics*. Available at http://rodrik.typepad. com/dani_rodriks_weblog/2007/08/leadership.html, accessed 6 April 2010.

————. 2007b. *One Economics, Many Recipes: Globalization, Institutions, and Economic Growth*. Princeton, NJ: Princeton University Press.

Rostow, W.W. 1960. *The Stages of Economic Growth*. Cambridge: Cambridge University Press.

Sachs, J. 1997. 'Nature, Nurture and Growth', *The Economist*, 343(8021): 19.

Sachs, J.D., W.T. Woo, and X. Yang. 2000. 'Economic Reforms and Constitutional Transition'. SSRN eLibrary. Available at http:// papers.ssrn.com/sol3/papers.cfm?abstract_id=254110, accessed on 8 April 2010.

See, H.P. 2008. 'Moral Character and Effective Leadership: With Reference to Chinese Leadership Style', *Centre for Malaysian Chinese Studies Bulletin*, No. 4. Available at http://ssrn.com/abstract=1496232.

Solow, R.M. 2000. 'Notes on Social Capital and Economic Performance', in *Social Capital: A Multifaceted Perspective*. Washington DC: World Bank Publications.

Stewart, F. 2000. 'Income Distribution and Development', *documento preparado para la Décima Reunión de la Mesa Redonda de Alto Nivel sobre Comercio y Desarrollo de la UNCTAD: Orientaciones para el Siglo XXI, Bangkok, Tailandia*.

Stiglitz, J.E., 1996. 'Some Lessons from the East Asian Miracle', *The World Bank Research Observer*, 11(2): 151–77.

————. 1998. 'Towards a New Paradigm for Development: Strategies, Policies, and Processes', *Prebisch Lecture*, 19. Geneva: UNCTAD.

————. 2000. 'Scan Globally, Reinvent Locally', in Diane Stone (ed.), *Banking on Knowledge: The Genesis of the Global Development Network*. London: Routledge.

————. 2002. 'Development Policies in a World of Globalization', paper presented at the seminar 'New International Trends for Economic Development' on the occasion of the fiftieth anniversary of the Brazilian Economic and Social Development Bank (BNDES), Rio Janeiro, 12–13 September 2002.

————. 2006. *Stability with Growth: Macroeconomics, Liberalization and Development*. New York: Oxford University Press.

Tallberg, J. 2006. *Leadership and Negotiation in the European Union*. Cambridge: Cambridge University Press.

Thalayasingam, P. 2007. '*Unpacking Foreign Aid to Sri Lanka*', Forum on the Future of Aid Opinion Piece, November.

United Nations Development Program (UNDP). 1990. *Human Development Report 1990*. New York: Oxford University Press.

————. 1995. *Capacity Development for Sustainable Human Development: Conceptual and Operational Signposts.* UNDP: New York.

————. 1996. *Human Development Report 1996.* New York: Oxford University Press.

————. 2003. *Development Effectiveness Report 2003: Partnership for Results.* UNDP Evaluation Office: New York.

Waglé, S. 2001. 'Social Capital and Development: A Survey', unpublished draft, UNDP, New York.

Williamson, J. 1994. *The Political Economy of Policy Reform.* Washington DC: Institute for International Economics.

Woolcock, M. 1998. 'Social Capital and Economic Development: Toward a Theoretical Synthesis and Policy Framework', *Theory and Society,* 27(2): 151–208.

————. 1999. 'Learning from Failures in Microfinance: What Unsuccessful Cases Tell Us about How Group-based Programs Work', *American Journal of Economics and Sociology,* 58(1): 17–42.

————. 2000. 'Managing Risk and Opportunity in Developing Countries: The Role of Social Capital', in Gustav Ranis (ed.), *The Dimensions of Development,* pp. 197–212. Yale: Center for International and Area Studies.

World Bank. 1995. *Annual Review of Evaluation Results,* Report No. 15084. Washington DC: World Bank.

————. 1996. *Annual Review of Evaluation Results,* Report No. 16110. Washington DC: World Bank.

————. 1997. *Annual Review of Development Effectiveness,* Report No. 17196. Washington DC: World Bank.

————. 2000. *World Development Report 2000/2001: Attacking Poverty,* 1st edn. Washington DC: World Bank.

Young, O.R. 1991. 'Political Leadership and Regime Formation: On the Development of Institutions in International Society', *International Organization,* 45(3): 281–308.

5

Understanding China and Its Transformation

Thirty years of reform in China is a fascinating story of how the largest country in the world managed to pull itself from dire poverty to growing prosperity and across the board improvements in the lives of people. With the overarching development vision consciously presented as a modernization drive, this period has produced a step-change in the attitudes of people, in their own expectations of progress, and positioned the country to reclaim its rightful place among the community of nations.

As earlier chapters have highlighted, China during this period has been 'undergoing a complex and interlocking set of changes: from a command to a market economy; from rural to urban; from agriculture to manufacturing and services; from informal to formal economic activities; from a fragmented set of fairly self-sufficient provincial economies to a more integrated economy; and from an economy that was fairly shut-off from the world to the powerhouse of international trade'

(Hussain and Stern 2006). It is likely that these macro-processes will continue for some time to come. Importantly, the relationship between Chinese citizens and their state has been evolving as well. The provision of social services, for instance, has moved away from state-owned enterprises (SOEs) and the government, even if there is renewed demand for a stronger role of the state in the provision of healthcare, education, and social insurance. Growing disparities, widespread concern about corruption, and elite capture in certain areas of the economy have raised new questions about the desirable role of the state and its institutions.

Part of the challenge of understanding China's development has been how to frame the purpose of development itself. It has been argued in earlier chapters that development of necessity has to go beyond an exclusive focus on economic growth, towards a broader understanding of people as both the means and the end of development. This view encompasses GDP growth rates, their distribution, but also the enhancement of capabilities of people to live better and fuller lives. In this vision, education, health, nutrition become as important as economic growth rates. The notion of 'development as transformation' goes a step further. It seeks to connect the growth process in China with society's capabilities, and assess how the productive forces interact with people and history as the country modernizes.

Previous chapters have tried to argue that standard explanations about China's performance are unable to fully capture the forces at play in its modernization. This chapter takes that next step in examining how these forces emerged and how the nexus between ownership, capacities, and policies led to the 50-fold growth[1] in per capita incomes since the late 1970s. A few propositions are presented that may be helpful in illustrating China's development path. These generally run counter to or fall outside the narrow realm of conventional economics. Taken together

---

[1] In nominal terms.

these propositions make a case of treating China's development as a study in transformation.

NATIONAL OWNERSHIP (AND LEADERSHIP)
A Few Transformative Propositions

i. In Chapter 4, we have advanced the proposition that national ownership of a developmental vision is a necessary condition for development. Strong, consistent leadership is required to sustain the vision.

ii. In a large country, ownership is particularly important at the local level.

iii. Transformation takes time, and long-term commitment to reform and development becomes essential for success.

iv. A clear, consistent vision is important, but detailed, rigid planning may not be helpful.

The ability to set strategic direction and define policy based on national conditions and realities, and their consistent implementation represent the foundation for successful development by making strategies and policies more relevant, accepted, and sustainable. This proposition implies that strong national ownership influences both growth and its sustainability (it represents a necessary but not sufficient condition). This chapter contends that such strong ownership is a critical factor in understanding Chinese progress. A related point is to assert that Chinese leadership and 'ruling elites' are committed to developmental progress over the long haul, that they are not seen as a 'grabbing' hand and that they see their legitimacy being intimately connected to whether progress is being made in the lives of the Chinese people.

Visioning

China presents an important example of strong national ownership on several levels. The nature of the reform process itself and the institutions that were created—pronounced as unorthodox by outside observers—illustrate amply, the independence of thought and implementation that Chinese leaders have displayed vis-à-vis traditional economic thinking and the policy advice received over the years.

Since the Communist Party took over in 1949, Chinese attitudes and policy setting processes have been influenced by a deep-seated desire not to repeat the nineteenth and early twentieth century experience when foreign powers were able to dictate terms to weak Chinese administrations. At the same time, Chinese leadership and its administration were eager to see and learn, but adamant in retaining the prerogative to adjust any lessons to their perception of the Chinese reality and the constraints therein implied. Nolan (2004) underscores the deep rooted nature of China's independent thought and polity, stretching many centuries.

Strategic Directions

The Four Modernizations, *Xiaokang*, the scientific approach to development are all terms which emphasize different aspects of the same vision. The remarkable feature of Chinese developmental direction since reforms were launched in 1978, has been one of consistency and adherence to Deng's vision of modernization and its focus on unleashing China's productive forces. In many ways, Deng Xiaoping set the standard for future leaders by articulating a middle path of a 'socialist market economy' as one of forging a 'third' way between capitalism and the Soviet style approach to a command economy. Since then, adjustments in policy or direction can be categorized as attempts to fine tune policies, respond to emerging challenges, and, drawing upon Chinese terminology, to 'respond to facts on the ground'. As growth accelerated in the 1980s and 1990s, so did disparities, and with it concerns about social stability. This in turn led to a shift in development strategy by early 2000s that put greater emphasis on the increasing the incomes of the poor, investing in agriculture and accelerating the development

of poorer provinces. Premier Wen Jiabao in his 2005 address to
the National People's Congress (NPC) signaled such a direc-
tional shift by stating that henceforth urban areas will support
rural areas, and industry would serve agriculture, a reversal from
earlier strategies. But the commitment to growth remained, and
to the Four Modernizations.

Using the Past to Serve the Present

How the reforms themselves were carried out also have their
own Chinese characteristics. Chinese reforms were characterized by local initiative and experimentation. New policies were
created and tested first as pilots. Deng Xiaoping's famous dictum
in the late 1970s of 'crossing the stream by feeling the stones', had
a profound influence. It provided the rationale for an approach
whereby no macro policy was subsequently introduced all in
one go without first being tested in different provinces and in
different situations. Only after some considerable analysis and
assessment, conducted by a range of policy groups and research
institutes connected to the State Council, of what worked and
what did not, did the successful aspects of an approach get scaled
up across the country and enshrined into national policy.

The waves of reform built on earlier successes and lessons were
drawn from polices that had not worked as well. For instance,
Qian (1999) notes:

> By 1984 the success of agricultural reform became apparent and
> extraordinary. Between 1978 and 1984 per capita grain production
> increased from about 319 kilograms to 400 kilograms, and
> production of other agricultural products increased even more
> because they were more profitable than grain. Correspondingly,
> per capita rural real income increased by more than 50% in
> the 6-year period. This is in sharp contrast with the stagnation
> of agriculture over the previous two decades. In comparison,
> the SOE reform was disappointing. The industrial sector
> was much too complicated, involving prices, taxes, finances,
> and enterprise employment, all of which were under central
> planning. Any significant reform would need a package to deal

with all these aspects. Encouraged by the extraordinary success of agricultural reform, in October 1994, the Third Plenum of the Twelfth Party Congress adopted a decision on reform of the economic system aimed at the urban area. This document made a significant ideology shift, from 'plan as a principal part and market as supplementary part' to 'planned commodity economy', which put plan and market on equal footing, if not put more weight on market. Zhao Ziyang, backed by Deng, became the main figure in the Party to engineer the reform, and he made 'dual-track market liberalization' and 'contract responsibility system' in SOEs as his two primary reform programs in this period.

This process of looking at facts was formalized as part of the 'scientific outlook on development', put forward by President Hu Jintao in 2003 at the Third Plenary Session of the Sixteenth CPC National Congress held in October 2003, where this term was officially adopted as one of the guiding principles for development in China.

Using the past to serve the present, *Gu Wei Jin Yong*, harkens to a longstanding cry in history for China's leaders to learn from the country's own past to define future policies and directions. The term '*Xiaokang*', is itself a Confucian phrase that refers to an 'all around well adjusted society'. Reaching the Xiaokang society by 2020 is now a national target for China's development (UN Country Team in China 2008). The Xiaokang vision is very similar to the global compact on MDGs reached at the United Nations in New York in 2000, to be attained by 2015. Both refer explicitly to, and set targets for, the measureable improvement in the lives of people.

A Strong Vision of Development

At the overall, strategic level, development strategy in China was not driven by any grand blueprint for reform. It was guided by an overarching vision of modernization and crucially was underpinned by social and political arrangements that encouraged participation and coalition building. Difficult questions of what kind of society the Chinese wanted for themselves and what they could realistically hope to achieve in a specific context were part of the constant dialogue and interaction on policies among different groups and constituencies. It was consciously recognized that there were clear trade-offs between a blueprint represented by the many plan documents and ground realities. This dynamic tension between what may be referred by some as best-practices and local realities is captured well by Rodrik (1999): 'Blueprints, best practices, international codes and standards, harmonization can do the trick for some of the narrowly 'technical' issues. But large-scale institutional development by and large requires a process of discovery about local needs and capabilities.'

Whether an intentional strategy towards a distant goal or an unintended *ex post* outcome of disagreements on the scope of reform, the gradual, step-by-step approach taken by China has been highlighted by many observers as a crucial reform aspect with intrinsic benefits.[2] And, importantly as some have observed that, intended or not, there was a certain 'ex-post coherence' of Chinese reforms (Naughton 2007).

Leadership

Articulating a vision is important and in that China has remained consistent over the reform period, but sustaining such a vision has been arguably even more challenging. At different points in the 1980s and 1990s, Deng's vision was severely questioned and tested. This period serves as a vivid illustration that leadership matters. Post-Tiananmen, the rise of conservative factions raised doubts about the future of economic reform in China. The abortive Soviet coup of 1991 and the collapse of the Soviet Union had strengthened the hands of Chen Yun and the leftist

[2] The unorthodox nature of Chinese reforms is captured well by Qian (1999) when he states, 'the Chinese path of reform and its associated rapid growth seem to defy the necessity part of the conventional wisdom. Although China has adopted many of the policies advocated by economists, such as being open to trade and investment and macroeconomic stability, violations of the standard policy prescriptions are also striking.'

ideologues at the expense of Deng and the reformers. Both in the media as well as within the party there was a concerted attempt to discredit Deng's policies of reform.

Deng realized that winning the political (and ideological) debate within the higher echelons of the party was difficult. He further recognized that communicating with the people directly was particularly difficult in Beijing due to the tight party control over the media. Deng's leadership ability showed in his ability to identify and carry out a strategy to garner support in China. More importantly, to paraphrase Caro's description (Caro 2002), Deng was able to focus on the key purpose of the reforms, amid the many proposed policies, the ones that would best accomplish a larger purpose, that is, to 'give the people economic space and the rest they could start doing by themselves'. Deng also recognized that he would need to mobilize support for his reforms by travelling around China and directly address his followers. Accordingly, he undertook the unprecedented 'Southern Tour' when he travelled to the Southern provinces in general and Guangdong and Shanghai in particular (Ash and Kueh 1996). A single leader, however charismatic and gifted is not enough to shift historical forces. Bringing along followers becomes necessary, both those directly in support and those referred to earlier as 'fence sitters'. As pointed out by Zhao (1993), while Deng's skill in choosing both the right time and place to take on the central party hierarchy was important, success would not have been possible without the support of his followers in the regions which had been the direct beneficiaries of the reforms. Deng emphasized the importance of broad-based economic development and reform to communicate with his followers and the lower level hierarchy in the party, using it as a way to criticize (and isolate) the ideological hardliners (Naughton 1993). The response to Deng Xiaoping's appeal by both his followers and non-followers was immediate. Deng's supporters used his Southern tour to mobilize opinion, lobby, and put pressure on the party hierarchy; thousands of cables and letters poured into Beijing party headquarters expressing support for Deng's policies.

Not surprisingly, Deng's Southern Tour is widely regarded as single-handedly shifting the political momentum decisively and irreversibly in favour of the continuation of economic reform in China.

Since then and following the departure of dominant leaders like Jiang Zemin, China has moved more fully towards a model of collective leadership which requires consensus on key policies and directions. Whatever the exact form of strategic decision-making, an abiding factor has been an absolute determination by China to take its own decisions based on their assessment of national conditions and requirements.

Local Ownership

China is a large, complex country. Ownership of reforms requires a buy-in at many levels. There are long traditions as well for China being fairly decentralized in economic terms, despite the more popular image of a powerful Beijing issuing instructions that are faithfully followed by the provinces. Even in ancient times this was the case, which is well captured in the Chinese saying, *tiangao huangdi yuan*, the sky is high and the emperor is far.

In the 1950s, Mao's reforms with the introduction of land reforms (covering land re-distribution and its use), initiated a process of economic decentralization. Specifically, in April 1956, at the meeting of the Political Bureau, Mao addressed the issue of central–local relationships. Once central leadership had been consolidated, it was Mao's view that local authorities should be given more powers so that they could have more independence and could do more things. He added that it was important to mobilize the enthusiasm both at central and local levels because China was a huge country, had a big population and faced a complex situation.

Some scholars hold the view that Mao ruled China through political centralization', but 'administrative decentralization' (Blanchard and Shleifer 2001). This laid a good foundation for the later reforms of Deng Xiaoping. It was only much later, in the early 1990s, during Zhu Rongji's premiership that attempts were made to re-centralize some economic functions, for instance taxation and fiscal arrangements, to ensure that the centre could keep a higher percentage of the revenues raised through taxation.

There is a group of arguments connected to this relatively large degree of decentralization that has characterized the Chinese reform process over the years. Qian (1999) notes that even in the early days 'the Chinese planning system was very much decentralized along regional lines, and local governments played an important role in economic decision-making and resource allocation. Related, central planning was usually crude, aggregated, and not comprehensive, and moreover, it was not "tight", meaning that plan fulfillment often was not a binding constraint.' These prominent features represented a significant departure from the textbook model of the 'Soviet system' and proved important for the evolution of reforms in China.

One aspect of decentralization was the level of grassroots initiative. The experimentalist approach of piloting and scaling up was characterized by a laissez-faire attitude to change that left considerable scope for change to happen spontaneously and organically.

Various reasons have been put forward by scholars to explain the absence of a comprehensive reform blueprint at the beginning of the reform process: The need to deal with a variety of urgencies in the wake of the Cultural Revolution; the lack of understanding and capacity of leaders to comprehensively plan for reforms; difficulty in reaching consensus given diverging interests across layers of administration and authority; the inherent difficulty in planning a process as complex as transition and so on (Garnaut and Song 2004).

Whatever the underlying reasons, this tolerance of heterodoxy gave reforms an enabling character, allowing initiatives to percolate from below. Those successful would be repeated by other provinces and, as evidence mounted, eventually enshrined in national policy. Experimentation would typically take place at the regional/city, sector, or enterprise level. In case of failure it would be stopped, in case of success it would be extended to other areas and enterprises. While sometimes suspicious of unconventional initiatives taken at lower levels, the Chinese leadership refrained from suppressing them—a tolerance that may well be their greatest contribution to the reform process.

McMillan (1994) notes that 'the government's role often has been to permit change rather than to initiate it. Many of the reforms, in particular in agriculture, were initiated at ground level and only afterwards ratified by the central government.' One example of this is the much discussed Household Responsibility System in agriculture, which as the earlier chapter has indicated originated spontaneously among farmers in Anhui province who signed makeshift contracts with their thumbprints in an unofficial pseudo-ownership scheme. Starting in 1978, the state took tentative measures to adjust rural policy (Naughton 2007). With expanded autonomy, a result of these adjustments, agricultural collectives began experimenting with more radical reforms. Similarly, the reform of SOEs started with local initiatives in Sichuan province, encouraged by the late Zhao Ziyang who was then Party chief of the province. As these reforms produced positive results, there was increasing support to extend and expand on these pilots. By 1981–2 the household responsibility system emerged as a national programme, which outlined the process of contracting land to households. Its spread was dramatic. By end of 1982, this organizational form had been extended to more than 90 per cent of Chinese agricultural households.

Long-term Commitment to Reform

As Chapter 4 highlights, strategies that can effectively deliver on 'development as transformation' may require: A coherent long-term development vision; *gradualism* in the application of development strategies as it reduces disruption and raises chances of success, or policy shifts that are given time for people to adjust to; and *pragmatic flexibility* in policies to meet needs as they emerge may be more effective than having a predetermined blueprint based on economic orthodoxy.

Transformation of society and the economy is inherently a long term, gradual process, and in China the astonishing changes that have taken place were allowed to take time. This gave both people and institutions a chance to keep up with changes and adjust their mindsets, preferences, and expectations at the relatively modest Chinese pace of policy reform.

In the party, there has been an ongoing struggle for the positioning of specific views in shaping development strategies and priorities for reform. Yet this struggle was not allowed to dislodge the essential directions of the reforms and developmental vision introduced by Deng Xiaoping in the late 1970s. Within the Party, there has been a core leadership that was deeply committed to improving long-term growth, and had a clear, pragmatic approach to development. The difficulties of the past, the unsettled situation during the civil war period, and the eventual triumph of the communist party had left an indelible impact on official attitudes and their commitment to economic and social progress of the people. If specific policies produced positive results, those policies were continued. The state in China was not as had been described in the literature as a 'grabbing' hand. In acting on its development vision, it was pragmatic and fairly consensus-based.

The role of the state also evolved during the reform period. During Mao's period the economy was controlled by a centralized political and administrative system. With the start of reform, the state became gradually less involved directly in the economy and the lives of people. New and revamped institutions were created to handle the requirements of law, trade, and the market-oriented economy. This did not mean however that the role of the state declined, instead it expanded into new areas while still keeping some old functions (Saich 2003: 33). Unlike most other countries, there is an important separation in the roles of the Party and the government, with the Party playing the lead role in setting overall policy and strategy, and the government as the body responsible for its implementation. There is a historical and cultural context here as well. In China there has been a long-standing acceptance of an 'active' role of the state, even in earlier periods. Without a strong state capability, it is felt that China would quickly descend into chaos and uncertainty (Nolan 2004). To maintain its legitimacy, periodic campaigns were launched by the party to combat corruption, to re-invigorate the commitment of cadres to the supremacy of the party, and to 'serving the people'.

In contrast to the political turmoil that accompanied transition in Eastern Europe and the Former Soviet Union (EEFSU), China's relative stability provided a predictable environment for investment, fiscal stability, and the gradual development of markets as well as a continued government presence strong enough to steer reforms and intervene to redress market or other performance failures.

Chinese development experience can be usefully characterized by the following:

- A strong vision of, and commitment to, development
- Local initiative and experimentation leading the way in much of the piloting
- Building constituencies for reform
- Part reformation was good enough—it was fine even if reforms worked only in one area of the economy
- The focus was on results and outcomes, rather than the means or even for that matter, principles

The term 'gradualism' or 'incrementalism' has been used by observers to characterize the nature and sequencing of reforms in China, even if there are continuing debates on whether gradualism should be defined in a narrow sense to refer to a situation where reforms require, predict, or create economic exigencies for further reforms, or a broader interpretation where the term 'gradualism' refers to giving sufficient time for policies and reforms so that they are better accepted by the people.

Huang (2002) makes a distinction between the different periods of reform. He considers the 'gradual' description of reforms fitting better with the reformist policies in the 1980s than those pursued in the 1990s, and that further it fits better the liberalization and opening up aspects of Chinese reforms. There is also the view that Chinese reforms occurred in fits and starts, otherwise the 1980s reform should have 'predicted' a deeper wave of reform in the 1990s, a comment which is probably true in the case of SOE reforms. SOE reforms in the 1990s most likely would have been different if the reforms were indeed about privatizing SOEs, instead the state took measures to strengthen their position and created incentives for them to become more competitive.

Whatever the term used, it should be noted that profound reform even at glacial speed overall inevitably contains dramatic micro shifts, such as the introduction of household contracts on farm land, creating a market track beyond the state one, introducing liberal local policies in SEZs, promoting incentives systems for SOEs, a merit based civil service code, removal of lifetime employment, and so on. Thus despite widespread Western criticism for reforming too slowly, the Chinese government has often been criticized domestically for moving too fast, as these mini-bangs create disruptive waves in the social, political, institutional, and organizational fabric of the country.

For instance, in the early 1990s, after economic overheating and the events at Tiananmen, there was a backlash against reforms by conservative factions. However their efforts at reversing reforms and re-nationalizing assets failed when the Governor of Guangdong province and the Mayor of Shanghai refused to turn in more revenue to the central government, with many others following their lead. Political deadlock ensued at the centre but did not impede further reform, as provinces simply pushed ahead on their own. Guangdong province took a lead in price liberalization, which led to near complete removal of the dual-price system nationwide by 1993.

The economic success of China has produced a virtual torrent of books and articles by economists promoting the virtues of a gradual approach as opposed to a 'big bang' set of policies introduced in Eastern Europe to mixed results. This conclusion however refers to one part of the overall argument. The reasons for China's success go much deeper. Four points can be highlighted.

Local Initiative and Experimentation

Perhaps the main argument related to this 'gradualism' or lack thereof is that it allowed a strategy of experimentation, whereby ideas and models could be tested within a limited scope out in the provinces—where innovative ideas also sometimes originated, another feature that will be touched upon below—and disseminated or enshrined in national policy only after having proven its worth.

Apart from avoiding costly mistakes and stimulating innovation, the scope for caution and step-wise decision-making afforded by this strategy also allowed the building of greater consensus and stronger constituencies around further reform. The fact that some reforms were never extended beyond certain localities did, however, sow the seeds of today's vast regional disparities. Harrold (1992) argues that:

> Perhaps the greatest advantage of the decentralization approach has been to create interest groups in favor of further reforms, and to foster a climate for reform initiatives and 'spontaneous' reform at the local level. Many central reforms are 'enabling', in the sense that they remove central prohibitions [and] local reforms frequently spread, [which] not only helps to build up increased confidence and interest in reforms, [but] also creates innovative approaches to reform.

One of the areas where this experimentalism is most obvious—and controversial—is that of institutions. In contrast to the commonly expressed view by more traditional economists that institutional innovation only held Chinese growth back, some have argued to the contrary, that such innovation was helpful or even necessary given Chinese conditions. Qian (2002) notes:

> Although building best practice institutions is a desirable goal, getting institutions right is a process involving incessant changes interacting with initial conditions. The difference between China and Russia is not at all that China has established best practice institutions and that Russia did not. The difference lies in the institutions in transition.
>
> To understand how reforms work in developing and transition economies, we need to broaden our perspective on institutions. It is not enough to study the familiar forms of conventional institutions found in the most developed economies as a desirable goal; it is also essential to study the variety of unfamiliar forms of institutions in transition. The distinction between the conventional, best practice institutions and the transitional institutions is important.

An important characteristic of the above process is that the distinction between top–down and bottom–up initiation becomes somewhat fuzzy and perhaps not even so relevant. Heilmann (2008) puts it succinctly, 'distinguishing between bottom–up (spontaneous) and top down (mobilization-style) initiation of experimentation is nearly meaningless since there is a strong element of both. Local initiative and central sponsorship, both were vital in the initial stage of major experimental efforts. Neither works without the other. The dynamics of the experimental process rest precisely on this interplay'. China's adaptive capacity in policymaking goes beyond local tinkering, it is probably better characterized as 'foresighted tinkering under the shadow of hierarchy, serving policy agendas that are constantly set and reset by higher levels' (Heilmann 2009).

China's institutional unorthodoxy will be discussed in greater detail later below.

Building Consensus for Reform: Growing Out of the Plan

A key aspect of China's gradual approach, important to eventual success, is that it provided a smoother and more easily acceptable

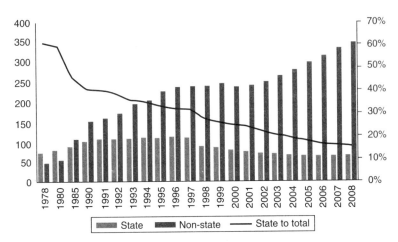

Figure 5.1 Dual-tracks in Non-agricultural Employment
Source: NBS. Based on Lau et al. (2000) and updated.

transition. In transition, there are inevitably, losers. Conducting reform without creating losers has been an implicit guiding principle since 1979, and the dual-track system (see Figure 5.1) is a concrete expression of that principle (Lau et al. 2000).

By allowing the economy to 'grow out of the plan'—in the famous words of Naughton (1994a)—this approach was less disruptive socially, economically, and politically than the *big bang* experiences of many other transition economies in Europe. It reduced opposition to change by providing security and compensation to potential losers, while also providing stability and the time to reorient preferences and expectations (ibid.).

Crucially, the competitive pressures from the expanding private sector is also cited by many observers as having a considerable impact in forcing efficiency improvements in the SOEs without the need for either privatization or large scale lay-offs.[3]

While it is generally acknowledged that maintaining job security and economic rents in the state sector also preserves

---

[3] See, for instance, Naughton (1994b), which shows that SOE output grew by 7.7 per cent per annum in 1978–91.

inefficiencies, the argument is made that more disruptive reforms would have created social costs important both in themselves and for their potential in eroding support for the reform process itself.

Along these lines, it has also been argued that the high household savings rates that made possible the rapid capital accumulation emerged partly as a response to a combination of fulfilled expectations and stable economic environment that was maintained throughout the period (Naughton 1994b). In this view, factor accumulation should not be taken at face value but examined more closely in search of underlying factors due to the characteristics of the reform process.

The Chinese dual-track system can be seen as implicit lumpsum transfers to compensate potential losers of reform. The product market in fact came close to full liberalization since resales, subcontracting, and purchases for re-delivery were permitted. Labour markets and real-estate markets however were not liberalized to the same extent.

This approach constrasts with the *big bang* approach which *inter alia* assumes a high degree of transferability of institutions from one society to the other, reflecting the underlying paradigm of modern economics—an equilibrium-oriented approach—which says 'get the prices right, and the rest will follow'. In reality, as the Chinese experience also demonstrates, social change is a highly complex, unpredictable phenomenon (Chen 1993).

Part Reformation

One aspect of gradualism was that some sectors were reformed while others were not; indeed many sectors were part-reformed along the lines of the dual-track system. Some observers have pointed to the fact that more marketized sectors and tracks have grown faster than non-marketized ones. While this is not surprising—since it is the main rationale behind marketization—it does not follow that expanding marketization to all sectors of the economy at once would have produced a better overall outcome.

Indeed, if the sequencing of reform across sectors has an impact on the stability of and support for the reform process itself, the opposite may be true.

The trial-and-error approach and the notion of path dependence are arguably key to understanding the 'socialist market economy' and guiding visions as well as the choices made by reformers. The unorthodoxy and pragmatism of this approach have been core features of China's reform process, and despite generating solutions seen as heretical by some it is hard to argue that they have not delivered—although counterfactual scenarios with still higher growth can always be constructed.

Economic theory has developed the concept of *second best* to describe solutions that are less than ideal but optimal given the constraints of a certain context. Irrespective of the general sense of imperfection that bedevils this concept, much of China's institutional reform can be usefully thought of in this way. Examples of such institutional *second best* solutions that increase efficiency in a non-optimal context include the pseudo-public ownership structure of the TVEs, the dual-track pricing system, and the fiscal contracting system.[4]

Qian (1999) notes that:

> Through experiments and innovations, a variety of transitional institutions emerged and many of them took unconventional forms. They were second-best arrangements but quite effective in providing incentives. As a result, China's reform in this stage was much deeper, more comprehensive, and more consistent than that in Eastern Europe prior to 1990, which helps explain why reform was a success in China but not in Eastern Europe.

Pragmatism (No 'First-best' Policies)

The gradual approach was in essence a reflection of the pragmatic nature of the Chinese leadership. Far from starting with a predetermined blueprint for reform or even a clear vision of

---

[4] As argued variously by Naughton (1996), Oi (1992), and Rawski (1999).

the end goal, the reformers began with the purpose of addressing a specific and limited set of increasingly obvious economic problems. The impact of the initial measures often gave rise to new issues which, however, were addressed with further reforms in a similarly pragmatic fashion. The leaders thus stepwise proceeded down a path of reforms never originally intended—in great contrast to the plans proposed for transition in EEFSU, often accused of being partly ideologically driven. This readiness of the Chinese leadership to respond to emerging issues with deepened reform has been outlined as an important part of it success (Naughton 1994b).

This pragmatism is arguably seen also in the relative tolerance for unexpected phenomena themselves, whereby the leadership accepted unorthodoxy and unanticipated developments as long as it delivered the results that were asked for—chiefly economic growth. Perhaps the most important example of this is the TVEs, whose major role in the growth of the 1980s and early 1990s was never anticipated by anyone, including Deng himself (Deng 1994).

Deng's dictums 'go a step and look for the next', 'feeling the stones to cross the river', and 'seek truth from the facts', all depict with clarity the very pragmatic thinking that has shaped China's approach to reforms. It is a pertinent and revealing exercise to compare this with Vaclav Havel's view of Eastern European reform experience that 'you cannot cross a chasm in two leaps' (Bhagwati 2004).

Another reason for this pragmatism may have been the perception that transition was impossible to plan, perhaps compounded by disillusionment vis-à-vis the planning system as a whole as the failures of the socialist economy had proven it's limitations.

The pragmatic, gradual approach has also implied responsiveness to unexpected needs and challenges. For instance, the competition engendered by the entry of non-state enterprises, starting with TVEs, propelled a variety of management reforms in the state enterprise sector (introduction of a profit tax, greater autonomy in production decisions, greater management freedom, and so on). Reforms at the corporate level in turn highlighted the need for and actively induced further adjustments at the macro level (Bajpai and Jian 1996).

This fits well with the notion of 'induced institutional change' put forth by several authors (Lin 2004; Chen 1993). China 'pragmatism' can thus be described as a needs-sensitive, results-based, and somewhat risk-averse approach to reforms. Rawski (1999) goes further to argue to that the most important feature of Chinese reform has been its interactive nature. Even the slogan 'crossing the river by feeling the stones' may give the wrong impression by implying a clear goal when none existed. Early reforms were tentative, partial, and consistently focused on enabling rather than compulsion.

CAPACITIES

Investing in capacity increases not only growth directly but also raises the prospects of successful development transformation. Several propositions can be highlighted:

a. The importance of *social policy*.
   Investing in human capabilities becomes almost a precondition to both start and sustain development progress.
b. The *state has an active role to play* in managing transformation by creating the corresponding capacities and institutions (*through public investment, influencing norms, and defining policies*).
   i. *Strong institutions* are necessary to successfully manage development transformation.
   ii. States need a strong *results-orientation*.
c. *Good social capital and cohesion* ensures continuity and stability in the flux of transformation and raises growth through cultural factors like work ethic and openness to change (*building constituencies for reform and compensating losers*).
d. *Strong or well-embedded social* capital reduces risk and other transaction costs. It enhances the flow of information and resources, reduces or controls individual divergence from the desired path.

Human Capability Formation

[A] country's potential for rapid growth is strong ... not when it is backward without qualification, but rather when it is technologically backward but socially advanced.

—Abramovitz 1986

Human development gains, particularly in health and education, provided an important part of the foundation on which economic growth was built. There are two parts of this argument: one, pre-reform human development gains were critical in enabling the post-1978 and later reforms to succeed, and two, investing in upgrading human capacities continued to be priority even as growth accelerated and incomes shot up. It gave the broad masses of Chinese people, especially its labourers and managers, the capability to respond effectively to new incentives and opportunities.

The theoretical link between human development (HD) and economic growth has been covered in the earlier chapter. There is however an important aspect of sequencing in the case of China. Given China's size and complexity, inevitably explanations about HD's contribution to growth are more nuanced. High HD investments in the 1950s and 1960s and the far reaching social reforms (leading to a different social context) strengthened the 'initial' conditions for the introduction of the Deng's market friendly reforms and policies. Several Chinese economists have highlighted this inter-dependence (Zhou 1984; Qian and Weingast 1996). Without Mao's radical policies, Deng's market friendly reforms may not have succeeded. For example, Qian and Weingast (1996) believe that 'although Mao did not decentralize for the purpose of promoting markets, his decentralization [measures] not only had lasting institutional effect but, retrospectively planted seeds for the later emerging federalism, Chinese style'.

Education

Education has been a traditional value in China. Investment in basic education has been a continuing priority from the start of the Peoples' Republic of China. A big part of the explanation of the Chinese success has been the rapid expansion of the education of people generally and the labour force specifically. In 1978, funds for basic education accounted for 2 per cent of GDP. By 2005 it was 2.5 per cent of a vastly expanded GDP. In absolute terms, there was a 60-fold increase in budgetary expenditures in basic education over the same period. In overall terms, China spends about 2.8 per cent in 2004 of GDP on education, even if this fell short of the 4 per cent of GDP target set in the 11th Five Year Plan (2006–10).

The link between education, equity, and modernization was explicitly reiterated by the 17th National CPC Congress in its call for a *Xiaokang* society. A key instrument of becoming a Xiaokang society was to 'give priority to education and turn China into a country strong in human resources. Education is the cornerstone of national rejuvenation, and equal access to education provides an important underpinning for social equity' (UNDP 2008).

A critical transformative measure by the government was to commit itself early on to the *right to education* by making 1–9 grade schooling compulsory. By 2004, almost 18 years after the passing of the Law on Compulsory Education, the nine-year commitment had been instituted in a high 92.6 per cent of the population. Enrolment rates of primary and secondary schools have been increasing over the years reaching almost 100 per cent in the late 1990s. At the national level, the completion rate of 1–9 years education was 75 per cent by 2001. Challenges of course remain. By 2003, China still had 381 counties that had not succeeded in making this commitment universally available.

Similarly, in the more than 60 years since the founding of new China, the *campaign to eliminate illiteracy* has never stopped. In 1964, from a high of 33.6 per cent of the population who could not read or write, a staggering 233 million people, illiteracy in China was reduced to 22.8 per cent in 1982, about 230 million people, and then brought down to 6.7 per cent in 2000, or 85 million people.[5]

---

[5] According to the Fifth National Population Census.

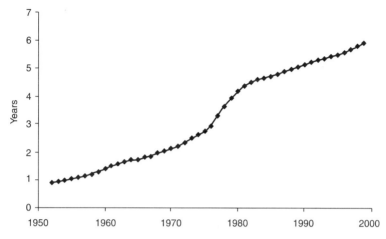

Figure 5.2 Average Schooling Years of China's Population Aged 15–64 (1952–99)
Source: Wang and Yao (2003).

The stock of educated people in China has gone up in all categories: primary, secondary, and junior college and above. By 1980, China had reached a respectable level of over four years of average schooling for the population (Figure 5.2), a valuable initial condition for the start of reforms. Most empirical studies on China that calculate the effect of education on economic growth do so in terms of wage differences of an educated person, with wages approximating to the marginal product of labour (and hence its contribution to growth). These studies produce a result that education at best contributes around 1 percentage point to the growth rate of China's GDP in the past (Perkins 2006). That this substantially understates education's contribution to economic growth is equally clear. Most of the models that measure such a contribution are unable to account for externalities inherent in the role of education, as people learn from each other, and the more educated they are the more learning that takes place. It also does not account for its influence on social capital, with education contributing to open to change attitudes, and a generally positive expectation of future progress.

In May 1985, the government's Reform of the Educational System stated that 'the responsibility for developing basic education will be handed over to local governments and nine year compulsory education will be universalized step by step' (UNDP 2008). While a welcome step in decentralizing authority for education, without a concomitant adequate fiscal support from the centre, it had a negative impact on poor counties' ability to sustain such a commitment. Between 1994 and 2001, town and township governments paid nearly four-fifths of China's compulsory education costs, while provincial governments paid about 11 per cent, county governments 9 per cent, and remarkably, central government less than 2 per cent. These concerns led to further reforms in 2005 which sought to provide a more sustainable basis of financing the nine-year commitment by setting up a more balanced provision of central and local funds.

In response to concerns about widening income disparities between urban and rural areas, much of the education spending was then targeted on rural areas. In 2006, 70 per cent of the government's new expenditures went to these areas. By 2007, the goal of universal primary school enrolment had been mostly realized, meeting one of the MDG targets several years in advance with some indicators in education comparable to or even exceeding those in industrialized countries.

However, there are continuing challenges. When comparing education expenditures as a percentage of GDP, China is still below that of the United States at 5.4 per cent of GDP and South Korea at 3.7 per cent of GDP. At the same time, a high 30 per cent of China's GDP is devoted to physical capital investment, a level very similar to that in South Korea. Further, its ratio of annual investment in physical capital to human capital is much higher than that of most countries around the world (Heckman 2003).

Health

Concerning health, China's average life expectancy has steadily risen from a relative high of 67.8 in 1981 to over 72.4 in 2007.

As with education, the big push forward in health indicators however took place earlier in the 1950s and 1960s, as Figure 5.3 brings out. Infant and maternal mortality rates have similarly sharply improved. And, as with education numbers, there are wide variations among provinces, with the maternal mortality rate (MMR) in Shanghai at 9.6 and Guizhou at 111.0, and between different categories of people, for instance, migrant women who represent only 10 per cent of urban pregnancies, account for two-thirds of maternal mortality.

While there has been an ongoing improvement in health outcomes over the reform years, there has not been a concomitant increase in health spending by the state.

From 1980 to 2000, as the result of growing dependence on markets and a delinking of social care provision from state supported work units, the Chinese state was spending a declining percentage of GDP on the provision of healthcare services. The reversal of the trend in the later years however only marginally reduced (by 10 per cent) the proportion spent by households on health, to 49 per cent in 2006 (as opposed to 21 per cent in 1980). China continues to under-spend on health. The 2003 SARS experience highlighted many of the challenges and shortfalls of the public healthcare system. The years of underinvestment in the sector showed in the inadequacy of the health sector response. In reviewing the health systems of the 191 countries,

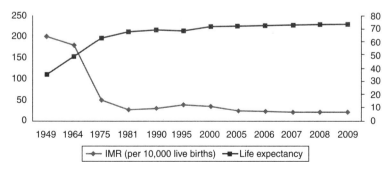

Figure 5.3 Infant Mortality Rates (IMRs) and Life Expectancy in China
Source: World Bank (2010).

WHO (2000) ranked China 144 in terms of overall performance and 188 in the equity of health financing.

These trends raise concerns for the future. In the 1970s, China, particularly its renowned barefoot doctor programme, was held up as model for developing economies for making basic healthcare widely available. But now it is regarded, including by its leaders and the wider public, as an extreme case of inequality in the provision of healthcare. The problem of inequality holds for both rural and urban areas. Recent surveys have shown that health costs may be responsible for 33 per cent of the newly poor. Some 80 per cent of the rural population and 50 per cent of the urban population are entirely uninsured for medical costs. These concerns have led to renewed state commitment for comprehensive health reform.

HD Gains and Their Contribution to Growth

Many commentators have pointed to the early emphasis of the East Asian states on universal education. For China, a 2001 World Bank paper studying the impact of human capital on economic growth concludes that human capital has contributed significantly to growth (Wang and Yao 2003). They however break human capital accumulation out of TFP, which they also find to be significant and contributing 2–3 percentage points to growth. This leads them to take the middle ground in the debate: Both factor accumulation and productivity growth have been very important for growth They conclude that the importance of factor accumulation seems to be decreasing and TFP will thus be the key driving force in future growth.

Similar conclusions emerge from a comparative analysis of India and China by Bloom et al. (2006). They point to rapid increases in life expectancy and declines in fertility in explaining growth, even if in both cases the magnitude of the effects is greater in the case of China than in India. Increase in life expectancy is taken as a proxy for population health. This finding confirms other studies, including a cross country study of growth rates by Bloom et al. (2004). This and other studies confirm that better health and nutrition led to substantial improvement in productivity, and hence growth, in China.

Initially, improvement of overall economic and social conditions which led to declines in mortality in India and China, including in infant and child mortality, led to large cohorts of young people. This 'demographic dividend' is credited for one-third of East Asia's economic miracle. The introduction of the one-child policy led to a sharp drop in fertility rates, and a sharp rise in the ratio of working to non-working age people, with a 2.5 peak level projected for 2010. India's demographics on the other hand moved more slowly, with its comparable peak of 2.1 expected in 2035. For India, the full value of its demographic dividend is still to be realized. China by contrast is now looking at a rapidly ageing population with over 400 million Chinese. By 2030, according to *Nature*, about 35 per cent of the population is projected to be 60 and above (Lutz et al. 2008).

There is yet another dimension here which connects human development investments to institutions and their effectiveness. According to the paper by Djankov et al. (2003), each community or nation faces a set of institutional opportunities, determined largely by the human and social capital of its population. The greater the human and social capital of a community, the more attractive are its institutional opportunities. Indeed Glaeser et al. (2004) argue that institutions have only a second-order effect on economic performance, with the first-order effect coming from human and social capital, which shape both institutional and productive capacities of a society. They consider the economic success of East Asia in the post-war era, and of China most recently, as a consequence of good-for-growth policies with human capital investment playing an important role, not of institutions constraining them.

The State, Bureaucracy, and Chinese Institutions

Among the central choices facing all societies is the role of government.
Economic success requires getting the balance right between the government

and the market.... this balance obviously changes over time, and will differ from country to country.

—Stiglitz (2006)

Development involves managing processes and addressing concerns that are dependent on the organizational and managerial capacities of various institutions in the state sphere, private sector, civil society, media, academia, or other social and political bodies. The state has the particularly important task to sustain efficient markets, prevent (or redress) market failures, avoid (or compensate for) negative externalities, and provide public goods. As Chapter 4 highlights, in transformation, different stages of development may require different capacities. What worked well previously may now fail and must be adapted to the new mode of production.

The Chinese government is seen as the embodiment of an active, developmental state. Its enthusiasm for development is seen as a critical factor in driving China's success. This activist role did not come by accident, as this change in behaviour of the Chinese government was an outcome of specific bureaucratic reforms which had a two-fold purpose: one, to change the human capital composition of the bureaucracy, with younger, more educated officials replacing older, more revolutionary cadres, and second, through extensive administrative and fiscal decentralization to empower lower level administrations (Li 1998).

There was an important sequencing dimension as well. In China, early institutional transformation crucially underpinned economic reform, as Deng saw the need to revitalize the bureaucracy as a necessary first step (Li 1998). But this fateful choice did more than that. It both reduced active opposition to the reforms, and created a constituency in favour of change, since the newly recruited officials owed their appointments to the leaders promoting change.

The sheer scale of the institutional change was staggering. In a short space of time, mostly over two to three years, China's bureaucracy was transformed (almost at all levels) as the Figures below bring out vividly. By 1988, a remarkable 90 per cent of officials above the county-level had been newly appointed after 1982; meanwhile in Russia, by contrast, local leaders remained largely the same people as before reforms (Frye and Shleifer 1997). Deng's rejuvenation of the government administration also increased the capacity of officials: the share of governors holding a college degree more than doubled while for ministers the share rose by 40 per cent.[6] Very similar results can be seen for provincial party secretaries, mayors, and department chiefs as well as down to county and division levels (see Figures 5.4 and 5.5).

This move resulted in both higher capacity and better alignment with reform objectives, as the younger and better educated cadres were more supportive of the reform process. Capacity upgrading has been and continues to be a priority.

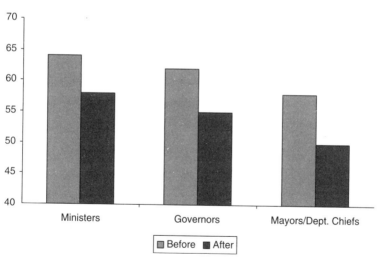

Figure 5.4 Average Age of Officials (Before and After 1982 Reforms, Years)
Source: Li (1998).

---

[6] The shares rose from 20 per cent to 43 per cent for governors and from 37 per cent to 52 per cent for ministers, as reported in Li (1998).

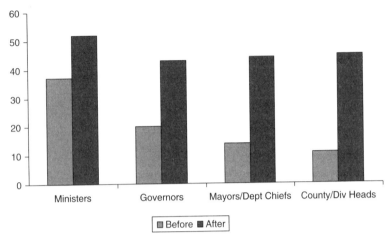

Figure 5.5 Share of Officials Holding College Degree (Before and After 1982 Reforms, per cent)
Source: Li (1998).

Education levels of officials have risen continuously over the entire reform period. Chinese bureaucracy has been designed for strong results orientation, linking career development to achievement of central objectives of modernization and economic progress (Howell 2004).

The outcome of this step and a series of related measures described below meant that the Chinese government has overall provided a relatively 'supporting hand' in furthering economic growth. Despite the lack of political liberalization, China's bureaucracy transformed itself into a force supporting economic reform and economic development. In the transformation framework outlined earlier, state attitudes go some ways in explaining development success.

Property Rights and Incentives

Institutions influence and shape incentives in human exchange, whether political, social, or economic. More specifically, the term 'economic institutions' is used to refer to property rights and the nature of markets. Property rights are considered the bedrock of economic growth and development. Economists contend that:

> Efficient economic organization is the key to growth; the development of an efficient economic organization in Western Europe accounts for the rise of the West. (North and Thomas 1973)
>
> [W]e have only to contrast the organization of production in the Third World economy with that of an advanced industrial economy to be impressed by the consequences of poorly defined and/or effective property rights. (North 1990)
>
> [I]ndividuals will not have the incentive to invest in physical or human capital or adopt more efficient technologies. Economic institutions are also important because they help to allocate resources to their most efficient uses, they determine who gets profits, revenues and residual rights of control. (Acemoglu et al. 2004)
>
> Property rights are considered a key aspect of market-supporting institutions. (Rodrik 1999)

By these statements, China is a major outlier. The Chinese experience provides compelling evidence for that discussion, by demonstrating that control rights and residual claims can generate incentives every bit as effective as formal property rights. The often heard counterargument that growth took place outside the state sector is somewhat misleading, since the collective sector was in many ways an extension of local governments, only with hard budget constraints and residual claim rights.[7] It can be pointedly argued—as this book does—that in the 'development as transformation' thesis, *ownership* of reforms may matter as much if not more than that of property. Similarly, privatization may matter considerably less than competitive pressure through domestic entry and opening to trade.[8]

---

[7] As shown by Naughton (1996), Oi (1992), and others.
[8] As argued by McMillan and Naughton (1992) and many others.

Lin (2004) argues that stabilization and liberalization can be implemented fairly rapidly whilst 'privatization may take a number of years to accomplish [and] the development of market-supporting institutions such as legal and financial systems, will take years or even decades. [Therefore] no matter what approach is adopted, the transition from a centrally planned system to a market system in any country in fact will necessarily be a gradual process.'

The argument has also been made that given the lack of standard capitalist managerial disciplines in the first phase of transition from a command economy, there is a need for the state to oversee managers, which is naturally easier in sectors that remain under state control. The Chinese experience would appear to present evidence that the managerial incentives can be adequate under such conditions, given the reasonably strong performance of the SOE sector in the reform period—while avoiding plundering of public resources in relatively anarchic states of interim transition such as that witnessed in parts of EEFSU (McMillan and Naughton 1992).

According to the same author, China's transition process can be best described as an 'induced institutional innovation' process, whereby incremental changes, 'cracks' into old institutional structures have 'self-propelled' more radical 'market-oriented' shifts, but in a non disruptive manner, in a way that left people with enough time to absorb, adjust to changes.

This is echoed by several studies, including Chen (1993), which argue that the decentralized change so typical of China's experience is effective because economic institutions by necessity must be self-organizing and develop in an evolutionary process. In the words of Harrold (1992), 'reforms in one area lead naturally to reforms in other areas, and indeed force those reforms by creating pressures for change [...] and policymakers have in general seen their interests served best by meeting such pressures with new reforms rather than by administrative protectionism, albeit sometimes with a considerable lag'.

Some interpret moves in recent years towards more traditional institutions—such as the constitutional revision in 2004 to give private property the same legal status as public property, the emphasis on rule of law and the many changes required by WTO accession—as *ex post* evidence of the validity of the *big bang* school of thought and the inevitable convergence with best practice institutions (Sachs and Woo 2003). This appears, however, to miss the point made by those suggesting that since institutions require time to change and the need for change was so great, gradualism was a core factor in success—which holds true even if one agrees that the standard set of neoclassical institutions are the only appropriate end goal.

Rodrik (1999) provides a useful analytical framework for looking at institutions and their role in market economies. What has driven growth in China has been the move towards a market economy. For such an economy to succeed, it has to rely on a wide array of non-market institutions to perform certain functions, generally to regulate or support markets. He makes the important point that 'institutional basis for a market economy is not uniquely determined' (ibid.).

Ownership reform in China has been less dramatic than some of the studies have characterized, certainly less than the proposed privatizations of most EEFSU countries. Farmers under the household responsibility still had to meet state mandated production targets. Under the reforms, managers in SOEs were allowed to retain a portion of profits, but the supervising entities could still transfer the devolved rights among the managers. It is therefore significant that several economists, including Naughton, find that the reforms 'have improved managerial performance in China's SOEs by strengthening incentives generated by pay and appointment mechanisms' (Putterman 1995).

Is a socialist market economy feasible? The reform of property rights in extending limited production rights pushed China into giving managers or farmers more autonomy in production decisions and in following market signals. Most studies confirm that shift did make a substantial contribution to economic growth. For the Household Responsibility System, studies claim that 78 per cent to 86 per cent of the growth in output can be attributed to the adoption of the household responsibility system. While the debate continues, both market liberation per se and the assignment of decision-making and revenue rights played key roles.

The debates about what all this means for the ownership and its importance to future growth however remain. One widely held view is that failure to give full land ownership to the farmer has held back agricultural growth. In industry, most authors concur that the 'non-state' sector is doing much better than SOEs. TFP, the famous residual, grew 2–3 times for the private sector than the SOE rate. But equally many have argued that the non-state sector covers a wide variety of 'ownership' rights. The abiding conclusion which can be reached is that 'reform of property rights in China has been gradual and limited. Agricultural land remains collective property, only some smaller state enterprises have been privatized and (the most significant) change in industrial ownership is the rise of TVEs, a form of organization closely connected with local public ownership' (ibid.).

Civil Service Performance

There are long antecedents of the civil service in China. The traditional Chinese state combined rule by a hereditary ruler with a professional civil service selected in most part through competitive examinations. Apart from creating a functioning bureaucracy, the Chinese civil service had an additional, important role—that of promoting a specific political or governing philosophy. An interesting parallel can be drawn with the joining of ideology with the implementation of reforms during the present communist period in China. There are countless references in Chinese history to the test of a ruler being 'whether he succeeds in promoting the welfare of the common people' (Nolan 2004). That a Confucian term, *Xiaokang*, is taken on as capturing China's current development vision is no accident and underscores the abiding nature of Chinese culture and reinforces the notion of 'learning from the past'.

Bureaucracy also functions in a specific cultural context. For a long period in China, many aspirants saw the civil service as a path towards personal prosperity and power. The civil service in China acted as a vehicle to link values and society. It allowed 'basic beliefs, operational values and social institutions to be integrated, mutually reinforcing' (Dernberger 1980) and well embedded in society. The numbers of candidates who passed the exams are staggering. Many more of course took the exam. Even in the eighteenth century, some 406,000 passed the local examinations, *shengyuan*. At the higher levels some 47,500 became eligible to join the civil service (Feuerwerker 1976). Equally, Confucian precepts contend that if the bureaucracy became corrupt, it loses its moral foundation. To serve the people requires winning their trust. And if trust is reduced between the people and the government, social disorder becomes the likely result. It reduces the legitimacy of government and 'the mandate of heaven' is removed from the Emperor (or ruling elite). Little wonder that one of the enduring slogans of Mao's period was for the Party to 'serve the people'.

In the more modern period, reform of the civil service dates from 1980, when it was felt that there was a pressing need to 'rejuvenate the leadership cadre and the system through which it was selected' (Howell 2004). Reforms included implementing a fixed tenure system that required retirement for most officials at age 60 for men and 55 for women and efforts to improve the quality of China's leadership, especially by recruiting younger, more educated officials.

Governing a country is as much a 'managerial' task as it is in setting a coherent vision. How was this done in China? The number of top 'managers/leaders' of the country are a relative modest 30 or so. These leaders/managers have to both take national decisions and manage/influence a large number of subordinates. Huang (1998) in his review of the organization of the Chinese government contends that the China managed well in 'aligning' civil servants to the expectations of the leaders. In particular, the Chinese political system was able to deliver on the appropriate mix of incentives and control measures that ensured that the 'right' people were selected to the top levels of the government. This is an important finding for a complex, large country like China which has some 28 ministries in the State Council, 31 provincial governments, 2,400–2,860 county governments, and some 30,000–40,000 township governments.

In the early 1990s, central party agencies directly appointed a large number of bureaucratic personnel, some 4,100 officials of them, who in turn then oversaw tens of thousands of officials (Burns 1994). Like business organizations, alignment problems occur when interests of the subordinates deviate from those of the leaders. That China did well in this context goes some distance in explaining how the country was able to achieve and maintain impressive economic and social results despite the enormous constraints presented by a high population and relatively poor resource endowments (Huang 1998, in his comments on promotion and leadership selection practices).

One aspect of the leadership selection practices was the emphasis placed on proven ability and being tested in a variety of situations. In the 1980s, for instance, the number of provincial bureaucrats who filled key central ministerial positions far exceeded that of ministerial bureaucrats. Two out of three party secretaries in the 1980s had extensive work experience in the provinces. These practices continue to this day. An outlier in this practice is the influential Ministry of Foreign Affairs which draws its ministers exclusively from its own ranks. Provincial or local level performance was considered critical. It was felt that performance of provincial cadres could be more readily and more objectively measured, and that 'performance of a bureaucrat in a provincial post reveals more information about his suitability as a national leader than the similar performance of a ministerial bureaucrat' (ibid.).

The 1990 reforms of civil service and the public sector were driven in part by the difficulty that central policymakers had in pursing economic reform. Even if many innovations were 'bottom up', with local leaders playing a critical role, reforms

themselves when extended nationwide were often watered
down as local leaders were more concerned about coping with
the tensions arising from policy implementation. A major shift
was in the selection of senior managers from those whose political background was appropriate to work-related abilities and
achievement. Performance appraisal of the civil servant in leading positions was further tightened around three broad tasks:
economic development, social and spiritual development, and
Party building. Due to the Communist Party of China's (CPC)
emphasis on economic growth, economic development became
the dominant task. Political careers and bonuses were linked
to the achievement of targets. Local leaders in turn could
'sub-contract' the targets to lower level officials (Chou 2005).

The public sector reforms since the 1980s also strengthened
bureaucratic accountability. Accounting and auditing systems
were substantially improved and upgraded. Starting in the early
1990s, accounting standards were increasingly brought closer to
international standards. According to experts, 'with one exception there are no significant differences between the Chinese
standards and International Accounting Standards' (Narayan and
Woolcock 2000).[9]

Peer feedback of performance, and more recently citizen
satisfaction about the provision of social services, all combined
to transform the civil service to a development driven service.
The strengthening of institutions created a more professional
home for civil servants and leading cadres less influential in the
well being of their subordinates. The system had some downsides
as well. It also created incentives for civil servants to 'manipu-
late' results and as such tended to dilute the intended impact of
reforms on administrative efficiency and government capacity.
Chou (2005) underlines as well the innate resistance to reform
in performance appraisal that disturbed 'organizational harmony'

---

[9] The exception requires that in China accountants and relevant authorities
agree on divergences from regulations and provisions for damaged or obsolete
inventories (Howell 2004).

or led to 'conflictual contexts'. Subordinates were prepared to provide positive feedback of their supervisors in their 'democratic' appraisals as long as their own faults were not brought to light. Ambiguity in parts of the appraisal system created space for local innovation but it highlighted the problems associated with reciprocity.

Capacity upgrading has been and continues to be a priority and education levels of officials have risen continuously over the entire reform period (Howell 2004). By 1998, nearly 90 per cent of bureau chiefs had graduated from university or community college. In 1980, more than 80 per cent of provincial/ministerial level officials were 60 years or older. By 1998, this percentage had dropped to about 54 per cent. The bureaucracy in particular has been designed for strong results orientation, linking career development to achievement of central objectives (ibid.). And, interestingly enough, the dual processes of economic decentralization and the decentralization of the personnel management system did not lead to a decline of the capacity of the Party to enforce reforms (Landry 2003).

The conclusion is that the Chinese government has both provided a 'supporting hand' in furthering economic growth and was strong enough to direct and guide the different waves of reform. In Russia, the big bang approach left a political/leadership vacuum and a weakened state. One consequence was that the state was captured by powerful interest groups and often functioned as a 'grabbing hand', suffocating growth and development (through corruption, nepotism, and so on). Another was that in many areas in Russia, government presence simply vanished, forcing people to rely on social networks and other informal systems.

Chinese Institutions, More Generally

The word 'institution' is here used to denominate intangible institutions rather than physical organizations. It thus encompasses the social rules, norms, and values as well as the economic, legal, and political fundaments upon which society is organized.

It does not, however, for the purpose of this section include organizational embodiments such as the judiciary, government administration, or the central bank system.

Excluding the narrowest of definitions, most scholars take a view of institutions as considerably more complex than individual pieces of legislation or regulation, encompassing individuals' norms, expectations, and responses. Rather than being an event that can be introduced at a given point in time, institutional reform is an interactive process that depends on both initial conditions and myriad choices made along the way. This means that they perforce evolve in a gradual, organic process that requires time— years and decades—to complete. Several authors have argued that such an interpretation fits well with the Chinese experience.[10]

As Chen (1993) notes perhaps the most important contribution of China's reform leadership was to refrain from making quick judgments or suppress 'illegal' practices. Instead, 'they let time be the judge. This tolerance of heterodoxy fostered innovation in institution-building. The 'gradualness' of China's reform, then, was not a conscious design of the central government, but rather the inevitable result of compromises among a myriad of conflicting proposals, through a long process of trial and error. China's success demonstrates the effectiveness of providing time for learning and adaptation'. Through experiments and innovations, inevitably a variety of transitional institutions emerged, with many of them taking on unconventional forms, perhaps more suited to the specific Chinese conditions. For instance, only gradually has the dualistic system been replaced with institutions that are perhaps closer to international standards. Qian (1999) again notes that 'this process is...different from some Eastern European countries in that the new institutions are built before the old ones are destroyed.'

Another example refers to fiscal decentralization. Lin and Liu (2000), while investigating the impact on growth rates of the

---

[10] See, for instance, Chen (1993), Lin (2004), Rawski (1999), Perkins (1994), and Qian (1999).

new fiscal arrangements initiated in the mid-1980s, draw two important conclusions: First is that institutional arrangements do matter, and second, a claim based on the data set that fiscal decentralization raised the growth rate in China by improving the efficiency of resource allocation more so than inducing additional investment.

Better performing institutions may improve growth by increasing the level of investment by, for instance, reducing the amount of red tape in setting up new enterprises, and increasing the efficiency of investment by enforcing well-defined property rights, though the latter has only a relatively weak empirical case (Aron 2000). Interestingly, Clague et al. (1996) find that the characteristics and stability of political regimes appear to be important determinants of the quality of economic institutions.

That Chinese institutions were different from those prescribed in standard economic textbooks is not debated. What has been is debated is their efficacy. Sachs and Woo (2000) claim that success in economic growth was the result of convergence of Chinese institutions to those in non-socialist economies, that since we all know what that future looks like, that is, functioning, efficient markets with secure property rights, there are real costs to the experimentation. Others like Qian and Weingast (1996) look at experimentation as the best possible strategy given the social and political circumstances, and as such are willing to live with the some of the allocative inefficiencies that may arise. For different reasons, both are unable to accept that these reforms allowed for transformation to take place, which in turn laid the base for further reforms. Allocative efficiency though useful as a concept, may be less important at early stages of development. Rodrik (1999) sees the debate between the 'big bang' and the 'gradual reform' advocates in a sense missing the point by not fully accounting for the institutional context. 'Big bang' worked for Poland because the 'country had already defined its future: it wanted to be a "normal" European society, with full membership in the European Union. Adopting European institutions wholesale was not only a means to an end; it was also the ultimate objective the country desired'.

Box 5.1 Unorthodox Institutions

The innovative *fiscal contracting*, with its high marginal retention rates for local government, aligned the interests of local governments with local business and played a fundamental role in turning local governments into 'helping hands' of local business. Local governments responded to incentives by supporting productive non-SOEs and reforming non-productive SOEs. (Note: the fiscal contracting was a variety of experimental bilateral arrangements between central and provincial governments on payments to the centre of certain fixed or increasing levels or shares of provincial tax revenues, varying across provinces. In the early 1990s, provinces retained nearly 90 per cent of local revenues on average and about 70 per cent of provinces were 'residual claimants' retaining 100 per cent at the margin.)

The early reforms (1979–93) often involved special *responsibility contracts* which both improved economic incentives for some agents (such as farmers or SOE managers) and let existing interests (rents) in the bureaucracy remain protected.

Township and village enterprises (TVEs) are another example that allowed market forces to work relatively efficiently despite the absence of secure property rights since they were owned by local government; it was also in the interest of both local and national government as it generated revenue for them; the pro-market incentives effect was strengthened with tax reforms making local government more dependent on TVE revenue to fund their budgets.

The *dual-track pricing system* was important in that it both forced farmers to sell a given quota of grain (and other products) to the state at a given price; but also allowed them to sell any surplus at market price. This price liberalization at the margin introduced market incentives and begun transformation of hearts and minds while also keeping the previous system in place alongside the market 'experiment'. The dual-track system was later applied to most other key economic reforms areas, including foreign exchange as well as labour, housing, social security, and ownership reforms.

SOCIAL CAPITAL (AND SOCIAL COHESION)

China has enjoyed strong social cohesion thanks to comparative ethnic homogeneity, historic equality, and lack of religious

sectarianism. The widespread awareness of the failures of the previous economic policies meant that mindsets were ready for change and engendered buy-in for the reforms. The above made society responsive to reform and new incentives. This responsiveness arguably outweighed market imperfections in promoting rapid growth.

Success of the reforms in the final analysis rests on people themselves, on their attitudes and behavior. The Chinese reforms demonstrate how reform cannot be viewed as a sequence of decisions by the state to which businesses and individuals respond, but rather unfolds as an organic process of interaction and feedback. In short, reform is a process, not an event (Rawski 1999). Relatively high faith by people in China in the higher levels of government and in the organizing functions of the political system helped to provide social stability during the reforms. Trust systems offset absence of formal contract enforcement and informal institutions were able to counter the constraints imposed by imperfect markets (namely, role of *guanxi*, 'friends first, business later').

Compensating Losers and Building Constituencies for Reform

A variety of observers have noted that one important component of the Chinese experience has been the limiting and compensation of losers, in effect engendering a reform process which can in large measure be seen as Pareto-improving.[11] All or most of the reforms in the first period can be categorized as win-win solutions, from the agricultural contracts (releasing underemployed agricultural labour and raising returns to the farmers who carry on) or the fiscal contracting system (giving local government 100 per cent retention at the margin but also providing the centre with increased fiscal uptake) to the buy-outs of the old guard to enable a government generational shift and the

---

[11] See, for instance, Lau et al. (1997, 2000) and Naughton (1996).

dual-track production system (maintaining rents and security in the state track while letting private and quasi-private initiative grow in the market track).

The initial rural reforms was a win–win for most parties which involved: Allowing farmers to retain the profits from all production in excess of their mandated quotas introduced incentives not only to enhance efficiency, but to support the reforms, while the rural bureaucracy was weak, and so reforms were implemented with little opposition. Later industrial reforms similarly introduced strong incentives for enterprises and their managers with profit retention, as well as for local governments through similar arrangements in the fiscal system. Thus several broad constituencies were created who, out of their own interest, gave their support to reforms, counterbalancing and outweighing the many vested interests that also existed.

The fact that lay-offs didn't start until 1993 is a good illustration of this (Gu 1999). While it was likely partly due to political disagreement among the leadership, it is hard to argue that the strategic implications in reducing disruption were not part of their decision.

Another telling example is the strategy of administrative rejuvenation pushed through by Deng Xiaoping in 1982. Realizing that the path of reform required government officials with different mindsets and skill sets than the typical peasant–revolutionary veterans found throughout the administration, Deng wanted to infuse it with younger and better educated staff. The problem was, of course, resistance on the part of those to be replaced, including many in senior decision-making positions.

By presenting new-age and educational requirements for officials alongside a one-time offer for those who accepting retirement to keep both incomes and perks, including housing, assistants, and security clearance, Deng, without conflict, dramatically transformed the government—removing those most likely to object to the reforms and making it better placed to manage the complex process on which China was embarking (Li 1998). As earlier noted, the average age of ministers and governors was lowered by six and seven years respectively, while their average tenure was reduced by one-third versus nearly half.[12]

Many observers have pointed out that the dual-track system was similarly useful because it improved efficiency while retaining existing economic rents, thus reducing opposition to reforms and allowing the process to move forward without disruption (Qian 2002; Naughton 1994b).

It has also been argued that the Chinese institutional innovations were beneficial partly by creating win-win solutions for all or most actors under a complex set of constraints, thereby improving the overall outcome in spite of certain remaining inefficiency—relative to theoretically optimal, but practically infeasible, Western institutions (Qian 2002).

Emerging Challenges to Social Cohesion

Despite the gradual process involved, adjustment was not painless. Large sections of society had to absorb the shock of the reforms. The pressure on society has intensified over the years. While average incomes have grown dramatically over the reform period, relative differences are increasingly wide and noticeable. Perceptions of unfairness have intensified over the years as disparities widen.

Not surprisingly, rising disparities have contributed to street protests and demonstrations as workers and farmers seek to convey their frustrations (Blecher 2004). A survey of Beijing residents in 2002 indicated that 80 per cent of those who responded believed that growing income differences were a major social problem.[13] Income inequality has widened substantially. Even more telling than the relative differences captured by the Gini coefficient (which went up from 0.30 in 1978, 0.382 in the late 1980s, to 0.447 in 2000), is the striking gap between rural and urban incomes (UNDP 2005). In comparing the latter, China has

---

[12] According to Li (1998), the average age of ministers fell from 64 to 58 and tenure from 6.6 to 4.4 years, while corresponding figures for governors was 62 to 55 and 6.4 to 3.8.

[13] By Beijing Social Psychological Research Institute.

become one of the most unequal societies in the world. In human development terms, life expectancy for rural residents is less than 65 years in Tibet, Guizhou, and Yunnan, but more than 74 years in Hainan and Jiangsu. Tibet and Guizhou have HDI levels comparable to countries in Africa, and Shanghai with Portugal. By contrast, for 2000, India has a Gini Coefficient of 0.325, Sweden 0.25, and Brazil 0.591 (UNDP 2005, 2008; see Figure 5.6).

And looking at the dispersion in progress among provinces, Figure 5.7 provides useful comparative data.

The relatively less well-off groups include the traditional working class and farmers. Between 1995 and 2001, SOEs laid off 37 million people—some 33 per cent of the total SOE work force. Over the same period, urban collectives laid off 55 per cent of their workers, a drop from 31 million to 13 million workers (Fewsmith 2004). Laid-off workers tend to be older, female, and lacking formal education. Securing new jobs for these workers has been an ongoing challenge, particularly in the old industrial areas of northeast China. Re-employment rates dropped from 42 per cent in 1999, to 9 per cent in the first half of 2002

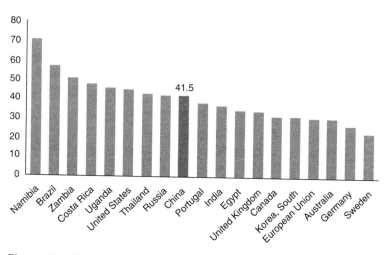

Figure 5.6 Gini Coefficient in Selected Countries
Source: CIA, *The World Factbook*. Available at https://www.cia.gov/library/publica tions/the-world-factbook/fields/2172.html.

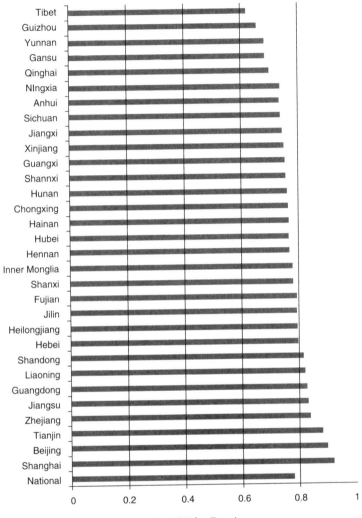

Figure 5.7 HDI by Province
Source: UNDP (2008).

(Gries and Rosen 2004). And what jobs they managed to find, did not provide either comparable wages or the social security afforded in their earlier jobs.

A similar picture emerges from the experience with TVEs, an engine which for a while drove development till the mid-1990s. Over a 10-year period, from early 1980s to 1990s, TVEs provided employment to some 100 million peasants. By 2001, the TVEs as a sector accounted for about 131 million jobs. There is a now a worrisome phenomenon of 'jobless growth' emerging. Whereas the Chinese economy has been rapidly growing, jobs have not kept up proportionately. Studies point to a declining ratio of new jobs for each unit increase in GDP (Hu 2004).

More important is the growing gap between skilled and unskilled workers, even in the urban sector. During the Maoist era, there was a rigid wage structure. The difference between highly paid and relatively low-paid workers was modest. But in the reform period, this wage structure has become marketized, and for people with skills, whether managerial or engineering or anything in short supply, the price has been bid up dramatically. The unskilled, entry-level wage, on the other hand, has been relatively flat. A lot of people have been able to move in from the countryside, so those wages have been slowly rising, but at nothing like the pace of wages for people with scarce skills (Lardy 2007).

Social tensions are clearly on the rise and there are increasing worries that there might be a growing large underclass emerging, formed of groups who are increasingly being locked out of China's prosperity. These particularly include the 200 million migrants in China who still are unable to exercise rights to social services due to the restrictions on residency. There are dangers of a vicious cycle working here, as migrant children get locked out of education opportunities and expensive healthcare.[14] A Chinese sociologist (Sun 2002) considers that China is in danger of creating a 'fractured' society as opposed to the stated goals of a harmonious society.

Concerns of about low incomes of rural communities and rising inequalities have however prompted new waves of reform. The first major reform in agriculture was of course the introduction of the household responsibility system which replaced the

---

[14] According to Liu et al. (2003) 'Medical expenditure has become an important source of transient poverty in rural China.'

People's Commune System to dramatic effect, as discussed earlier. China substantially reformed its marketing system for agricultural commodities and inputs generating a national network of wholesale markets with private merchants and prompted farmers to adjust their production activities in line with profit incentives (Watson 1988; Lin 1992). The success of the agricultural reform is also seen in the fact that China has maintained a grain self-sufficiency rate above 95 per cent in recent years (WFP 2009). Since 2000, China adjusted further its rural tax and fee system aimed at reducing the fiscal burden on farmers. Fees play a much larger role than taxes for farmers. In 1999, taxes were a modest rmb 48 billion of the total taxes and fees combined total of rmb 125 billion. A range of township and village charges were eliminated. Post-reform, the fiscal burden declined from rmb 125 billion to rmb 65–70 billion. By 2006 all agricultural taxes was eliminated, a process which started in 2003. The government then extended subsidies to a broader range of agricultural commodities. In 2008, farmers received more than rmb 100 billion as subsidy.

Progress was made as well on the sensitive issue of land rights. China's 2002 Rural Land Contracting Law is seen as a significant step forward in strengthening farmers' rights. This Law requires the government to issue contracts or certificates to all farmers outlining their rights to profits from their land parcels and to mostly shelter them from government intervention or real-location for 30 years. Further provisions were added in 2008, to ensure that compensatory arable land is provided in the first instance when agricultural land is taken over by local authorities for non-agricultural purposes. And, significantly, towards the end of the year, government unveiled a land reform policy to encourage famers to lease or transfer their land use rights under a yet-to-be-built land market.

These concerns about social stability appear to have had an effect as Chinese leaders recalibrate their development policies. Through regional development initiatives (Western Development and Dongbei strategies), increased investments in social services, and the above changes in agricultural taxation and related

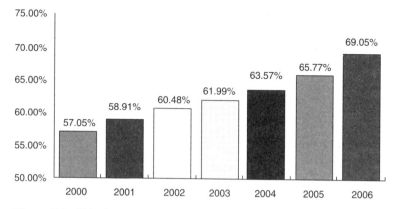

Figure 5.8 China's Progress in Building a Xiaokang Society
Source: Working Group of Institute of Statistics under the National Bureau of Statistics, *Statistical Report on Monitoring the Process of Constructing the Well-off Society in China*, 2006. Available at the website of National Bureau of Statistics, accessed on 21 November 2007.

fiscal measures, the gaps between the regions appear to be slowing down. For instance, Tibet's HDI, which was 57 per cent of Shanghai in 1990, rose to 70 per cent in 2003. More broadly, China has set up broad based indicators to measure progress on its vision of *Xiaokang*. The Xiaokang index created by the National Bureau of Statistics includes 25 indicators in six categories: economic development, creation of a harmonious society, quality of life, democracy and rule of law, science, technology, education, health, and the environment (see Figure 5.8).

The Dynamic between Social and Organizational Capital

Local Governments and Corporatist Aspects of TVEs

Did the state directly influence the creation of organizational capital in China? Local governments in particular played an active role in supporting TVEs, though their specific contribution to the development of such organizational capital remains debatable. TVEs however, in many ways fused local government to entrepreneurial action.

Walder (1995) argues that a combination of decentralization, opening of economic space for local commercial action, and the involvement of local bureaucrats in business created in effect a 'local-corporatist state' working under hard-budget constraints. Without entering into the debate about the usefulness of such a term, especially when extending the underlying logic of Walder's approach to the urban decentralized industrial state sector (Nee et al. 2007), fiscal decentralization in the early 1980s did serve to harden local governments' budget constraints. Generally, governmental support by definition tends to be about 'soft budget constraints' as there is always a bailout guarantee through higher level governments, extra-budgetary fees, tax increases, and public debt. However, a federal system in China in effect created incentives for competition among provinces and counties for mobile capital and labour resources. Local governments responded by providing a competitive local infrastructure and business environment (Qian and Roland 1998). Bailout of inefficient firms became, in a sense, unattractive.

Yet it is difficult to go further than that and claim that local authorities directly and successfully added to organizational capital at the firm level. All governments have multiple political, economic, and social objectives. In China, at different stages of reform, both the incentive for public officials to get directly engaged in commercial work and the outcome have varied. In rural China, in the initial stages of reform for instance, land was distributed directly to the farmers tilling the land. This form of limited privatization benefited the direct producers fairly equally. It led to rural, small households taking the lead in the expansion of the private non-agricultural sector. Walder (2002) claims that the reason why ordinary households benefited disproportionately from such reforms is that the rural administrative elite (officials) had more attractive alternatives with good salaries in their government positions and potential managerial positions in the expanding public enterprise sector. State capture was limited. The government elite and their relatives avoided movement into private enterprise, while private entrepreneurs avoided—or were excluded from—movement into the government posts. A different situation obtained in the 1990s, when

> rural governments began to privatize their public firms...the implications of privatization shifted rapidly, as the managers of public enterprises and the relatives of cadres moved into private enterprise at rates higher than all others. When they did so, they began with assets much larger than those held by the household entrepreneurs who pioneered the rural private sector. In short, the social impact of privatization shifted as the process changed qualitatively through time, and the benefits shifted decisively from ordinary households to rural administrative elites. (ibid.)

Potential conflicts of interest between firms and public officials are also well documented in China.

> Conflicts of interest, for instance, emerge in the cases of firm extensions across community boundaries, shifts of production sites and the downsizing of firm employment. In each of these cases, the goals to maximize local revenues and wage labour naturally collide with a firm's objective of profit maximization. Also frequent extension of government help in case of labour unrest and local demonstrations, confirms that governments never act independently of non-economic goals, so long as they wish to secure broad social consensus. Finally, the capability of government officials to act as entrepreneurs hinges on the solution of the asymmetric information problem between principal and agent. In other words, we suspect it is the state bureaucracy's capacity to set up and maintain an institutional environment that offers conditions favorable to private capital that explains the success of a developmental state in promoting transformative economic growth. (Nee et al. 2007)

Other terms have been used as well to describe the nature of this public–private partnership at the local level in China. Zheng (1994) refers to 'developmental localism', and Oi (1995) suggests a model of 'local corporatism' which under the particular circumstances—including important information asymmetries and unfair advantages in the form of soft credit, subsidies, and guaranteed markets that public enterprises enjoyed—was more efficient than purely private forms of ownership would have been in promoting economic growth, especially in a transition environment that early reform–China represented. Young (2000) however considers this as local protectionism with its attendant costs. Whatever the term, what is clear, is that led by local governments, this model led to a massive upsurge of a hybrid rural industry (TVEs) on the edges of agriculture and state industry. Local officials were directly engaged in encouraging and ensuring the success of these enterprises. Much of the production during the early stages of reform required little expertise and start up costs, entry barriers were low. This may 'explain why China has been able to pursue a development strategy without an elite central bureaucracy of the type that exist(ed) in Japan and Singapore' (ibid.).

The Role of Guanxi and Informal Networks

Guanxi is about deepening social relations. It is a longstanding Chinese practice that cultivates mutual interest and benefit. It is also not culturally unique to China. It exists in some form or the other in most societies. Whereas it is associated with corruption by some, in China it generally does not carry negative connotations. Gift giving in particular is seen as a way of deepening guanxi. Our interest here in guanxi is for a different reason, to see what role it might have played in the conduct of reforms in China. Xin and Pearce (1996) build on the work of Putnam et al. (1993) and Nee (1992) to posit that 'managers cultivate personal connections to substitute for reliable government and an established rule of law'. Drawing upon interviews with executives in both Chinese state-owned and private companies, they draw the conclusion that deepening gaunxi was a way to 'compensate for (the) lack of formal institutional support'. And, as expected, private sector executives relied 'significantly more on building connections with government officials to defend themselves against threats like appropriation or extortion' (ibid.). By this reasoning, with more established systems of market governance, the role of guanxi in future Chinese development should decline over time.

In empirical studies at the firm level, Park and Luo (2001) note that guanxi makes an observable difference in 'establishing external relations and legitimacy and positioning competitively in the market' more so 'than in improving internal operations'. Importantly in their study, guanxi does not appear to be a significant influence on profits (ibid.), even if costs are high in cultivating and maintaining guanxi. Their study confirms earlier findings that in a transition economy with ambiguous property rights and weak legal systems, guanxi becomes a way to overcome institutional and strategic disadvantages, in particular by developing better links with authorities who have control over resources.

It is possible however to take a different, perhaps broader, perspective by looking at the positive roles played by guanxi in strengthening trust, and how trust is likely to be the 'glue' that enhances business generally, rather than, for instance, to rely excessively on expensive and conflict oriented legal systems. Guanxi type systems can be viewed as legitimate alternatives to Western market systems, since much of the global world values trust in doing business. Lovett, Simmons, and Kali (1999) consider that the Chinese economy is not just moving towards market capitalism but rather towards a relationship-based 'network capitalism'.

The Chinese Diaspora and FDI

The importance of the Chinese diaspora in Southeast Asia, described by political scientist Gordon C.K. Cheung (2004) as a 'virtual nation', wherein economic as well as social capital flow in broadly based regional and increasingly global networks. Kao (1993) considers the size of the Chinese business located outside the People's Republic of China (PRC) as the world's fourth economic power, after the US, Europe, and Japan. It is a 'network of entrepreneurial relationships' that share a common culture (ibid.).

This diaspora has played an important role in China's development, in at least two ways: first, as a provider of capital for a country strapped of such resources in the early years of reforms and, second, in helping upgrade skills and methodologies which enabled the Chinese economy to catch up in a relatively short period with global product standards, technology, and innovation. They also introduced new business models that allowed China to leapfrog traditional approaches to business plan development and fixed capital constraints. For instance, Li Ka-shing, the richest man in Asia, convinced Deng Xiaoping in building a bridge across the Hongkong straits linking the island to the mainland financed upfront by Hongkong money, with the investment recovered over the years through toll taxes or other revenue generation schemes. Once the model demonstrated its usefulness, thousands of bridges and highways were built using the same model. Similar innovation has characterized the recent dramatic spike in Chinese investment, both public and private, in areas like Africa and elsewhere. Chinese companies are agile and able to draw on extensive national and international Chinese networks. Chinese companies depend less on data and feasibility studies than on intuition, party guidance, and a firm grasp of the technical aspects of the planned investment (Chen 2001).

The Chinese diaspora was responsible for much of the early FDI flows coming into China. FDI flows from the ASEAN (essentially from five countries—Philippines, Thailand, Malaysia, Singapore, and Indonesia) accounted for a peak of almost $11 billion in 1995, and were still over $3 billion annually during 2000–1. The Chinese diaspora were among the first investors that took the risk and responded almost immediately to China's open-door policy (Shambaugh 1995), with initial investments in the four special economic zones: Shenzhen, Zhuhai, Shantou, and Xiamen. Ethnic ties served as a lubricant for the strengthening of social relations and networks that encouraged investments in the mainland from the Chinese diaspora.[15] Yet, however dense

---

[15] Most Chinese diaspora in Southeast Asia are from Fujian, Hakka, Chaozhou, and Guangdong.

social ties are, they do not substitute for managerial competence or technological learning, this form of social capital plays a role of supplementing more traditional forms of capital and know-how. 'In this context effective guanxi plays the role of lubricant which enhances the transaction, not the glue which fixes the transaction'.(Smart and Hsu 2004).

The role of FDI in Chinese development is not without some controversy. Huang (2003) sees the high levels of FDI more a reflection of China's weakness as an economy rather than its strength. Foreign firms play a large role in the economy not because all of the foreign firms are: 'the world's best practice forms but because they are uniquely positioned to exploit many of the business opportunities in China created by China's inefficient economic and financial institutions' (ibid.). However, it is difficult to contest that organizationally and in terms of product standards, Chinese firms and the Chinese economy generally were quite far off from the competitive standards of the global economy. Crucially, these early FDI flows provided information about world market conditions and the expertise and contacts so vital particularly for export markets (Smart and Hsu 2004). They linked mainland firms to global networks and helped them understand the implication of quality and product standards. Even Huang accepts that the early deficits in rule of law and lack of properly functioning markets in China would have deterred most foreign firms from entering China's 'murky business environment' (ibid.). The outlier of course was investment from the Chinese diaspora, who were willing to take risks for a variety of reasons, including the sense of ethnicity and a desire to help China in its emergence as a trading and manufacturing power. This was not the only difference between Chinese diaspora FDI and non-Chinese transnational corporation (TNC) FDI. Western TNCs were generally larger in firm size and tended to invest in the big cities, whereas Hong Kong and Taiwanese investors were open to investing in the countryside, though transportation linkages remained important since many of their investments were in the export sector.

In summary, overseas Chinese capital played a key role in China's linking up to the global economy and in being a source of much needed capital especially in the early years of reform.

Corruption—How Does It Function in China?

Corruption tends to occur in two situations: one as an opportunity, especially in situations where state officials have extensive economic and regulatory powers, and second, where there is a motivation brought upon by factors as diverse as relative impoverishment and changing values. Sun (1999) contrasts the different experiences of Russia and China on corruption, and attempts to answer the question as to why China has had a less pernicious outcome on economic growth. China's gradual reforms allowed the state to remain in control over economic and political decisions and their implementation. Unlike Russia, in China there was no vacuum in the economy that was filled by mafia type organizations. The two-track approach also put most of the new opportunities in the non-state sector. What corruptive practices existed in the non-state sector were directed towards seeking the support of powerful officials or state institutions so that the 'playing field' was more level. The growing alignment of interests among local officials and private businesses, particularly in the area of real estate,[16] provided strong incentives for public officials to support market outcomes and firm profitability.

Corruption also reduced the opposition to reform. Rent seeking became the price for 'institutional stability, but may be a necessary price' (ibid.). Rent seeking has been the dominant form of corruption in China, with a 20–30 per cent premium exercised as a result of the two-track system. Between 1987 and 1989 over '70 percent of cadre economic crimes were linked to the two track system' (Sun 1999). With the 1992 financial reforms and curtailment of the range of goods being regulated, the corruptive impact of the two-track system also correspondingly declined.

---

[16] This represents an important source of revenue for municipalities.

The difference in opportunities and incentives for corruption in China and Russia are linked not only in the reform model pursued but also to the nature of the state itself. 'The structure of government institutions and the political process are important determinants of levels of corruption. Weak governments that are unable to control their agencies experience high levels of corruption' (ibid.). The Chinese state remained strong, and at the core, its leadership was fairly uncorrupted. Periodic campaigns were conducted to root out corrupt officials, and harsh sentences meted out to those found guilty of corruption. Private sector tycoons were not exempt from state scrutiny as demonstrated in the recent imprisonment in 2009 of leading Chinese entrepreneurs such as the Chairman of Gome, the largest electronics retailer in China.

In 1988, with the creation of the Centre for Reporting Economic Crimes, a vast monitoring system was set up, with local branches nationwide. There is also increasing commitment to strengthened transparency in government. Citizen complaints are regularly attended to and income disclosure mechanisms have been instituted across government. Most of these anti-corruption mechanisms were not present in Russia. For senior party leaders and the Party in China, cracking down on corruptive practices has become a necessary part of the arsenal of measures shoring up the legitimacy of the Party itself. It is an interesting statistic that on average two-third of the crimes in financial institutions were committed by employees under 35 years of age with little direct experience of party discipline (ibid.) (see Figure 5.9).

Finally, in an econometric analysis by Iliev and Putterman (2007) of the importance of social capability and related 'soft' factors in the economies of Communist and post-Communist states, property rights appeared to be at least somewhat more secure and corruption under somewhat better control in China (corruption index 0.30) than in Russia (1.01), which they felt might be one factor behind the far larger flow of foreign investment into the former than the latter.

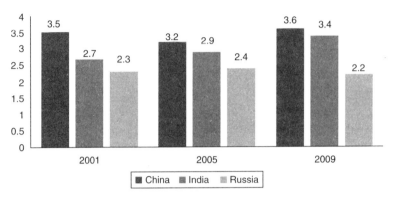

Figure 5.9 Corruption Comparisons among China, India, and Russia (Higher is Better)
Source: Transparency International (2009).

POLICIES (AND THE SEQUENCING OF REFORMS)

In severe crises, growth rates achieved in the past do not preserve stability. Short-term government rescue schemes cannot compensate for social inequality and social tension that has accumulated over decades.

—Heilmann (2009)

The past does not guarantee the future.

—Chinese proverb

A few key propositions can be highlighted:

a. *Functioning markets* are an essential aspect of the measures required to sustain growth.

b. *Aligning incentives* and the context to the development vision is a crucial task for effective transformation (and growth).

c. Sequencing matters, a lot. For instance, that bureaucratic reform preceded economic reform in the early 1980s was critical to final success.

d. At times institutional/organizational reform is more important for transformation (and thereby growth) than detailed policies.

e. Investing in infrastructure and public goods generally becomes essential to kick-start broader, sustained growth.

The 'Right' Policies: Some Observations

There is widespread agreement that the 'right' policy and institutional environments are crucial to fostering economic growth and development. Unfortunately, however, there is equally widespread disagreement about the right policy mix and the most appropriate institutional framework. This disagreement is not necessarily a bad thing; on the contrary, if one believes in ownership and the importance of local context, it arguably serves the interests of developing countries very well that there is no longer a predetermined consensus on specific policies and institutions or their order of introduction.[17]

Getting policies 'right' raises an equally important issue of getting 'the policy process right'. Heilmann (2009) considers that the pragmatic nature of policymaking in China represents an unusual combination of extensive policy experimentation with long term policy prioritization, a process which he characterizes as 'maximum tinkering under uncertainty'. He presents reform in the urban state sector as an instructive example. Chinese policymakers were well aware from the start that complementary reform packages would be the right way to deal with the administrative and welfare impact of SOE reform. But they could not arrive at a consensus of what the state sector would look like at the end of the transformation, since sweeping privatization had few supporters. Losing control was an abiding concern. Unlike what occurred during Brezhnev's Soviet Union, this did not produce a policy deadlock, and instead piecemeal restructuring was initiated. In order to deal creatively with uncertainty, political actors of necessity purposefully tinkered with diverse policy measures and institutions, and adapted them to their concrete

---

[17] Many have argued that conditionality of aid has been a failure. Donor-induced policy change has not worked, whether because the recommendations were not appropriate or due to the fungibility of resources intended to support the policy change. The conclusion that many donors are drawing is to work instead through governments according to their own priorities through direct budget support or to leave the government entirely and work instead with civil society.

conditions, thereby finding out what could work at acceptable costs. Observers have likened the management challenges of China's political economy as 'rebuilding the ship at sea'.

Finding the Balance: Markets and Incentives

That markets and incentives play a key role is not in question, rather what appears inadequate are explanations as to why they have worked so well in one context or country and not in the other.

Between 1978 and 2004, the promotion of private business took place in what has been described as a 'curbed policy subsystem' by Heilmann (2008). For ideological reasons, private business was one of the least acceptable emerging elements of China's reforming economy. At the beginning it was mostly tolerated as long as it did not pose a major policy risk (Naughton 2007). The success of the Wenzhou District experimental zone influenced the national debate, even if there were occasional ideological setbacks. A key institutional innovation was the registration of private companies as 'collective' enterprises to conceal the true extent of the private sector, thereby reducing some of the political pitfalls involved in an open promotion of the private sector. Only in 2001 did Jiang Zemin cement the legitimacy of the private sector with the 'Three Represents' philosophy which formally allowed socially progressive entrepreneurs to become members of the Communist Party. Private enterprise and private property did not enjoy full legal protection until very late in 2004, almost 25 years after reform first started.

Incentives however seemed to work. Reform aimed at decentralizing ownership and control rights such as decentralizing the right to set wages, make production decisions, and appoint new managers, created strong incentives for managers and employees to learn and to work hard. Using an extensive data set about changes in SOEs, Xu (1997) found that productivity and growth rates improved significantly with the above incentives. Yet reform measures such as increasing profit-retention rates and adopting performance contracts did not appear to have influenced productivity that much. Decentralization alone, for instance, accounted for a large 42 per cent of productivity growth in SOEs in the 1980s.

While accepting the unorthodox nature of Chinese policies and reforms, many observers like Huang (2008) still credit the growing role of markets and incentives as the real drivers of Chinese economic progress. He furthers underscores that it is the expansion of private ownership that should be viewed as the primary source of China's economic miracle, that indeed strengthening of property rights and private entrepreneurship provided the real stimulus for high growth. There is some credibility in the latter point about entrepreneurship, though as has been well documented in this book and elsewhere that China's path in developing property rights has been highly specific and unique.

Each wave of reform took a step forward in empowering large numbers of people, providing opportunity and access to markets. The relatively low inequality at the onset of reforms, the first bursts of income growth in the agricultural sector, the role of the TVEs functioning mostly in rural areas and small towns, all unorthodox in nature, led to a broad-based growth of the Chinese economy in the early years of reform. Inequalities got accelerated only later in the 1990s and 2000s. Market forces and entrepreneurship, if not ownership in the traditional sense, have become essential features of the Chinese economy. Over 70 per cent of new growth is now contributed by the private sector (Fan 2005). Even more, SOEs as well are increasingly functioning within a market environment. Competition is particularly intense for the domestic market between global companies and subsidiaries of foreign companies. These are the intended outcomes of specific reforms and opening-up policies.

Qian and Xu (1993) in commenting on market performance, and the transformative implications of specific policies, compare 'privatization' with 'denationalization of the state', they point to the importance attached by Chinese officials to enhancing the forces of production, exactly the point underscored by Deng in his explanation about the Four Modernizations. Denationalization covered successful non-state enterprises taking over or merging with state enterprises, converting state enterprises into joint ventures with domestic or foreign non-state enterprises, and reorganization of state enterprises into joint stock companies. In fact, a considerable part of FDI went into heavy industry SOEs. This experience in China is somewhat similar to Taiwan and South Korea (Lau 1992) where the reduction of the public enterprise sector was achieved mainly through the growth of the private sector, rather than privatization of state enterprises.

While the debate about what drives China's progress is likely to continue, it is worth reiterating that: one, most observers accept that China has become a predominantly market-driven economy. It represents a substantial change from where the economy was in 1976, when Mao died; two, observers continue to disagree about what drives Chinese growth. Is it high savings rates? Are the 'animal spirits' of the Chinese responsible as the economy got opened up? And so on. Today most products and services in China are sold at market-determined prices, even if the caveats are equally important. For instance, land remains state property, utility prices are set by the state and so on; second, that markets are very competitive, a consequence of the openness of the economy, with many suppliers and producers competing often at relatively thin profit margins, and a large FDI sector, a phenomenon more important since the 1990s, which produces one-third of the output and is active in both domestic and international markets. Many Chinese prices are converging with international prices. In 2005 imports were equal to 30 per cent of GDP, which is high in comparison to Japan (10 per cent) and the US (about 17 per cent). Equally, China at 25 per cent scores high when comparing shares of foreign companies in industrial output in the EU and the US (about one fifth) (Lardy 2007).

There is a larger role for incentives in transformation. Walder (1995) raises a particularly important point that incentives matter in a more general way for a transition or developing economy, since a society itself is in transformation. Incentives have to be regularly adjusted not merely for individuals and firms but also for government agencies and public officials themselves. But incentives may not be sufficient for successful economic growth. Depending on the specific conditions, more direct support may well be justified so that local producers are not left exclusively to their own devices. Oi (1995) goes on to emphasize that the corporatist strategy pursued in China effectively 'spread(s) risks and resources to maximize local community interests', underlining the fact that such an active public–private partnership role of the state was an important ingredient for China's success. Policy options therefore have to go beyond the traditional infrastructural support role, to include market development and promote information and technology.

Macroeconomic Policies Should Facilitate 'Transformation' and Growth

Social Policy

One important conclusion coming out of the empirical work by Ranis and Stewart (2006) is that due to the strong interrelationship between economic growth and human development, countries must promote both in order to sustain either. Economic growth provides the resources needed for significant investments in human development; but growth is also not sustainable without such investments. There are links as well in specific areas also. For instance, keeping inflation low, a traditional focus of macroeconomic policies has a human developmental aspect as well, since high inflation tends to hurt most the poor and disadvantaged (Elson and Cagatay 2000).

In terms of social policy, China's population at the outset of reform was far more educated and in better health than comparable countries. Average schooling in the adult population rose from less than one year in 1950 to four years in 1980 and six years in 2000. Without the foundation laid by Mao, Deng's reforms could not have been so profoundly successful. Different trajectories are possible. In 1960, Egypt had twice the per capita income of China and about the same level of childhood mortality. In the period until 1980, Chinese heavy investments in improving health and education outcomes for the entire population saw child mortality drop to levels which compared well with most other developing countries. Economic growth, however, was slow and erratic as the economy remained mostly under the plan. Egypt, meanwhile, saw steady economic growth and moderate but sustained improvements in child mortality. In the period since 1980, Egypt has put greater emphasis on improving health outcomes on a broad basis, and child mortality has accordingly fallen faster than in the first period. Economic growth has seen steady but modest progress. China, meanwhile, experienced a combination of a very rapid economic growth and slower improvements in infant mortality. What is interesting about this analysis is the sequencing of policies and the resulting dynamics in economic growth and mortality rates. Crucially, in spite of starting from a level half that of Egypt, China ended the period with both a higher level of GDP per capita, lower mortality levels, and a trajectory of considerably faster ongoing growth. Another comparison is with India. In 1979, at the start of reforms, China had a life expectancy of 68 years, compared with only 54 years in India. Yet the relative neglect of public health over the years, and an embrace of private sector incentives in the provision of healthcare in China, led to an situation that despite rapid, and sustained growth over decades, life expectancy only went up marginally, but still high of 74.5 years in 2010 (CIA, *The World Factbook*). India is now at 66.5 years (ibid.), the gap between the two countries has narrowed significantly. This raises the need to align better social policies and investment in societal capabilities so that the basis for future growth can be continued to be secured.

Monetary Policy

Since the early 1990s, monetary policies in China have focused on maintaining low inflation and price stability, and promoting economic growth and structural change.

In practice the number one objective has been to ensure a minimum growth rate of 8 per cent. The second objective was to keep inflation at around 3 per cent. While in theory there might be short term trade-offs between the two objectives, authorities saw the two objectives as mutually reinforcing in the long run. Growth has been accompanied by low inflation in China. The third objective has been to maintain stability of the exchange rate. The peg of the RMB to the US dollar, and now more recently to a basket of currencies, has been an effective tool for some time now in maintaining such stability. Recent capital liberalization and the appreciation of the RMB to the dollar for the 2004–8 period has made monetary policy more challenging to reconcile these different objectives.

Relatively simple macroeconomic rules were followed: Evidence suggests that when the growth rate is above 10 per cent, Chinese authorities accelerate their 'cooling' efforts without waiting for inflation to accelerate. Conversely, when the economy is in a downturn, that is, growth rate is less than 8 per cent; authorities adopt expansionary policies to stimulate the economy. There were situations however where it was quite difficult for the authorities to make the right call. If growth rates dropped to 9 per cent but where inflation rates were still high, decision-makers had considerable difficulty in judging whether the inflation rate would fall further, without the further tightening of macroeconomic policy. Two examples can be highlighted: In 1997, when the growth rate was dropping and overcapacity was clearly visible, authorities were reluctant to simulate the economy, as they were concerned about inflationary resurgence. Only when it was already too late was the action taken to shift the earlier contractionary economic policy to an expansionary one. This was one of the factors which led to a slowdown in growth as well as a six-year period of price deflation. The second example refers to early 2003, when there was emerging evidence that the economy was heating up. Yet the authorities were reluctant to adopt a tighter macroeconomic policy. They were not certain that the economy had in fact turned around and that a tight macroeconomic policy should be adopted. As a result, 'the government refrained from taking action for the fear of killing off the recovery which was in its initial stage. Only later when the government was convinced that the turn-around had happened, were actions taken. Even so, the government is still very cautious in its tightening for fear of overkill' (Yu 2008).

Over the years, the arsenal of monetary policy instruments has varied as the economy was opened up and markets increasingly driven by price signals. Since 1998, the emphasis has been on using interest rate changes, often with limited impact (McKinley 2003). More often than not, monetary policy was often the first candidate to achieve the macroeconomic policy goal of tightening or loosening.

A consistently expansionary policy can have other risks. However, a quick review of China's debt accumulation history during the last 10 years of an expansionary fiscal policy shows that China's debt balance/GDP ratio has remained generally less than 20 per cent. Many economists (Hofman and Wu 2009) have argued that if we take into consideration the so-called contingent liabilities, China's debt balance/GDP ratio is much higher, maybe as high as 100 per cent. But these fears may not be entirely warranted as long as certain assumptions hold. As Yu (2008) notes:

> the Chinese government's ability to repay debts is much higher than it appears. However, whether China's fiscal position is sustainable depends on the dynamics of the debt balance/GDP ratio. There are two factors which determine the dynamic path of the debt balance/GDP ratio: the growth rate and the budget deficit/GDP ratio. As long as China can maintain a relatively high growth rate of 7–8 percent, and a budget deficit/GDP ratio of less than 3 percent, following the passage of time, the debt balance/ GDP ratio would converge to a limit of less than 40 percent. Incorporating contingent liabilities into the debt balance would merely influence the initial condition of the dynamic path of the debt balance/GDP ratio, and it would not change the

limit to which the debt balance/GDP ratio converges. As long as the Chinese government can avoid making fatal mistakes in coordinating macroeconomic policy and economic restructuring so as to maintain a decent growth rate and a relatively low budget deficit, China's fiscal position will be sustainable. Therefore, there is ample room for the government to use expansionary fiscal policy to counterbalance any negative impact on the growth by a tight monetary policy.

In more recent years, monetary policy has been increasingly driven by the growing balance of payments surpluses. Since the early 2000s, these growing surpluses combined with easy domestic liquidity have fueled an investment boom. In 2004 and again in 2006 the authorities took a number of administrative measures to control investment demand—notably that of SOEs, and provided banks with 'guidance' to reduce lending growth, especially to sectors such as real estate that the government was seeking to slow down. The often contradictory short-term challenges of keeping growth moving and keeping a lid on inflation are captured by the dilemmas that this situation presents for monetary policy. The authorities have been generally reluctant to raise interest rates, fearing that this may affect long-term investment decisions. Since 2006, China has adopted an increasingly flexible exchange rate partly to respond to global concerns about China's undervalued currency and to slow balance of payment inflows. Furthermore, authorities also employed more traditional measures such as increasing reserve requirements to absorb liquidity and slow down domestic money growth (Hofman and Wu 2009).

The Fiscal Influence of the State

China's extraordinary progress is connected to the role public finances have played in the arsenal of policy measures. Fiscal policy has played and continues to have a significant influence on the China's economy and society. Indeed, as the economy grew, so did the state's ability to invest further in the economy and society.

Over the years, there have been large ebbs and flows in the relationship between national income and revenue, some which are difficult to fully understand when comparing it with international experience.

> In the first 17 years the revenue/income ratio dropped by almost 21 percentage points from 31 per cent in 1978 to 11 per cent in 1995. The subsequent 9 years to 2004 saw a close to 9 per cent rise. The magnitudes of both the rise and fall are huge by international standards and have gone together with a fundamental transformation of the economy. (Hussain and Stern 2006)

In part this reflected the many waves of reform which required different levels of fiscal support. Yet in all of this, reflecting their sense of fiscal probity, Chinese leaders have kept deficits generally low—only in a few years did they reach 3 per cent of GDP (see Figure 5.10).

In the early years of reform, with price liberalization, and the rise of private sector firms, the tax base gradually got reduced.

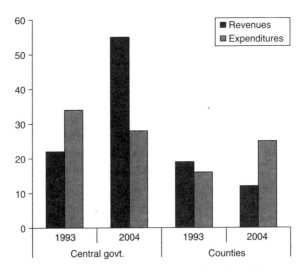

Figure 5.10 The Fiscal Capacity of Central and Local Government
Source: NBS (2006).

This was coupled with an intergovernmental fiscal system that provided incentives to local governments to grow but encouraged them to use fund transfers as 'extra-budgetary funds' often outside the purview of the central government.

> By the mid-1990s general government revenues had fallen to 11 percent of GDP (down from more than 31 percent in 1978) and the central government share of these revenues had dropped below 30 percent. Meanwhile, extra-budgetary funds had become as large as budgetary funds. Although budget deficits remained small, quasi-fiscal operations through the banking system were substantial, about 5 to 7 percent of GDP. (Hofman and Wu 2009)

The 1994 financial sector reforms were important in that they tried to reverse the situation: they led to a gradual increase in the share of government revenues in GDP (20 per cent of GDP in 2009), and an increase as well in the central government share of those revenues from less than 30 per cent in 1991 to almost 55 per cent in 2002.

China's government expenditures were concentrated on building infrastructure, reforming SOEs, developing the social security system, science and technology, education, agriculture, and development of the western regions. A virtuous cycle can be noted. The growth in overall income and a stronger tax collection effort led to rapid increases in tax revenues relative to the increase in interest payments. Interestingly enough, it appears that the result of a long-term expansionary fiscal policy has been to improve rather than deteriorate China's fiscal position (Yu 2001).

Figure 5.11 also brings out some of the structural changes in the state's fiscal expenditures, particularly noteworthy is the relatively high shares of economic development in total expenditures for much of the reform period. Only after 2002, did this share drop below 30 per cent. Correspondingly the state increased its expenditures over the years on social, cultural, and educational development.

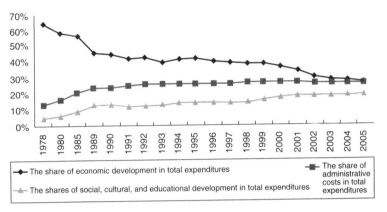

Figure 5.11 Structural Changes in the State's Fiscal Expenditures (1978–2005)
Source: UNDP (2008).

Chapter 3 highlighted that at the start of the 1994 financial reforms, provinces 'collected most of the taxes but the central government was responsible for close to half of the expenditure', clearly an unsustainable situation (Hussain and Stern 2006). With the far reaching 1994 financial reforms, this pattern was reversed. The central government now 'raises over half of tax revenue but is responsible for only 28% of the total expenditure' (ibid.).

Many observers like Hussain and Stern (2006) contend that fiscal reform has not been rapid enough, the banking sector remains weak, and that it has lagged behind market reform. Others like Brean (1998: 49) provide an interesting counterfactual by contending that had this been done with corresponding pressure on inefficient SOEs, China would have faced untold social and economic instability. China took on financial reform with a close eye to progress on the real economic front.

Administrative measures as opposed to more indirect measures remain important, for instance, in 2004 and 2006 in guiding investment demand and in the management of China's exchange rate policy, though in recent years in China there is growing recognition and some progress of the need to move deeper fiscal reform. The central government can potentially play a larger role in dealing with regional inequalities, as it is now in a better position than before in redistributing resources from richer to poorer regions. For a variety of reasons, especially given the growing concern about inequalities, leaders recognize that, as in the earlier decades of reform, fiscal policy has a crucial role to play in generating the improvements in social services such as health, education, and social protection, and in providing stronger support to migrants who now struggle to access social services due to the *hukou* restrictions, and in building a more just and harmonious *xiaokang* society.

Public Goods and Policies Focused on Transformation

Besley and Ghatak (2006) make an important distinction between public goods that support markets and those that augment. The mere existence of public goods does not imply useful provision of government services. Government failure may be as important and as possible as market failure. A basic market-supporting public good is of course the provision of law and order which enable markets to function and 'rights' to be protected. Some legal systems do it better than others. Market-augmenting public goods are closer to what is listed in standard textbooks: they include health and education whose provision can bring benefits to society. Depending on the country and institutional context, infrastructural services such as postal and telecommunication services and rail and air transportation may or may not be provided by the state.

Another way of looking at public goods is to categorize them in terms of their impact on 'transformation'. Building new roads to connect people with markets can have a powerful transforming effect on the lives and incomes of people in the region. Adding an additional lane to an already existing two-lane highway may expand trade and commerce but may not have the same transformative value as the earlier example. Similar criteria can be drawn in terms of how pro-poor specific public goods might be (Fan 2004). The right of access to health, for instance, requires a state commitment to ensuring the provision of basic healthcare, even if the actual provision may require a mix of state and private sector roles.

The role of public goods in driving China's transformation was critical (see Figures 5.12 and 5.13). Policy and institutional reforms were combined with massive public investments in roads and other key infrastructures. The ensuing rapid economic growth led to transportation shortages and congestion problems and increased the demand for roads. Responding to these challenges, starting in 1985, the government gave high priority to road development, particularly the construction of high-quality roads such as highways and freeways. While the construction of high-quality roads has taken place at a remarkably rapid pace, the construction of lower-quality and mostly rural roads has been relatively slow.

Using provincial-level data for 1982–9, Fan and Chan-Kang (2005) extend earlier work by Fan et al. (2002) and conclude that road development, together with agricultural R&D, irrigation, education, electricity, and telecommunications, made significant contributions to economic growth and poverty reduction.

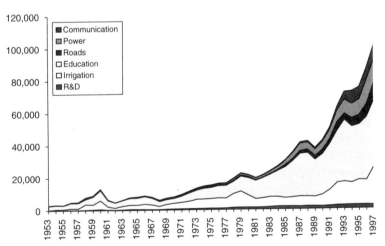

Figure 5.12 Public Spending in Rural China (1953–97) (million 1990 Yuan)
Source: Fan et al. (2002).

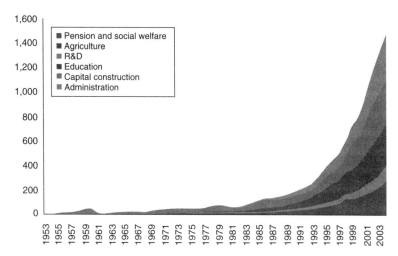

Figure 5.13 Public Spending on Main Sectors (1953–2004) (billion Yuan)
Source: NBS (2005).

But, as expected, there were considerable variations in terms of their impact on development for different types of roads and between regions. Low-quality (mostly rural) roads in particular had much higher cost–benefit (four times larger than for high-quality roads). Investment in low-quality roads generates high returns both to agricultural GDP and to rural non-farm income and is significant in reducing poverty. Another key finding of the study is to present evidence of a potential trade-off between growth and poverty reduction when investing in different parts of China. Road investments yield their highest economic returns in the eastern and central regions of China while their contributions to poverty reduction are greatest in western China (especially the southwest region), implying the need for a differentiated approach to public good investments.

> Without this essential public good, efficient markets, adequate health care, a diversified rural economy, and sustainable economic growth will remain elusive. Effective development strategies require good infrastructure as their backbone. The enormous benefit of rural roads that the study reveals for China holds true for other countries as well. Investment in rural roads should be

a top priority to reduce poverty, maximize the positive effects of other pro-poor investments, and foster broadly distributed economic growth. (Joachim von Braun, Director General, IFPRI, in the Foreword to Fan and Chan-Kang 2005)

Sequencing Reforms: Policies, Institutions, and Capacities

Institutions and policies are profoundly joined at the hip. One cannot succeed without the other. Yet, there are interesting questions of sequencing which China's experience brings out forcefully. Without committed people with the right attitudes, policies themselves may stand little chance of having the intended impact. Deng's decision to revamp the government administration very early in the reform process arguably laid the foundations for the remaining changes the ruling elite intended to introduce. By removing those of the old guard who could be expected to object on political grounds to his policy direction and who were often peasant revolutionaries with low levels of modern education, Deng created a younger, more open, and better educated government bureaucracy both more likely and more able to support him and like-minded leaders in the new course for China.

In turn, opening up markets has, for instance, created in China an 'effective' demand for stronger, more transparent rules and better regulatory institutions. In the first phase of China's reforms, getting the fundamental institutional setting right through profound structural change mattered more than specific policies, given the need for workable solutions to a radically different mode of production. The 'right' policies may be useless or even harmful in the 'wrong' institutional context. In the later period, getting policies right has become of increasing importance as the institutional framework has matured. As many have recognized, the current resource intensive growth pattern has become increasingly expensive to maintain. In order to raise the efficiency of production, China now has a challenge to get both policies and institutions aligned and 'right'.

★★★

Many of the China economists, grappling with making sense of its developmental progress in the context of traditional economic theory, see China's case as an important study of transitional economics, mapping the journey from a highly planned economy to a market oriented economic system obtaining in developed countries, such as the US. China's extraordinary success and those of other Asian countries like South Korea and Japan have evinced keen interest from policymakers, students, and business people from all over the developing world to see what lessons of their success are potentially transferable to their own economies and societies. The global context itself is rapidly changing as well, as new trading and investment 'powers' led by China, Brazil, and India are creating new opportunities for the developing world. Not only does this add to trade and capital flows, but it also provides for greater policy space and freedom for many developing countries in choosing their development partners and in matching needs and resources in the way they see fit.

This chapter has presented a transformation narrative of China's development since reform and opening up starting in the late 1970s. It is clear that history and institutions matter. So do capacities and policies. It is the mix of all these which produce specific development outcomes. Sustaining these development outcomes requires committed leadership and a coherent long-term vision. While some of these factors can arguably be seen as given, such as geography and resource endowments, this chapter has posited that as China's experience demonstrates there are few issues that are not amenable to policy or administrative reform, that it is for instance possible to set up systems and incentives that encourage people to work hard and prosper and for the government to become an active agent of change.

In China, as has been well documented, initial conditions were favourable at the start of reforms in several key respects: human capabilities were relatively high, there was a relatively equal distribution of income and wealth—Mao's reforms in the 1950s and 1960s had dramatically swept aside the inequities of the past—and leaders and the people were both ready for change, mostly a result of the failed policies of the earlier periods, particularly the long, difficult experience of the Cultural Revolution. All these factors combined to create a 'great pragmatism' among Chinese leaders and people alike. These were important strengths. In the economic sphere, there was little external debt, due to the austerities practised during Mao's period. Whyte (1995) also considers that China emerged from collectivization with a much higher capacity for small-scale rural entrepreneurship. Others like Oi (1995) are of the opinion that Mao's political system had a strong administrative strength that was available to later leaders when pro-growth reforms and policies were adopted.

However, it bears repetition that not all this, even these initial strengths were all the result of past historical conditions. A telling example is the orientation of the bureaucracy. For instance, the 'active development role of the bureaucracy' was the intended result of the early 1980s administrative reforms introduced by Deng Xiaoping and his government. The role of the state was particularly decisive. There was a decisive move toward merit and ability in bureaucratic career patterns and a generational shift in the bureaucracy. The evaluation system for party officials strongly encouraged growth. Not only did the state function as a 'helping hand', but through extensive decentralization and an emphasis on results, there was incentives for strong public private partnerships at the local level, giving rise to terms like 'local corporatist state' to capture this phenomenon whereby private and quasi-private firms were actively supported by local authorities. This active support was supplemented by equally active efforts to 'grow the market' with orders from the different parts of the state providing the first basis of entering a market. Hybrid forms like TVEs prospered and drove Chinese development particularly in the rural areas for much of the 1980s and the 1990s. But in time these forms were recast or reinvented into new corporate arrangements, at times with FDI investment, to become more competitive and benefit from the increasingly market-driven environment.

In the broad sweep of Chinese reforms, there was particular interest in introducing new incentives that influenced behaviour of all different segments of society: consumers and producers of course, but also government officials, managers of public enterprises, and private entrepreneurs. Conscious policies were directed to deepen competitive pressures and the role of the market in wide areas of the economy. Public ownership was maintained, but successive waves of reforms ensured that SOEs also had to perform in the market, and operate under increasingly 'hard' budget constraints.

With the large and rapidly growing rural economy in the 1980s and 1990s, incentives for government cadres were created as well, to share in the prosperity from growth. As highlighted in this chapter, their interests were not confined to public ownership. The rapid growth in the private sector created opportunities for them as well, and later 'privatization' or 'restructuring' of public enterprises such as TVEs near the end of the second decade of reform, created additional opportunities.

> A large new class of independent entrepreneurs now dwarfs those with political connections and rivals them in wealth. We have also seen that asset-stripping in this setting has been restricted and delayed due to the continued viability of the party-state, and that to the extent that it does occur, it is a gradual process that will take place over a generation or more. (Walder 2003)

The 1994 reforms of the fiscal and intergovernmental fiscal system gradually increased the share of government revenues in GDP (to some 20 per cent of GDP now), and also increased the central government share of those revenues from less than 30 to almost 60 per cent. Like other developing countries, some of the elements of China's success appear the standard ones: liberalization of the price system, opening up for trade and foreign investment, commercialization of the financial sector, and privatization of the economy—all while maintaining a reasonable level of macroeconomic stability. However, the way in which China pursued these reforms has been radically different from most other developing economies: it pursued reforms in a gradual, experimental way, by using decentralization and incentives to reform local governments and to provide time and space for people's attitudes to adjust to new expectations. Importantly, and again consciously, it undertook measures to ensure that change, to the extent possible, was a win-win proposition for most segments possible. Maintaining and protecting social cohesion was a high priority.

China also grew rapidly because it was able to sustain its reforms over long periods of time. Even when confronted with challenges such as the Tiannamen Square incident, it responded by deepening reforming. Other countries' reform processes saw more swings in the pendulum, in part driven by the political cycle inherent in the short-term nature of most elected governments. Above all, China was able to develop domestic capacity to design and drive home-grown reforms suited to its conditions.

Even in the early period of reforms, China's was able to raise the finance needed for its capital-intensive growth, through use of creative business models and in close partnership with overseas Chinese capital. A closed capital account and increasingly strong banking supervision reduced the risks of potential financial crises, a lesson that China learnt well from the Asian financial crisis in the 1970s, when open capital accounts devastated domestic economies of many Asian economies with the flight of global capital flows away from those countries.

And, despite journalistic accounts to the contrary, China has pursued a determined effort to reduce corruption in government and society. The country has, overall, avoided state capture and concentration of power by building institutions within the party and government that have in the large part put a check on power abuse and corruption. Equally, encouraged by a decentralized, federalist environment, the active competition among regions has tended to limit such opportunities of rent seeking and encouraged institutional innovation.

Not all policies and reforms were of course helpful. Many of the emerging challenges have arisen in part due to the rapid growth itself. Concerns about sustainability, inequity, and the environment have been dominating official debates on new policies and reforms. The next chapter takes these issues, as it outlines China's prospects for the future. Will growth continue? What are the transformative forces likely to be in play in the future and so on? As China grows richer and policy objectives are no longer exclusively about growth, what are the likely policy trade-offs as efforts are made to ensure that the benefits of reforms are spread more equitably and that development can be sustained over time.

REFERENCES

Abramovitz, M. 1986. 'Catching Up, Forging Ahead, and Falling Behind', *Journal of Economic History*, 46(2): 385–406.

Acemoglu, D., S. Johnson, and J.A. Robinson. 2004. 'Institutions as the Fundamental Cause of Long-run Growth', NBER Working Paper.

Aron, J. 2000. 'Growth and Institutions: A Review of the Evidence', *The World Bank Research Observer*, 15(1): 99.

Ash, R.F. and Y.Y. Kueh. 1996. *The Chinese Economy under Deng Xiaoping*. New York: Oxford University Press.

Bajpai, N. and T. Jian. 1996. *Reform Strategies of China and India: Suggestions for Future Actions*. Harvard: Harvard Institute for International Development, Harvard University.

Besley, T. and M. Ghatak. 2006. 'Public Goods and Economic Development', in *Understanding Poverty*, pp. 285–302. New York: Oxford University Press.

Bhagwati, J.N. 2004. *In Defense of Globalization*. New York: Oxford University Press.

Blanchard, O. and A. Shleifer. 2001. 'Federalism With and Without Political Centralization: China versus Russia, *IMF Staff Papers*.

Blecher, M. 2004. 'The Working Class and Governance in China', *Governance in China*, pp. 193–206. Lanham, MD: Rowman and Littlefield.

Bloom, D.E., D. Canning, L. Hu, Y. Liu, A. Mahal, and W. Yap. 2006. 'Why Has China's Economy Taken Off Faster than India's?', in *Pan Asia Conference*. Available at http://scid.stanford.edu/events/PanAsia/Papers/papersonly.Html, accessed on 20 June 2010.

Bloom, D.E., D. Canning, and J. Sevilla. 2004. 'The Effect of Health on Economic Growth: A Production Function Approach', *World Development*, 32(1): 1–13.

Brean, D.J.S. 1998. 'Financial Perspectives on Fiscal Reform', in Trish Fulton, Jinyan Li, and Dianqing Xu (eds), *China's Tax Reform Options*, pp. 47–56 Singapore: World Scientific.

Burns, J.P. 1994. 'Civil Service Reform in China', *The Australian Journal of Chinese Affairs*, 2(2): 44–72.

Caro, R.A. 2002. *The Years of Lyndon Johnson: Master of the Senate*. New York: Knopf.

Chen, M. 2001. *Inside Chinese Business*. Boston: Harvard Business Press.

Chen, P. 1993. 'China's Challenge to Economic Orthodoxy: Asian Reform as an Evolutionary, Self-organizing Process', *China Economic Review*, 4(2): 137–42.

Cheung, G.C. 2004. 'Chinese Diaspora as a Virtual Nation: Interactive Roles between Economic and Social Capital', *Political Studies*, 52(4): 664–84.

Chou, B.K. 2005. 'Implementing the Reform of Performance Appraisal in China's Civil Service', *China Information*, 19(1): 39.

Clague, C., P. Keefer, S. Knack, and M. Olson. 1996. 'Property and Contract Rights in Autocracies and Democracies', *Journal of Economic Growth*, 1(2): 243–76.

Deng, X. 1994. *Selected Works of Deng Xiaoping, 1982–1992*. Beijing: Foreign Languages Press.

Dernberger, R.F. 1980. *China's Development Experience in Comparative Perspective*. Cambridge, MA: Harvard University Press.

Djankov, S., E. Glaeser, R. La Porta, F. Lopez-de-Silanes, and A. Shleifer. 2003. 'The New Comparative Economics', *Journal of Comparative Economics*, 31(4): 595–619.

Elson, D. and N. Cagatay. 2000. 'The Social Content of Macroeconomic Policies, *World Development*, 28(7): 1347–64.

Fan, G. 2005. 'China is a Private-sector Economy'. Available at http://www.businessweek.com/magazine/content/05_34/b3948478.htm, accessed on 24 May 2010.

Fan, S. 2004. 'Infrastructure and Pro-poor Growth', Réseau du CAD sur la réduction de la pauvreté: Agriculture et croissance favorable aux pauvres, Paris.

Fan, S. and C. Chan-Kang. 2005. *Road Development, Economic Growth, and Poverty Reduction in China*. Washington DC: International Food Policy Research Institute (IFPRI).

Fan, S., L. Zhang, and X. Zhang. 2002. 'Growth, Inequality, and Poverty in Rural China: The Role of Public Investments', Research Report, International Food Policy Research Institute (IFPRI), Washington DC.

Feuerwerker, A. 1976. *State and Society in Eighteenth-century China: The Ch'ing Empire in Its Glory*. Ann Arbor: University of Michigan Press.

Fewsmith, J. 2004. 'Elite Responses to Social Change and Globalization', in Jude Howell (ed.), *Governance in China*. Oxford: Rowman and Littlefield.

Frye, T. and A. Shleifer. 1997. 'The Invisible Hand and the Grabbing Hand', *The American Economic Review*, 87(2): 354–8.

Garnaut, R. and L. Song. 2004. *China: Is Rapid Growth Sustainable?* Australian National University: Asia Pacific Press.

Glaeser, Edward L., Rafael La Porta, Florencio Lopez-de-Silanes, and Andrei Shleifer. 2004. 'Do Institutions Cause Growth?', *Journal of Economic Growth*, 9(3): 271–303.

Gries, P.H. and S. Rosen. 2004. *State and Society in 21st Century China*. London and New York: Routledge.

Gu, E.X. 1999. 'From Permanent Employment to Massive Lay-offs: The Political Economy of "Transitional Unemployment" in Urban China (1993–8)', *Economy and Society*, 28(2): 281.

Harrold, P. 1992. *China's Reform Experience to Date*, World Bank. Available at http://ideas.repec.org/p/fth/wobadi/180.html, accessed on 19 May 2010.

Heckman, J.J. 2003. 'China's Investment in Human Capital', *Economic Development and Cultural Change*, 51: 795–804.

Heilmann, S. 2008. 'Policy Experimentation in China's Economic Rise', *Studies in Comparative International Development (SCID)*, 43(1): 1–26.

———. 2009. 'Maximum Tinkering under Uncertainty: Unorthodox Lessons from China, *Modern China*, 35(4): 450.

Hofman, B. and J. Wu. 2009. 'Explaining China's Development and Reforms', Paper Submitted to the Growth Commission, World Bank Resident Mission, Beijing.

Howell, J. 2004. 'New Directions in Civil Society: Organizing around Marginalized Interests', in J. Howell (ed.), *Governance in China*, pp. 143–71. Rowman & Littlefield Publishers, Inc.

Hu, A. 2004. 'Economic Growth and Employment Growth in China (1978–2001)', *Asian Economic Papers*, 3(2): 166–76.

Huang, Y. 1998. 'The Industrial Organization of Chinese Government', MA Working Paper Boston, Harvard Business School.

———. 2002. 'Did the Chinese Government Pursue a Gradualist Reform Strategy in the 1990s?', in China Transition Workshop.

———. 2003. *Selling China: Foreign Direct Investment during the Reform Era*. Cambridge, Mass.: Cambridge University Press.

———. 2008. *Capitalism with Chinese Characteristics: Entrepreneurship and the State*, 1st edn. Cambridge Mass.: Cambridge University Press.

Hussain, A. and N. Stern. 2006. 'Public Finance: The Role of the State and Economic Transformation in China: 1978–2020', *Comparative Studies*, 26: 25–55.

Iliev, P. and L. Putterman. 2007. 'Social Capability, History and the Economies of Communist and Postcommunist States', *Studies in Comparative International Development (SCID)*, 42(1): 36–66.

Kao, J. 1993. 'The Worldwide Web of Chinese Business', *Harvard Business Review*, 71(2): 24–38.

Landry, P.F. 2003. 'The Political Management of Mayors in Post-Deng China, *The Copenhagen Journal of Asian Studies*, 17: 31–58.

Lardy, N. 2007. 'China Economy: Problems and Prospects', in *Footnotes*, Newsletter of the Wachman Center, Foreign Policy Research Institute.

Lau, L.J. 1992. *Macroeconomic Policies for Short-term Stabilization and Long-term Growth of the Chinese Economy*. Asia/Pacific Research Center, Stanford University.

Lau, L.J., Y. Qian, and G. Roland. 1997. Pareto-improving Economic Reforms through Dual-track Liberalization, *Economics Letters*, 55(2): 285–92.

———. 2000. 'Reform without Losers: An Interpretation of China's Dual-track Approach to Transition', *Journal of Political Economy*, 108(1): 120–43.

Li, D.D. 1998. 'Changing Incentives of the Chinese Bureaucracy, *American Economic Review*, 88(2): 393–7.

Lin, J.Y. 1992. 'Rural Reforms and Agricultural Growth in China', *The American Economic Review*, 82(1): 34–51.

———. 2004. 'Lessons of China's Transition from a Planned Economy to a Market Economy', *Distinguished Lecture Series*, 16.

Lin, J.Y., F. Cai, and Z. Li. 1996. 'The Lessons of China's Transition to a Market Economy', *Cato Journal*, 16(2): 201–31.

Lin, J.Y. and Z. Liu. 2000. 'Fiscal Decentralization and Economic Growth in China', *Economic Development and Cultural Change*, 49(1): 1–21.

Liu, Y., K. Rao, and W.C. Hsiao. 2003. 'Medical Expenditure and Rural Impoverishment in China', *Journal of Health Population and Nutrition*, 21(3): 216–22.

Lovett, S., L.C. Simmons, and R. Kali. 1999. 'Guanxi versus the Market: Ethics and Efficiency', *Journal of International Business Studies*, 30(2): 231–2.

Lutz, W., W. Sanderson, and S. Scherbov. 2008. 'The Coming Acceleration of Global Population Ageing', *Nature*, 451(7179): 716–19.

McKinley, T. 2003. *The Macroeconomics of Poverty Reduction*, Initial Findings of the UNDP Asia-Pacific Regional Programme. New York: UNDP.

McMillan, J. 1994. *China's Nonconformist Reforms*. Institute on Global Conflict and Cooperation, University of California.

McMillan, J. and B. Naughton. 1992. 'How to Reform a Planned Economy: Lessons from China', *Oxford Review of Economic Policy*, 8(1): 130–43.

Narayan, D. and M. Woolcock. 2000. 'Social Capital: Implications for Development Theory, Research, and Policy', *The World Bank Research Observer*, 15(2): 225–49.

National Bureau of Statistics (NBS), China. 2005. *China Compendium of Statistics 1949–2004.* Beijing: China Statistics Press.

Naughton, B. 1993. 'Monetary Control and China's Most Recent Macroeconomic Cycle', *China Economic Review*, 4(2): 231–4.

————. 1994a. 'Chinese Institutional Innovation and Privatization from Below', *The American Economic Review*, 84(2): 266–70.

————. 1994b. 'What is Distinctive about China's Economic Transition? State Enterprise Reform and Overall System Transformation', *Journal of Comparative Economics*, 18(3): 470–90.

————. 1996. *Growing Out of the Plan.* Cambridge, Mass.: Cambridge University Press.

————. 2007. *The Chinese Economy: Transitions and Growth.* MIT Press.

Naughton, B. and D.L. Yang (eds). 2004. *Holding China Together: Diversity and National Integration in the Post-Deng Era.* New York: Cambridge University Press.

Nee, V. 1992. 'Organizational Dynamics of Market Transition: Hybrid Forms, Property Rights, and Mixed Economy in China', *Administrative Science Quarterly*, 37(1): 1–27.

Nee, V., S. Opper, and S.M. Wong. 2007. 'Developmental State and Corporate Governance in China', *Management and Organization Review*, 3(1): 19–53.

Nolan, P. 2004. *Transforming China: Globalization, Transition and Development.* London: Anthem Press.

North, D.C. 1990. *Institutions, Institutional Change, and Economic Performance.* New York: Cambridge University Press.

North, D.C. and R.P. Thomas. 1973. *The Rise of the Western World: A New Economic History.* New York: Cambridge University Press.

Oi, J.C. 1992. 'Fiscal Reform and the Economic Foundations of Local State Corporatism in China', *World Politics: A Quarterly Journal of International Relations*, 45: 99–126.

————. 1995. 'The Role of the Local State in China's Transitional Economy', *China Quarterly*, 144: 1132–49.

Park, S.H. and Y. Luo. 2001. 'Guanxi and Organizational Dynamics: Organizational Networking in Chinese Firms', *Strategic Management Journal*, 22(5): 455–77.

Perkins, D. 1994. 'Completing China's Move to the Market', *The Journal of Economic Perspectives*, 8(2): 23–46.

————. 2006. 'China's Recent Economic Performance and Future Prospects', *Asian Economic Policy Review*, 1(1): 15–40.

Putnam, R.D., R. Leonardi, and R.Y. Nanetti. 1993. *Making Democracy Work*. NJ: Princeton University Press.

Putterman, L. 1995. 'The Role of Ownership and Property Rights in China's Economic Transition', *The China Quarterly*, 144: 1047–64.

Qian, Y. 1999. 'The Process of China's Market Transition (1978–1998): Evolutionary, Historical and Institutional Perspectives', *Journal of Institutional and Theoretical Economics* symposium on 'Big-Bang Transformation of Economic Systems as a Challenge to New Institutional Economics', June, pp. 9–11.

————. 2002. 'How Reform Worked in China', SSRN eLibrary. Available at http://papers.ssrn.com/sol3/papers.cfm?abstract_id=317460, accessed on 25 May 2010.

Qian, Y. and G. Roland. 1998. 'Federalism and the Soft Budget Constraint', *American Economic Review*, 88(5): 1143–62.

Qian, Y. and B.R. Weingast. 1996. 'China's Transition to Markets: Market-preserving Federalism, Chinese Style', *Journal of Economic Policy Reform*, 1(2): 149–85.

Qian, Y. and C. Xu. 1993. 'Why China's Economic Reforms Differ: The M-form Hierarchy and Entry/Expansion of the Non-state Sector', *Economics of Transition*, 1(2): 135–70.

Ranis, G. and F. Stewart. 2006. 'Successful Transition towards a Virtuous Cycle of Human Development and Economic Growth: Country Studies', SSRN eLibrary. Available at http://papers.ssrn.com/sol3/papers.cfm?abstract_id=920603, accessed on 21 May 2010.

Rawski, T.G. 1999. 'Reforming China's Economy: What Have We Learned?', *The China Journal*, 41: 139–56.

Rodrik, D. 1999. 'Institutions for High-quality Growth: What They Are and How to Acquire Them', prepared for delivery at the IMF Conference on Second Generation Reforms.

Sachs, J.D. and W. T. Woo. 2000. 'Understanding China's Economic Performance', *Journal of Economic Policy Reform*, 4(1): 1–50.

————. 2003. 'China's Economic Growth after WTO Membership', *Journal of Chinese Economic and Business Studies*, 1(1): 1–31.

Saich, T. 2003. 'Reform and the Role of the State in China', in Robert Benewick, Marc Blecher, and Sarah Cook (eds), *Asian Politics in Development: Essays in Honour of Gordon White*. London: Frank Cass Publishers.

Shambaugh, D.L. 1995. *Greater China*. Oxford: Oxford University Press.

Smart, A. and J.Y. Hsu. 2004. 'The Chinese Diaspora, Foreign Investment and Economic Development in China', *The Review of International Affairs*, 3(4): 544–66.

Stiglitz, J.E. 2006. *Making Globalization Work.* New York: W.W. Norton & Co.

Sun, L. 2002. 'The Sociology of Practice and the Analysis of the Practical Process of Market Transition', *Social Sciences in China,* 23(4).

Sun, Y. 1999. 'Reform, State, and Corruption: Is Corruption Less Destructive in China than in Russia?', *Comparative Politics,* 32(1): 1–20.

Transparency International. 2009. *Corruption Perceptions Index 2009.* Available at http://www.transparency.org/policy_research/surveys_indices/cpi/2009, accessed on 10 June 2010.

UN Country Team in China. 2008. *China's Progress towards the MDGs 2008 Report,* Beijing. Available at http://www.undp.org.cn/modules.php ?op=modload&name=News&file=article&catid=18&topic=4&sid =4354&mode=thread&order=0&thold=0, accessed 19 May 2010.

United Nations Development Program (UNDP). 2005. *China Human Development Report 2005.* Beijing: China Translation & Publishing Corporation.

———. 2008. *China Human Development Report 2007/08.* Beijing: China Translation & Publishing Corporation.

Walder, A.G., 1995. 'China's Transitional Economy: Interpreting Its Significance', *China Quarterly,* 144: 963–79.

———. 2002. 'Markets and Income Inequality in Rural China: Political Advantage in an Expanding Economy', *American Sociological Review,* 67(2): 231–53.

———. 2003. 'Sociological Dimensions of China's Economic Transition: Organization, Stratification, and Social Mobility', *Shorenstein APARC.*

Wang, Y. and Y. Yao. 2003. 'Sources of China's Economic Growth 1952–1999: Incorporating Human Capital Accumulation', *China Economic Review,* 14(1): 32–52.

Watson, A. 1988. 'The Reform of Agricultural Marketing in China since 1978', *The China Quarterly,* 113: 1–28.

WFP. 2009. *China—A Report on the Status of China's Food Security,* United Nations World Food Programme—Fighting Hunger Worldwide, China Agricultural Science and Technology Press. Available at http://www.wfp.org/content/china-report-status-chinas-food-security, accessed on 24 May 2010.

WHO (Word Health Organization). 2000. *The World Health Report 2000: Health Systems—Improving Performance.* Geneva: WHO.

Whyte, M.K. 1995. 'The Social Roots of China's Economic Development', *The China Quarterly:* (144): 999–1019.

World Bank. 1995. *Bureaucrats in Business.* Washington DC: World Bank.

———. 1996. *From Plan to Market.* New York: Oxford University Press.

———. 2010. *World Development Indicators.* Washington DC: World Bank.

Xin, K.R. and J.L. Pearce. 1996. Guanxi: Connections as Substitutes for Formal Institutional Support, *Academy of Management Journal*, 39(6): 1641–58.

Xu, L.C. 1997. *The Productivity Effects of Decentralized Reforms: An Analysis of the Chinese Industrial Reforms*. Washington DC: World Bank Publications.

Young, A. 2000. 'The Razor's Edge: Distortions and Incremental Reform in the People's Republic of China', *Quarterly Journal of Economics*, 115(4): 1091–135.

Yu, Y., 2001. 'A Review of China's Macroeconomic Development and Policies in the 1990s', *China and World Economy*, 6.

————. 2008. 'Chinese Macroeconomic Management: Issues and Prospects', *China, Asia, and the New World Economy*, 1: 254–74.

Zhao, S. 1993. 'Deng Xiaoping's Southern Tour: Elite Politics in Post-Tiananmen China', *Asian Survey*, 33(8): 739–56.

Zheng, Y. 1994. 'Quasi-corporatism, Developmental Localism, and Behavioral Federalism', PhD dissertation, Princeton University.

Zhou, T. (ed.). 1984. *Dangdai Zhongguo de Jingji Tizhi Gaige (Economic System Reforms in Contemporary China)*. Beijing: China Social Science Press.

6

Prospects for the Future

The past 30 years of reforms and China's rapid growth have dramatically reduced poverty and raised living standards. China is now the second largest economy in the world,[1] up from the 10th largest in 1978. China's GDP share of the world economy has increased sharply, from 1.8 per cent in 1978 to 6.42 per cent in 2008. China has moved from the low to the lower-middle level in both income and human development categories. Lifestyle patterns, in which people formerly emphasized basic food and clothing, now include growing and increasingly sophisticated consumption levels and patterns. Human capabilities have increased not only as a result of the strides made in education, income, and health—the three elements of the Human Development Index (HDI), but also as a consequence of increased freedom of choice. The Chinese are now free to choose their employers, choose a place

---

[1] See World Bank, World Development Indicators database.

to live, and have the freedom to set up a business and become an entrepreneur.

Amidst these laudatory achievements and pundits talking up the emergence of China as a world power, it is easy to forget that China remains a developing country—there are still 100 countries ahead of China in per capita terms. Estimates indicate that China has 250 million people living below $1.25 per day in 2005 Purchasing Power Parity (PPP) dollars (World Bank 2009), and that life remains a struggle for a large number of people. There are, for instance, a staggering 400 million people who exist on incomes between $1 dollar and $2 dollar per day. In 2007, 251 million people were without access to an adequate supply of safe drinking water and other basic public infrastructure. Poverty is particularly severe in the remote areas where natural conditions are hard, and in fragile ecosystems as people residing there face growing pressure from changes in the climate. Migrants, some 150 to 200 million of them, constitute a particularly vulnerable group, as they do not have as yet the right to receive the same social services and social security benefits as official urban residents (UN 2008).

According to the 2007–8 *China Human Development Report* (*HDR*), some 52 per cent of the improvement shown in the HDI from 1980 to 2005 can be attributed to gains in GDP, 18 per cent to positive changes in life expectancy, and 30 per cent to education. But as the government itself recognizes, this unprecedented economic growth has come with a hefty price tag in terms of environmental degradation, inequality, and social insecurity.

WILL CHINA KEEP ON GROWING?

This is an important question, both for China and the rest of the world. While most observers consider that China will keep on growing for the foreseeable future, their reasons for that prognosis differ widely, not unlike their explanations for its past success. It is a question that preoccupies many analysts and policymakers, both in China and elsewhere, often tinged with a concern about the implications of what the rapid rise of China portends for the existing world order.

Will the Chinese bumblebee defy the laws of economic gravity once again? China has already grown faster and longer than the other fast growing Asian countries. Japan, Korea, and Taiwan all grew fast, particularly in their initial periods of rapid development, that is, in the 1960s and 1970s, but China has managed to grow consistently at high rates over the last three decades. Will the presumed policy distortions finally slow down its growth trajectory? So the critical questions are: will the past continue into the future? Are there extraordinary challenges which need to be addressed? Are there 'forks in the road' which require Chinese leaders to revisit their development vision and its execution?

There are different ways of addressing this question.[2] One is simply to extrapolate past growth rates into the future. Other assessments compare how far the Chinese economy has come in its structure of production. Yet other projections highlight the policies needed to ensure the continuance of high growth rates in the decades ahead. Most observers are optimistic about China's future. The reasoning for this optimism is based on the view that the growth drivers involved in China's transformation are as relevant today as they were earlier in the progress in China, and that with the right policies, there is strong likelihood of meeting the *Xiaokang* target of quadrupling income levels by 2020 (with 2000 as the base). There is an assumption here that, as before, the government and the ruling Chinese elite will remain fully engaged in ensuring the betterment of the lives of the Chinese people and in driving the broader development agenda of the country.

There is equally an assumption that there is growing willingness to take on the issues of inequality and social welfare that are beginning to fray social bonds and reduce social cohesion.

---

[2] See, for instance, Holz (2005, 2008); He and Kuijs (2007); Brandt et al. (2007); Bottelier and Fosler (2007); and Perkins (2006).

And that not only there is now a political imperative but also sufficient fiscal space to address income and social disparities.

There is a minority view as well. Some observers consider the future of China as bleak. They consider that the Chinese economy is built on a house of cards, an economy which is likely to collapse at any moment. In his book on China, Gordon Chang (2002) announces the coming collapse of the country, and yet others like Lester Brown, given China's scale, worry about who will feed its large population (Brown 1995). Even well wishers who accept that China has made real progress consider that the policy distortions inherent in the Chinese economy have not prepared the country well to successfully deal with any big shocks. Their reasoning is best captured in the following:

> Monetary policy is typically the first line of defence against such shocks but, with monetary policy constrained by the objective of maintaining a tightly managed exchange rate, it can best play a very limited role. There appears room for fiscal manoeuver since the explicit levels of the fiscal deficit and government debt are quite low, but this may be deceptive as there are large contingent liabilities in the state owned sector banking system and huge unfunded pension liabilities. The financial system is still dysfunctional in many ways and may not be deep or robust enough to withstand a significant shock (Prasad 2007).

This concern is echoed by He and Kuijs (2007) who take the view that given the current policies, continuing high growth in China (which is inefficient) would require even higher savings and investment rates. The authors undertake a general equilibrium analysis to model how a desirable policy package could rebalance China's economy and how this could then enable China to grow rapidly. They see the downsides to China's current growth path which they consider as unsustainable: overly high saving and investment, high resource and energy intensity, environment concerns, the limited role of domestic consumption, and a large external imbalance. They accept that the government is not an idle spectator in these issues, and that a scenario based on the past is unlikely to hold. While projections are notoriously uncertain, and often just wrong in the case of China, they make the important point, that even within a neoclassical framework with specific policy adjustments, high growth rates over the long term are likely to hold for China.

An important point raised by these China well-wishers is to highlight the fact that the Chinese economy is getting more complex and integrated into global trade and financial systems, and as this happens the authorities have to be particularly mindful of external shocks, so that they can be planned for and better managed. The global financial crisis of 2008 was the first major test for them, which by most accounts Chinese authorities have passed with flying colours. Rebalancing the economy and creating a harmonious society are high priorities of the government. The debate remains as to what are the next wave of reforms and the desirable policy options.

SOME PROJECTIONS

Some macro numbers can be helpful, particularly to illustrate the likely changes in the future for China and its role in the world economy. A simple extrapolation into the future of past real GDP growth trends indicates that the size of the Chinese economy will surpass the US economy in PPP terms sometime between 2012 and 2015. By 2030 or thereabouts, China is likely to be the world's largest economy in nominal terms as well (Holz 2005, 2008).

Many economists consider that China is still at an early stage of development, and that by comparing China with other more advanced countries, particularly countries like Japan and South Korea, it is possible to develop a future growth scenario that can measure how far China can grow and the period of time required to 'catch up' with these countries (Table 6.1). For instance, Chinese per capita growth rates (in PPP terms) of 590 per cent between 1978 and 2009[3] are comparable to the

---

[3] Calculated by author with compound rate of 6.1 per cent.

490 per cent for 1950–73 for Japan and 680 per cent for South Korea over 1962–90 (Wolf 2005). In this context, desirable policy measures are all about enabling the removal of constraints that prevent well-established development patterns from unfolding. Over time, labour shifts from low productivity agriculture to higher productivity industry and services. Based on China's 1978–2002 rate of agricultural labour decline, and allowing for some of the inherent uncertainty of such comparisons, China has several decades to go before reaching the 10 per cent (of total labour force) threshold at which Japan and Korea appear to bottom out (Holz 2005). Hence the unfolding of this structural shift is likely to remain a source of economic growth for some time to come. It is however worth reiterating that China has already been growing at a faster clip for a longer period than Japan and South Korea. We are in some ways in uncharted waters here.

Different models can be drawn upon to project future trends for China, based on 'traditional economic growth and trade theories covering issues of structural change, catching up and factor price equalization'.[4] Most of them essentially sketch out the 'catch up' potential of China. For instance, China per capita incomes still only represent a modest 5 per cent of the US level. 'Moreover, compared to Japan and Korea at a comparable level of development, China is now more open to foreign direct investment (FDI) and technology, while globalization makes import

---

[4] A common approach is to decompose GDP growth. Some models assume that the production function will remain stable, a difficult assumption at best given that continuing transformation is all about changing the production conditions. Others make assumptions about how long China is likely to continue with high savings and investment rates. Still others rely on calculating the growth of labour and other variables, referred to as the income approach. This is based on estimates about China's future labour force based on what is known about the amount and distribution of the current labour force. Future GDP levels are derived from this based on the assumption that present and future demographics in the form of quantity and quality of labour are sufficient for this purpose. Adjustments are made to calculate GDP levels per economically active labourer. Another way of looking at future growth is to compare China with other development trajectories, and to see whether the removal of barriers to economic transition to the next stage of development will provide the impetus to further growth (Holz 2005, 2008).

Table 6.1 Sectoral Developments in China, Japan, and South Korea (1960–2001)

China	1960	1970*	1980	1990	2000
Share in employment					
Agriculture	80.8	68.7	60.1	50.0	
Industry	...	10.2	18.2	21.4	22.5
Services	...	9.0	13.1	18.5	27.5
Share in value added					
Agriculture	...	...	30.2	27.1	15.1
Industry	...	...	48.2	41.3	45.9
Services	...	...	21.6	36.7	39.0
GDP per capita, ratio US (2005 $)	...	0.7	0.8	1.4	2.9
GDP per capita, ratio US (curr $)	3.2	2.2	1.6	1.3	2.7
I/Y ratio	...	...	20.0	24.2	33.2
GDP growth (10 years backward)	...	4.7	6.3	9.4	10.5
Labour productivity growth (10 years backward)	...	...	...	6.0	8.0
Japan					
Share in employment					
Agriculture	...	...	10.4	7.2	5.1
Industry	...	...	35.3	34.1	31.2
Services	...	...	54	58.2	63.1
Share in value added					
Agriculture	...	5.2	3.6	2.5	1.4
Industry	...	44.4	40.4	39.2	32.2
Services	...	50.3	56.0	58.3	66.5
GDP per capita, ratio US (2000 $)	...	96	106	118	108
GDP per capita, ratio US (curr $)	16	39	75	107	108
I/Y ratio (10 years bw)	35.6	34.1	29.9	29.0	

(Continued)

Table 6.1 (continued)

Japan	1960	1970*	1980	1990	2000
GDP growth (10 years bw)	10.5	4.5	4.0	1.4	
Labour productivity growth (10 years bw)				2.7	1.1
South Korea					
Share in employment					
Agriculture	...	...	34.0	17.9	10.9
Industry	...	...	27.8	35.4	28
Services	...	...	38.2	46.7	61
Share in value added					
Agriculture	...	...	...	...	4.3
Industry	...	23.7	32.5	37.3	36.2
Services	...	...	...	...	59.5
GDP per capita, ratio US (2000 $)	...	11	14	23	31
GDP per capita, ratio US (curr $)	5	5	13	25	28
I/Y ratio	...	20.3	29.0	31.0	35.0
GDP growth (10 years backward)	9.4	7.3	8.7	6.2	
Labour productivity growth (10 years bw)	5.7	3.6	5.8	4.5	

Source: He and Kuijs (2007), NBS, USDA, IMF, and author's estimates.
Note: *Some of the data pertaining to Japan is for 1971..

of technology and ideas easier. This is probably another reason why growth of labour productivity and TFP in China now are higher than in the countries then' (He and Kuijs 2007). The key, of course, is the likely forces that have a bearing on increases in labour productivity. 'Catch-up' is influenced by factors like better technology and best practices, or a better educated labour force. These forces combined with high levels of investment and savings set a strong foundation for continuing growth (see Table 6.2a).

A similar conclusion is reached when looking at factor price equalization, which essentially states that skill-specific wages should equalize between countries over time, given a certain set of assumptions. An inverse U-shaped relationship can be posited as labour productivity initially rises with an increase in wages, and then declines as the returns (or relative returns) to capital 'equalizes' with the returns obtaining in advanced economies such as the US. If China were to follow the patterns of Japan and South Korea, then there is compelling evidence to indicate that China is still at the beginning of this U-shaped universe, that the 'potential for economic growth from relatively low labor costs will continue for another thirty years' (Holz 2005).

Most observers generally concur that China's economy will exceed that of the US in PPP terms in less than 10 years, and in per capita terms much later, some 30 to 40 years in the future (Table 6.2b). But this storyline is an aggregate one. Holz (2005) adds an important dimension in these comparisons by pointing out that 'the coastal areas, especially the fastest growing five provinces together with Shanghai, with a population exceeding that of the US, may catch up in as little as two decades'. A more recent book by Arvind Subramanian, *Eclipse* (2011), goes further and concludes that the Chinese economy is already number one based on PPP estimates. By 2030, per capital income levels in China would be half those in the USA.

Table 6.2a Comparing Projections on Chinese Growth

	Projection Period	Average Annual Growth (%)	When China Overtakes US
Holz (2008)	2005–25	7.0–9.0 (2005–15)	2010 (in PPP)
Maddison(2007)	By 2030	4.98 (2003–30)	Before 2015 (in PPP)
Keidel (2008)	By 2030	…	Before 2030
Fogel (2006)	By 2030	8.0	
Xinhua News Agency (2008)	By 2030	8.0	
Wang et al. (2007)	2006–20	7.8 (2006–10) 5.9 (2010–20)	
He et al.(2007)	2010–20	Baseline scenario 8.3 (2010–15) 7.0 (2016–20)	

Table 6.2b Comparing Projections on China's Real GDP Growth (2006–30)

	Global Insight	Economist Intelligence Unit	Goldman Sachs
2006–10	8.6	8.0	7.1
2011–15	7.2	5.5	5.8
2016–20	6.4	4.4	5.0
2021–25	6.1	4.5	4.5
2026–30	n.a	4.7	4.1

Source: Holz (2008); Maddison (2007); Keidel (2008); Fogel (2006); Wang et al. (2007); He et al. (2007); and Elwell et al. (2007).

A BROADER PERSPECTIVE

These projections, though helpful, are illustrative at best. They outline the potential of growth for China in the years to come. A better question then to ask is whether these scenarios are likely to take hold? And if so, what are the essential elements of the economy and society which require attention. As with the explanations about China's past success, taking on a broader perspective can be helpful in identifying key factors that are likely to drive future growth and development in China. That China and other East Asian countries like Japan and South Korea have been able to grow rapidly over many decades can present useful lessons for other developing countries. The interesting bit is to tease out the underlying reasons for such success, and examine the 'drivers' and reforms that are likely to influence future development outcomes.

Like others, this book takes an optimistic view about China's future. There are then two set of issues to address: the first are the set of long term 'drivers' or forces that are likely to influence China's future growth and the second are the challenges that need to be addressed so that not only China continues to grow but also that the growth can be sustained and the population at large benefits from that growth.

The Continuing Drivers of Growth (and Modernization)

Ongoing Commitment to Reform and a Developmental State

There are few signs that the Communist Party of China (CPC) and the Government are in any way likely to change their development orientation. As has been argued in earlier chapters, producing better development results constitutes an essential part of the legitimacy for the Party. This combination of a strong state and increasingly better policies has produced stellar results over the 30 years of reform, so why fix something that is not broken! More specifically, several points can be made: one, as the 11th Five Year Plan (2006–10) explicitly states, the state remains committed to further reforms and continuing high growth rates. Second, in the run-up to the next Five Year Plan (2011–14), and as China gears up for its next stage of reforms, it is equally clear that some features key to previous success would need to be revisited. Policies have already moved in the right direction (*Xiaokang*, five balances, new socialist countryside, reducing disparities). There is also widespread acceptance that administrative structures need to be reorganized in order to raise efficiency and effectiveness, enhance transparency, and promote greater participation.

The broad reform orientations are now well embedded in Chinese thinking. The Chinese leadership continues to be committed to the notion that China is a market economy, and that obstacles to the efficient functioning of markets should increasingly be reduced in the future. As highlighted earlier, the Chinese economy is increasingly market and incentive driven, and that this movement will continue into the future, especially with the growth of the services sector. This is pertinent for the future, as manufacturing is currently the largest sector. In 2006, for instance, in compliance with WTO commitments, China allowed foreign banks to compete on an equal basis with domestic banks, and there is now 'increased competition in insurance, securities, asset management and telecommunication' (Lardy 2007). As Figure 6.1 highlights there is still some distance to go in determining the preferred balance between public and private sector roles. What is particularly pertinent is the growing policy commitment that competitive forces are relevant to the public enterprises as well. This has translated into a hardening of budget constraints—even if these constraints are presently stronger in the case of banks but less so with the government (Garnaut et al. 2006).

Clearly along the way, many aspects of the development model would need to be revisited. Rising income inequalities and the protection of the environment in particular make this a political imperative. One important dimension of change is likely to be a retooling of the balance between the centre and the provinces. The 1994 reforms made an important correction by reinforcing the fiscal position of the centre. The 'unfunded' mandates of local governments in the delivery of social services now require a further rethink about the degree of fiscal decentralization. China has to institute more robust policies that aim at equalizing health and education outcomes among provinces and counties. That and delivering on the stated policy commitment to provide

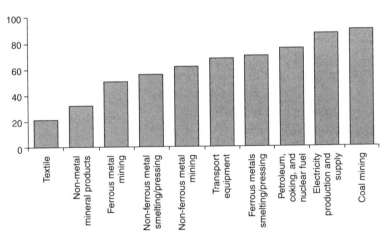

Figure 6.1 Shares of the Government in Different Industries and Sectors (2005)
Source: National Statistics Bureau of China and Citigroup estimates (2010).

social security to all Chinese citizens as a matter of right, is likely to go some distance in making a dent at the high and still growing income inequality in China.

Production Efficiencies, Openness, and Globalization

China is moving rapidly to upgrade its production capabilities across the board. That in many areas it remains inefficient provides at the same time that much additional space for China to 'catch up'. The focus on past Chinese levels of inefficiency has obscured the emergence of a new storyline—the rapid growth in productivity in recent years, since 2000 onwards. Bottelier and Fosler (2007) argue that in fact this more recent fast productivity growth is probably the defining factor underlying China's growth success and the emergence of an increasingly large trade surplus from the second half of 2004 onwards (see Figure 6.2).

One key aspect of this drive for efficiency is the continuing commitment in China to openness and globalization. Going global, *zouchuqu*, is already having a significant impact on production efficiency in China. One indicator of the potential power of this

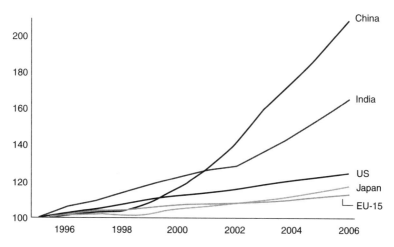

Figure 6.2 China's Productivity Growth (1995 = 100)
Source: Bottelier and Fosler (2007).

phenomenon is brought out by an IMF study (Tseng and Zebregs 2002) which presents evidence to claim that FDI, in fact, has generated most of the observed efficiency gains, even if inward FDI accounted for only 5 per cent of GDP in the second half of the 1990s. According to them, FDI has raised 'TFP growth in China by 2.5 percentage points per year during the 1990s'. The share of foreign-owned companies in gross exports is close to 50 per cent. While these estimates may be debatable, it does underscore the important roles played by best practices and competitive forces in the rapid rise in productivity that China has been experiencing. In fact it could be argued that the long-term future of China is intimately connected with its push to go global. This is not just for the frequently quoted reasons—that it's growing manufacturing capacity can only be sustained by overseas demand—but more fundamentally, to position China as a global economic player and to bring greater efficiencies and economies of scale in domestic markets as well. These forces are likely to continue and intensify in the future.

There is much room for 'catch up' in production efficiency levels. At the macro level, one measure of factor efficiency is the 'incremental capital output ratio' (ICOR). China's ICOR is around 5, in comparison to 3 for Japan in the 1950s, and between 2 and 3 for South Korea in the 1970s. There is much evidence that Chinese resource efficiency can be substantially improved. China, for instance, uses two to three times more water and fertilizer in agriculture than the world's average. Well structured incentives and policies now need to be considered that actively promote the conservation and use-efficiency of resources. The other unsustainable dimension is the energy intensity of production: China uses four and a half times as much energy per US dollar of output as the US (at market exchange rates) and seven and a half times as much as in Japan (He and Kuijs 2007), though figures are more comparable when PPP adjustments are made.

This 'going out' has been embraced enthusiastically by Chinese firms. Chinese participation in global supply chains and networks are likely to enhance domestic capabilities as Chinese firms and individual engineers, scientists, designers, managers, and so on, sharpen their skills by working in global business networks. Organizational capital gets deepened as best practices and high product standards get internalized. These links will continue to channel up-to-date technologies and best practices into domestic industries, given the openness of the Chinese economy and the growing sophistication of Chinese consumers. These pressures will help reinforce the continuous improvement of product standards, and greater sophistication of production processes (Ding et al. 2009).

This 'going out' has other dimensions. It covers newly competitive industries that cater to transnational markets. Take the example of auto parts. Two-way trade in automotive products doubled between 1995 and 2000, and then quadrupled to $29.6 billion in 2004. Trade in auto parts rose even faster, five-fold with 2000 as the base. Chinese firms are increasingly supplying both domestic and foreign markets, often in partnership with global firms. Chinese firms are being courted to assemble vehicles in countries like Russia, Iran, Egypt, and Malaysia (Li 2005).

There is increased Chinese participation as well in global Research and Development (R&D) networks. Volkswagen, for instance, plans to 'develop, assemble and sell a hybrid minivan in cooperation with a Chinese automaker' because of 'the Chinese industry's rapid advance into a complex technological area of automotive design' and because Chinese 'government ministries have been heavily subsidizing research into hybrid-propulsion and fuel-cell vehicles' (Landler and Bradsher 2005). Whereas for years many of China's best and brightest left for the US, particularly to work in high-tech industries and institutes, there is now a reverse flow which is gathering momentum. A recent illustration captures this well. The first chief technology officer of Applied Materials, a major Silicon Valley firm and the biggest supplier of the equipment used to make semi-conductors, solar panels, and flat display screens, is moving to Beijing. Applied Materials has just built its newest and largest lab in Xian. Companies, entrepreneurs, and engineers all over the world are being drawn to

China as it gears up to develop a high-tech economy, with plans to compete globally in high-tech products and services.

China is also entering a new phase of growing interdependence and dependence on imported energy and materials. Two aspects are particularly noteworthy here: China now imports one-third of its crude oil and over half of its iron ore. By 2020, China is projected to import 60 per cent its crude oil and 40 per cent of natural gas needs. The Chinese government and Chinese firms are increasingly scanning globally to secure long-term access to resources, to ensure that they don't become binding constraints to China's future. The emergence of China as a major manufacturing platform, often in partnership with manufacturers located elsewhere in Asia has in turn created new opportunities beyond those narrowly focused on meeting orders from global firms. Related to this is the emergence of China as a growing source of overseas investment (See Figure 6.3). While accurate data on annual Chinese outward investment flows is difficult to find, the growth is however dramatic. From a low base in 2003, it jumped four-fold by 2005. Anecdotal evidence suggests that this growth

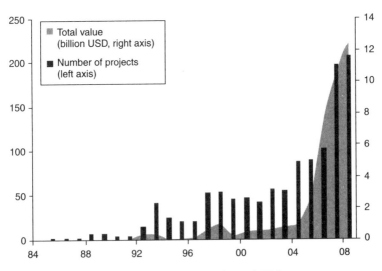

Figure 6.3 China's Outbound FDI
Source: Alon et al. (2010).

if anything has accelerated with China going across the globe to secure resources and strengthen its competitive position.

The structure of trade is rapidly changing as well with the emergence of new trading partners and opportunities for China. In 1999, trade between China and Africa was $2 billion. By 2008, the trade volume had reached a remarkable $108 billion. And surprisingly, a phenomenon which caught most observers by surprise, China is now the largest trading partner of India. 60 per cent of Chinese exports now go to countries in the Asia and Pacific region. Developing countries are increasingly exporting to, and investing, in each other (UNCTAD 2004). China is fast becoming a lead investor and trade partner in most countries in Africa.

Urbanization and Unification of the Rural and Urban Economies

Broad societal forces are still in play in China. In the next 20 years, China plans to move a staggering 350 million people from rural to urban areas, a figure larger than the current population of the US. The share of the urban population is still less than 50 per cent (*People's Daily* 2009, a percentage below most developing countries in Asia. Urbanization is associated with rising incomes, as migrants make their journey in search for a better life. This societal force coupled with the political and economic imperative of raising incomes and efficiencies in agriculture and the rural sector presents both challenges and opportunities.

Many aspects of the rural economy remain within the planned system. Farmers still have to meet overall production targets for specific crops, particularly cereals, and rural migrants still need to be mindful of *houkou* restrictions. Removal of some of these impediments is likely to produce a new round of growth opportunities. The basic business model in agriculture, hitherto small farmer and household driven, may need to be expanded to include more modern forms of commercial agriculture, including large-scale operations. There is much domestic policy discussion about land titles and how tradable they should become.

Prudence requires a careful review of this issue before enacting sweeping changes in land entitlements for farmers—there are, for instance, 300 million or so farmers in China. Given China's specific conditions and its sheer scale, there are likely to be some significant constraints which would have to borne in mind. For instance, if Chinese agriculture becomes fully commercial, in line with the situation pertaining in South Korea and Japan, the shift in agricultural production is likely to be towards high-value crops such as fruits and vegetables. This shift may increase agricultural incomes but the implications for food security and for world prices of food commodities may be sizeable. Current Chinese demand for cereals alone is greater than the total world trade in cereals.[5] As before, a step by step approach may be warranted.

A related challenge refers to Township and Village Enterprises (TVEs) which remain an important source of jobs in the rural areas, though much reduced in employment generation and share of the economy from its highpoint in the 1980s and early 1990s. A revisiting of the TVE model for a new generation may offer new opportunities with stronger links to regional markets and agricultural processing. The New Socialist Countryside (NSC) launched in 2006 highlights some of these challenges and opportunities. For example, in 2004, despite its reduced size, over 22 million TVEs employed 139 million people and generated 4,182 billion Yuan in added value. TVEs created jobs for about 30 per cent of rural labourers in 2006. A vibrant TVEs sector is seen as an essential part of the new socialist countryside. TVEs are expected to provide competitively priced goods and services in many sectors, for example, agricultural products processing, construction, industry, transportation and communications, commerce and catering.[6]

---

[5] For example, according to FAOSTAT, in 2007 Chinese demand for cereals was 386.4 million tonnes, while the export of cereals of the whole world was only 323 million tonnes.

[6] See, for instance, the Special Report on 'Rural Development Building a New Socialist Countryside'. Available on the Chinese Government's official web portal, Gov.cn, at http://www.gov.cn/english/special/rd_index.htm.

On the other side of the equation, this large population transfer to urban areas is likely to produce a huge growth stimulus. It would necessitate the construction of new towns and cities and the upgrading of existing urban areas and provide China with a significant opportunity to consider energy efficient, low-carbon pathways, which in turn can increase overall efficiency and reduce energy intensity of production and help reinforce China's position globally as well.

Challenges

Sustainability

China's large population makes its per capita endowment of many essential resources, particularly land and water, substantially lower than the world average. Rapid growth has put these resources under pressure and has produced serious environmental challenges. That Chinese growth is resource dependent and inefficient in many ways is well documented. Sustainability concerns about resource use and environmental degradation are now high on the policy agenda of the Chinese leadership.

The large challenges pertaining to the environment and natural resources cannot be overstated. Air, water, and other forms of pollution are endangering people's lives and health, and compromising future productive capacities. Ecosystem degradation, such as through soil erosion, desertification, the loss of forests, and the reduction of biodiversity puts sustainable development at risk. Agriculture is an area of particular concern. Although China has made great progress in providing its population with basic food and clothing, ensuring food security in the future will remain a daunting task, given the potential for crop failures and reduced fertility due to climate change and climate-related droughts, floods, and other natural disasters. One estimate puts a potential 38 per cent reduction in agricultural yields per acre as a result of climate change (UNDP 2010).

Further, poor people in China tend to live in ecologically fragile regions (Greenpeace and Oxfam 2009). The quality of infrastructure, education, health, and basic social services is generally low for China's poorest populations, rendering many with weak capacities to cope with exogenous shocks whether they emanate from the economy or climate change. The poor are also most at risk from food insecurity, and are more dependent for livelihoods on primary agriculture and fisheries—industries that are highly affected by changes in temperature, rainfall, and other natural conditions.

Equally, energy efficiency and environmental protection are now the subject of growing policy attention. Importantly, performance incentives are being aligned to promote these objectives. For instance, performance assessment of government officials has been broadened to include measures of energy efficiency, environmental protection, and social development, a shift away from the earlier exclusive focus on GDP growth. China has set ambitious targets on energy conservation, dramatically expanding the share of renewable in the total energy mix (17 per cent by 2020), and reducing by 40–45 per cent the carbon intensity of its production by 2020. China is now the first or second country globally in new and renewable energy such as wind, solar, and biomass. Cities as diverse as Tianjin, Beijing, and Guiyang are aiming to move rapidly towards a low-carbon economy. Increasingly, Chinese planners are recognizing that countries with high levels of human development have two different patterns of per capita emission: one pattern represented by European countries and Japan, with relatively low per capita carbon emissions and the other represented by Australia, Canada, and the United States, where per capita emissions remain high. Even within China, as the China 2010 *HDR* brings out, there is considerable potential at the provincial level in decoupling economic development from carbon emissions (Figure 6.4).

China's future population growth is expected to peak around 2030. Even if per capita emission were to remain unchanged, population growth will drive up total carbon emissions. For China to shift to a low-carbon economy would require changing both the structure of investment and consumption, so that

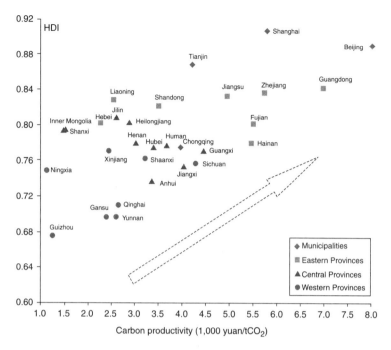

Figure 6.4 Carbon Productivity and China's Provincial Human Development Index Rankings (2007)
Source: UNDP (2010).

future patterns become more sustainable and less resource intensive. This is a large challenge since China is still in a phase of rapid development in heavy and chemical industries such as machines building, steel, building materials, and chemicals. The proportion of energy-intensive industries overall is still rising. This combined with investments in infrastructure as a result of China's rapid urban growth pose particular policy challenges. Equally, coal which is abundantly found in China is likely to remain the dominant source of energy for some time to come. In 2007, it accounted for 69 per cent of China's energy output.

Reinvesting in Societal Capabilities

The 2007–8 national HDR highlights the pressing need to reinvest in providing social services to the 1.3 billion people of

China, and to re-examine the role of the state in the provision of these services.

As highlighted in earlier chapters, while per capita social spending has risen sharply, the burden has shifted from the state to households, who saw their share in social spending increase from 20 per cent in 1978 to as much as 60 per cent in 2000. The social security system, still in its initial stages, covers only a quarter of the eligible population and remains insufficiently funded. The end-result is that households have had to save more. Consumption has declined from 66 per cent of incomes pre–reform to 50 per cent in 2006. While clearly the push on exports worked well for China in recent years, there is now need for a shift in future growth strategies. The global imbalances (which are likely to persist for some time), the sharp drop in global demand for China's products, and climate change all now require new thinking beyond the current stimulus package and future investments, issues that are more fully covered later.

Government has had a long-standing but still unmet commitment to raise the ratio of fiscal spending on education to 4 per cent of GDP. This has to be coupled with reforming the way education is taught in schools, with greater emphasis on creativity and less on rote learning as China gears up to take its rightful place as one of the leading economic powers. That considerable progress has been made was reviewed in the previous chapter. In summary, by 2007, the nine-year compulsory education system had covered 99 per cent of the Chinese population. Since 2000, the primary school enrolment rate has been consistently above 99 per cent, while the middle-school gross enrolment rate rose from 88.6 per cent in 2000 to 98 per cent in 2007 (Chinese Ministry of Education). In 2007 and 2008, China waived tuition and miscellaneous fees for rural and urban students receiving compulsory education.

In health, again to summarize, China has made impressive achievements in the last three decades, as is evident from longer life expectancies, which rose from a low of 35 years before 1949 to 73 years in 2000, exceeding the world average level of

67 years (WHO 2009). Even more recently, maternal mortality rate
has continued to drop, from 53 per 100,000 in 2000 to 36.6 per
100,000 in 2007, a level less than one-tenth of the 2004 average
mortality rate for developing countries (Chinese Ministry of
Health 2008). But, despite these achievements, as Chapter 5
points out, the health sector overall and access to basic healthcare
in particular needs drastic reform. There are large inequalities
in health outcomes among provinces, between urban and rural
areas, and different income groups. Access to healthcare for the
poor is restricted and there are growing environmental health
concerns. The 2005 life expectancy in Beijing, Shanghai, and
other locations in the eastern, more developed regions was in
excess of 80 years, while that of Guizhou was below 70 years.
The mortality rate of children under age five in Qinghai was
3.5 per cent, nearly seven times that of Beijing at 0.51 per cent.
Beijing, Shanghai, and Tianjin are the regions with the highest
level of education, with literacy rates among people over age 15
exceeding 96 per cent, while for Gansu, Qinghai, Ningxia, and
other places in the western region, the rate is about 80 per cent.

A key question is what should be the role of the government
in the provision of these services. An emerging answer to the
question is that the government has the primary responsibility
for the provision of basic social services. This sentiment and the
findings above are now well accepted by the government, and
reforms have been initiated (Ho and Nielsen 2007).

There are reasons to be optimistic. China's finances are in
good shape. Besides the US$ 3.3 trillion in reserves, China has
low inflation, a low national debt, and tax receipts in excess
of 20 per cent ratio of GDP. All these factors bode well for
taking additional measures that can help rebalance the economy
between exports and domestic consumption and fix the social
sectors. The time is ripe for innovative policies and thinking to
steer China towards a sustainable economy and society. And with
the challenges of climate change in front of us, China can seize
the opportunity to become a competitive low-carbon economy.
Importantly, keeping in mind that 60 per cent of China's trade is

within Asia, China can contribute to regional recovery as well. Recent decisions by the Chinese leadership to provide substantial credit lines to Indonesia (US$ 15 billion) and Central Asia (US$ 10 billion), are indicative of mutual interest this implies and the growing Chinese willingness to seize the moment. If its neighbours become prosperous, then China's own future can be more sustainably assured over the long term.

Indeed, China's ability to expand coverage of quality social services can no longer be considered a purely domestic concern. Achievements in these areas are not only prerequisites for further development in China, they are also crucial if Chinese domestic consumption is to increase and for the necessary rebalancing of the world economy is to occur in the wake of the global financial crisis. Such a need to transform China's development pattern has been explicitly recognized by China's leaders, most recently at the December 2009 Central Economic Work Conference.

Reducing Disparities and Reinforcing Social Cohesion

In Chapter 5 we touched upon some of the emerging challenges to social cohesion. As evidence of persistent disparities, the 2007 Human Development Index, an indicator that combines measurements of income, health, and education, varies widely across different regions of China. The highest ranking, for Shanghai, was 44 per cent higher than the lowest ranking, in Tibet. The index for the eastern region was visibly higher than for the western region (see Figure 1.2). The level of human development in Beijing, Shanghai, and other regions is on par with the Czech Republic, Portugal, and other countries with a high HDI, while the low level of Guizhou and the western region are similar to that of the Democratic Republic of Congo and Namibia (UNDP China 2008). Disparities like these extend across all aspects of human development in China. Data from UNDP and the Asian Development Bank (ADB) show that China is in danger of becoming one of the most unequal countries globally, with large rural–urban income gaps and one of the most uneven income distributions of Asian countries. The Gini Coefficient rose from 40.7 in 1993 to 47.3 in 2004 (UNDP 2008; ADB 2007). According to UNDP estimates, the income gap between rural and urban areas in China is now among the highest in Asia and threatens future development (Chinese Ministry of Foreign Affairs and the UN System in China 2008). Income differences between urban and rural areas, and between the eastern and western regions are particularly stark. In 2007, the per capita GDP of Shanghai reached 65,347 yuan, while that of Guizhou was nearly 10 times lower at 6,835 yuan.

In China, improvements in overall human development coexist with worsening disparities, despite impressive rates of growth in GDP. Finding jobs, accessing medical services, and attending schools have become the 'three big mountains' for much of the Chinese people. Converting income growth into sustainable progress in human development for all Chinese citizens is one of the country's major challenges in the decades ahead (UNDP 2010), complicated by growing costs from high environmental pollution and resource degradation. The negative impacts of climate change could make this task even more formidable.

Rising disparities and concerns widely aired in the media about well-connected elites suborning power and position for personal economic benefit are having knock-down effects on trust in government, in social cohesion, and China's social capital generally. The government has tried to respond at the policy level to these concerns, with landmark statements from 2005 onwards, though the real challenge lies in their effective implementation. While most surveys still show relatively high trust in government (especially in comparison with other leading economies), figures compiled by the State Council also show that every year over 3 million people are involved in direct action (strikes, demonstrations) conveying their displeasure about some of the state of affairs, with a particular focus on local land disputes (Lum 2006).

With a growing urban population, the Chinese Government has been obliged to make large investments in urban infrastructure. Consequently, public expenditures on rural medical, educational, and other sectors have lagged behind, reflecting in poorer education, health, and other key human development indicators. Chinese society is also rapidly evolving. Dialogue and debate are now constants for any policy proposal prepared by the government. Civil society is rapidly developing. By some estimates there are now close to half a million NGOs of all kinds,[7] even if the overall policy framework governing this development remains embryonic. The ability of civil society and social partners to contribute to China's development, particularly at the grassroots and local levels is being recognized. The 17th National Communist Party Congress explicitly mentioned the importance and value of civil society contribution to the 12th Five Year Plan currently under preparation. On gender equity, despite much progress, there is in fact a growing challenge. There are persistent gaps in the areas of economic empowerment, political participation, and societal attitudes. What is particularly worrisome is China's imbalanced sex ratio at birth, 120 boys to 100 girls in 2007, an imbalance that has arisen over the last decade as a consequence of market liberalization, boy preference, and economic pressures due in part to the under-provision of social services and social security in rural areas.

Is Demography Destiny?

It is difficult to dispute the common sense conclusion that population control has indeed played an important role in the rise of living standards in China. As stated in Chapter 1, estimates indicate that without the limits established on population growth in China, the Chinese would have numbered in excess of 1.5 billion people by the beginning of this century, with the attendant challenges that this number represents for resource pressures and living standards.

A few years ago, studies (Srinivasan 2006) comparing China and India received widespread attention, since they indicated that

---

[7] Estimated by China's Ministry of Civil Affairs, 'Briefing on the Development of China's Civic Affairs 2009'. As of the end of 2009, there were 0.431 million of social organizations in China.

in the long run, India was likely to outstrip China in aggregate income since it had a larger cohort of young people entering the labour force. In some ways there is a mechanical aspect to this demographic effect. The generation between 15 and 64 is more likely to be working and when this proportion of the population increases, it reduces the ratio of dependents to non-dependents. Equally with development, female participation in the labour force rises, making the working population even larger in size. There are observable impacts as well on savings as people age— the young and the old spend, and those who are in the middle tend to save, and on human capital. The latter though difficult to estimate may well be the most important, as living longer lives can have a profound influence on 'attitudes about education, family, retirement and the role of women' (Bloom et al. 2003).

This demographic dividend was seen as essential to East Asia's success, accounting for as much as one-third of that growth (Bloom and Williamson 1998). Recent estimates suggest the total dependency rate in China will further decline from 42.6 per cent in 2000 to 38.8 per cent in 2013. Therefore it is likely that the demographic dividend will continue to make a contribution to China's economic growth. The turning point is estimated to take place in 2013 or so, when the demographic dividend at least in principle starts shifting to becoming a demographic debt.

Most industrial countries have benefited from the demographic dividend, but this extra source of growth eventually ceases as the demographic transition is completed. The experiences of industrial economies suggest that this source of growth can be replaced by other factors, such as fuller employment and increased productivity through improved education and health levels and more efficient institutional environments.

For China, the task is to fully utilize its current human potential and prepare the country for a rapidly ageing society. This is generally done partly by increasing labour force participation which in China over the last years had declined from 73 per cent in 1997 to 64 per cent in 2004 with the shedding of labour in the public sector (Cai et al. 2008). The current levels of employment and the economic working population indicate that a demographic dividend still exists. The more effectively labour is utilized, joined with continuing high saving rates, the longer the demographic dividend can be maintained. One important reform to extend this dividend over time is by reducing the institutional barriers that still exist in the labour market, particularly those concerning migrant labour from rural areas. Under current projections,[8] the ageing population will continue to increase in the coming decades, which makes the creation of sustainable pension systems an important part of future reform. While creating more work opportunities remains a high priority for Chinese policymakers, this issue will need even more focused policy attention as the population ages. Raising the retirement age may have to considered in the distant future, inter alia to reduce the dependency of older people on social pensions. Finally, perhaps the time has to come to revisit the current population policy so that apart from other considerations measures can be taken to prevent the Chinese population from ageing too rapidly.

Macroeconomic Policies

From the creation of capital markets to the establishment of a country-wide social security system, what has taken the west centuries has been condensed into decades in China.

—Holz (2008)

China, the Global Economy, and the Post-London World More than a year and a half after the G20 Summit in London, there are increasingly evidence of a strong economic recovery in China, as well quicker recovery than expected in other major developing countries such as India and Brazil. Did the G20 meeting help? While the G20 may have fallen short of expectations with regard to commitments to a low-carbon future and the developing world, the fact is that the world, certainly the developed portion of the world, has benefited from the additional

---

[8] See World Population Prospects: The 2008 Revision Population Database.

US$ 1 trillion in stimulus spending. In the medium term, the world stands to benefit from the reform of the International Monetary Fund (IMF) and the World Bank and the agreement to regulate financial markets. The last months have also highlighted the rise of new major players on the global scene, portending broader shifts in global economic and political influence.

In the run-up to, during and following the G20 Summit, China is actively contributing to global conversations about the next steps on global financial architecture. Just days before the G20 Summit, on 23 March 2009, China's central bank governor called for 'an international reserve currency that is disconnected from individual nations and is able to remain stable in the long run' (Zhou 2009). At the G20 Summit itself, after calling for global cooperation and pledging to provide the IMF with US$ 40 billion, China reiterated its longstanding position on making the governance of the IMF and the World Bank more representative of the world we live in.

While the reality that China has some US$ 2.4 trillion in foreign reserves helps, the realization of these aspirations partly depends on the effectiveness of the policies being pursued by China as it seeks to maintain overall growth, balance the structure of its economy, and be a positive influence in bringing Asia and the rest of the world in its wake.

Domestic Demand or Exports: Finding the Balance   Exports alone account for one-third of China's GDP. Recent ballooning of exports and trade surplus has given a sense that growth in China is export-led and that this cannot be sustained in the future. Keidel (2008) contends to the contrary, that domestic factors were in fact far more significant over the past years. In his detailed study of the facts on the ground, Keidel concludes that shifts in investment and consumption have been the forces primarily responsible for China's growth, with the trade surplus of lesser importance.

The slowdown in growth during 2008 and the collapse in China's exports at the end of the same year led to calls to reconsider what was seen as an export-led model and focus on stimulating domestic demand instead. A UNESCAP paper (2009) called for countries pursuing export-led development strategies to 'diversify markets and products and strive towards a sustainable balance between domestic demand and exports'. Similar calls have been made by Chinese economists. These views have fallen on receptive ears. Li Daokou, the director of the Department of Finance at Tsinghua University and member of the Peoples Bank of China's Monetary Policy Committee argues that China's economic structure has now entered a period of transformation of its production, with a growing shift away from a focus on exports towards greater emphasis on domestic consumption (*China Daily* 2009). To illustrate this, he pointed to the fact that 'economic growth of China's inland western and central regions, which relied less on export, had exceeded that of the coastal areas in the first quarter (of 2009), reflecting a strong pull from domestic consumption and investment' (ibid.). At the national policy level, Premier We Jiabao (2009) also declared that 'we should focus on restructuring the economy, and make greater effort to enhance the role of domestic demand, especially final consumption in spurring growth' (*Xinhua* 2009).

Among all the impediments to balance the economy, the undervalued Renminbi (RMB) exchange has received most critical attention, a topic which is reviewed in more detail later. Observers like Goldstein and Lardy (2009) and Krugman (2010) have taken the view that the continuing undervaluation of the RMB makes it difficult for the Chinese government to pursue its aim of reducing reliance on investment demand and external demand on sustaining growth.

It is increasingly accepted by Chinese policymakers that further investment in social services and the creation of a sound social security system in particular are critical for making individuals and households feel more secure in their spending, which is in turn helpful to reducing savings and boosting household consumption (ADB 2010). Equally it has to be accepted that transformation cannot happen overnight. As Chen Deming

(2009), the Minister of Commerce, said recently 'expanding the domestic market would be slow and limited … maintaining foreign demand would actually buy time and earn resources for economic development, create wealth, as well as provide sufficient capital for China's social welfare net, all foundations for economic transformation' (*The Economic Observer Online* 2009).

China's RMB—Is It Too High?   The other hotly debated topic is the alleged undervaluation of the RMB. There are several issues connected to the RMB revaluation debate: (i) RMB as a store of value, (ii) the likely influence of RMB appreciation on the Chinese economy, and (iii) China as a currency manipulator and its role in the imbalances of the global economy.

Mundell (2005, 2009) has consistently argued the merit of fixed exchange rates, so that the currency in question can act as a store of value, which in his view is essential for the stability of the global trading system. In his view the basic role of exchange rates is to allow for the exchange of goods and services from one country to the other. Large swings in the US dollar and RMB rates are potentially damaging for China, bring great uncertainty to Sino-US trade, and reward speculators. Consistent with this line of reasoning, Mundell opposed RMB's devaluation in the early 1994 and its revaluation in recent years.

The second issue concerns China's increasingly large size of reserves, and an undervalued RMB. It is worth reiterating that China's large reserves, now $3.3 trillion dollars by the latest count (early 2012), are however of recent origin. They started climbing dramatically only 2003 onwards, and for reasons which were mostly domestic in origin. RMB exchange rates played little role. In 2003, the potential impact of the SARS (Severe Acute Respiratory Syndrome) outbreak on the economy prompted the government to overreact. Authorities pursued an easy monetary policy and pumped in liquidity into the economy. Very quickly this stimulus led to inflationary pressures on housing and food. In response, the government tightened up credit and curtailed investment. Through 2003, exports and imports were in approximate balance. By mid-2004, domestic tightening led to a drop in import demand, opening up a surplus. Interestingly a similar scenario took place in 2009 as the sharp drop in global demand triggered by the financial crisis led to a steep drop in exports. The knock-down effects of the global crisis also led to a sharp drop in imports as the financial crisis led firms to cut back their imports. The net result was that the trade balance remained in surplus, and reserves continued to increase.

Despite the welcome news of a rebound in the Chinese economy, a chorus of complaints is being aired about China's role in reinforcing imbalances in the global economy. Countries like the US and economists like Krugman (2010) have vehemently argued that RMB undervaluation is adding to these global imbalances. No doubt there are valid arguments on both sides. However perspectives seem to depend very much on the geographical location from which the problem is viewed. At the aggregate global level, of course, if one country keeps accumulating reserves, primarily by consistently running a trade surplus, then other economies have to be in continuing deficits. In some ways this debate has descended into a zero sum discussion. If the Chinese revalue, they slow their exports, which account for one-third of the economy, and add to unemployment, a politically challenging outcome. Equally in the short term the consequent slowdown in Chinese growth would dampen the prospects of global growth and economic revival, and lead to loss of investor confidence worldwide. Parts of the domestic economy would be particularly hurt. Labour-intensive exports in China have for instance thin profit margins, reportedly between 3 per cent (*Reuters* 2010), and an appreciation unless well-orchestrated is likely to devastate large swaths of the coastal export-driven economy.

The current global crisis did not of course originate in China. Individual central banks, without multilateral agreements and coordinated action are unlikely to make much headway in meeting the challenge of keeping a balance between importing and exporting countries. The 2008 London meeting was an attempt to help such coordinated actions. UNCTAD (2010) has argued that both absolutely fixed rates and fully flexible rates are suboptimal approaches. According to UNCTAD, experience suggests that these 'corner solutions' add to volatility and uncertainty and aggravate global imbalances. Further, it is difficult to explain away the basic fact that between mid-2005 and mid-2008, the RMB appreciated by 22 per cent against the US dollar but China'a external imbalances continued to widen rapidly, and equally the US trading position did not much improve. In this context, Mundell echoes an argument made by a number of other prominent economists, such as US Federal Reserve Chairman Alan Greenspan and fellow Nobel Prize-winner Joseph Stiglitz. They contend that while a revaluation would make Chinese goods more expensive in the US, American consumers would just buy imports from other low-cost countries instead. In that case the US trade deficit with China might fall, but the size of its overall trade deficit would not.

That there are likely domestic downsides to a significant revaluation of RMB is clear to Chinese policymakers. Dani Rodrik (2009) estimates that an 'appreciation of 25 per cent—roughly the extent by which the RMB currently is undervalued—would reduce China's growth by somewhat more than two percentage points'. He goes on to argue that WTO accession constrains China's industrial policy by putting limits on promoting specific industries through tariffs or domestic content requirements, making the policy choices to free up the RMB politically difficult. Another argument advanced in playing down the role of exchange rates is that productivity growth in China has accelerated since the turn of the century, and this is the more important factor in explaining China's international competitiveness than the exchange rate (Bottelier and Fosler 2007).

A broader, more global perspective is clearly needed that puts economic recovery and stability as the primary objectives. A multilateral solution is needed for global stability and a balanced world. RMB changes on their own, unless they are part of an overall package, are unlikely to achieve much. As Michael Spence (2010) noted in an article in the *Financial Times* 'the west is wrong to obsess about the renminbi' (*Financial Times* 2010).

2009–10: Growth Rates and Financial Stimulus Most importantly, a slowdown of this magnitude would put China below the 8 per cent growth threshold that its leadership apparently believes is necessary to avert social strife. The same scenario has repeated itself in 2012, with the National People's Congress formally adopting in March a lower growth rate target of 7.5 per cent. No one knows where the 8 per cent figure really comes from, and many experts believe that China's society and polity are capable of handling much lower growth. But, even if political implications are put aside, it would be a tragedy if the most potent poverty-reduction engine the world has ever known were to experience a notable slowdown.

Ever since the Chinese Government announced that it aimed to achieve an 8 per cent growth rate in 2009, there have been on-going discussions on the sufficiency of the two-year $587 billion stimulus package. And the package is a story in itself as it came after a dramatic change in economic conditions. As China-watcher Barry Naughton observed (Naughton 2009), the 'speed and intensity of changing economic conditions in China during 2008 has rarely, if ever, been matched in world economic history'. Yet the Government was able to respond swiftly. As late as June 2008, responding to concerns about inflation, the central bank had raised the commercial bank reserve requirement twice within 10 days to restrain monetary growth. By the end of October, the economic policy regime completed a U-turn as the Government announced the 4 trillion RMB package on 5 November.

Unlike other countries where the speed and severity of the crisis took governments by surprise, Chinese authorities were well aware of the emerging financial storm and decided to pro-actively ease monetary policies since mid-2008.

> Initially, this involved a tradeoff between cushioning the downturn on the one hand and preventing inflation expectations, which were still relatively high, from becoming entrenched on the other hand. As inflation started to fall toward the latter half of 2008, inflation concerns faded and monetary policy moved into an easing mode, with a relaxation of credit controls and cuts in interest rates and

reserve requirements. The government also announced policies to support the property sector, exempt interest income from taxation, and increase VAT rebates for exports of various products. (Arora 2009)

Total exports more than halved, from USD 131 billion in May 2010 to USD 65 billion in February 2009. In the first months of 2009, the real estate industry showed zero growth over the year before. Despite these setbacks, the fact is that the Chinese economy is still growing and there is consensus that it will continue to do so in the foreseeable future. But will the stimulus package be sufficient to increase consumption, generate employment, and achieve the 8 per cent target in the short-run, as well as lay down the foundation for a more balanced consumption-led rather than export-dependent growth?

In this regard, traditionally there are three considerations: the size of the stimulus package—the bigger the better; its composition—tax cuts versus spending; and the extent of frontloading—the sooner spent by the consumer the better. In the case of China, the extent that the stimulus package actually encourages consumption and addresses the lack of confidence of households in the social security and pension systems is likely to be critical. From what can be gathered, the Chinese stimulus package is equal to 4–5 per cent of 2008 GDP, with an exclusive reliance on spending. Reportedly, 70 per cent comes from local governments and lending by state banks, with the balance coming from the central government.

- The stimulus package appears to be in line with traditional approaches, with some 63 per cent consisting of spending on transportation infrastructure and earthquake reconstruction, and 10 per cent for low-income housing—which are long gestating expenditures.
- In regard to laying the foundation for consumption, the government is spending 4 per cent on healthcare, education, and cultural services and 5 per cent on providing rural households with subsidies (possibly in the form of vouchers) for purchasing motorcycles and home appliances, scrapping

old vehicles and upgrading to light trucks and small engine cars, along with subsidies to farmers for important materials, e.g., grain, petroleum, nonferrous metals, and specialty steel products.

As a whole, it appears that the stimulus package seems to be working, partly because the Chinese government has a range of fiscal, monetary, and administrative instruments which few other governments relying more on traditional macro-economic instruments can access at this point. In fact, many advanced countries are seeking to extend the reach of their policy instruments so that they too can influence the level of credit and incentivize the nature of its use. Investment and retail spending are growing, and car sales are up. Bank lending is expanding (total lending went up from RMB 772 billion in December to RMB 1,662 billion in January). Even energy use is up.

Figure 6.5 shows the impact of the financial crisis on GDP growth rates, which had declined to 6.8 per cent and 6.1 per cent in 2008 Q4 and 2009 Q1, respectively. The stimulus led to a rebound starting 2009 Q2 at 7.9 per cent to 2009 Q4 at 10.7 per cent, making the 2009 annual growth rate reach 8.7 per cent,

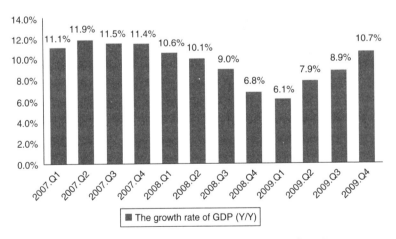

Figure 6.5 The Year-on-Year Growth Rate of GDP
Source: National Bureau of Statistics (2010).

exceeding the 8 per cent target set by government at the beginning of the year.

Though overall inflation continues to be low, concerns are mounting on possible asset bubbles particularly for housing. Due to these concerns, the People's Bank of China has raised on several occasions the deposit reserve requirement (RER), for instance, in January and February 2010. The RER is now currently a high 16.5 per cent, which is also high when compared to RERs of other major economies, for instance, 2 per cent in the Eurozone, 5.75 per cent in India, and 10 per cent in the US.

And there is good news on the overall fiscal status of the central government. Despite the large stimulus package, the deficit as a percentage of GDP remains low, especially in comparison to other large economies, especially those in advanced economies. Goldman and Sachs (cited in Batson 2010) nonetheless have pointed that banks' loan books could be hiding an additional 20 per cent of government debt since most of their lending was going to SOEs or local governments.

The fiscal status of the central government when compared to other large economies seems good as well: the deficit—the worst in years, due to the stimulus package spending—is still under control, only 2.2 per cent of the GDP. And the deficit of the main Western countries is much higher than China's (see Figure 6.6).

Monetary growth may increase inflationary pressures and the risk of an asset bubble down the road remains a concern, but it helped ensure that China's economy did not fall into a vicious downturn when the financial crisis hit. Other policy moves aimed at boosting demand in the housing and auto market also proved effective.

But China's crisis management is only part of the story. It does not explain why other countries that took even stronger measures failed to generate a similarly rapid recovery, or why China's government seems to have more room than others for policy manoeuver. China's budget was actually in surplus and its government debt-to-GDP ratio was only 21 per cent before the

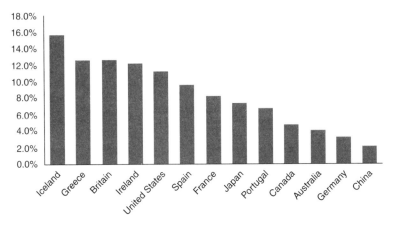

Figure 6.6 Deficit as a Percentage of GDP
Source: OECD (2009).

crisis (now it is about 24 per cent); much lower than any other major economy. That gave Chinese policymakers freedom to spend money to confront the crisis. Moreover, the level of non-performing loans in Chinese banks was quite low when Lehman Brothers collapsed, which allowed Chinese policymakers to let it increase in order to battle the crisis

On the downside, there are two major concerns. For one, more clarity is required to determine how much spending is true addition, and how much would have been spent anyway. Also, with only 4 per cent for healthcare, education, and cultural services and 5 per cent to provide rural households subsidies, the proposed expenditures should be seen as a down payment on additional measures needed to shift the Chinese economy away from a reliance on exports to a focus on internal markets, and to scale up investment in the social sectors.

There also some traditional concerns about an expansionary fiscal and monetary policy for medium to long-term economic prospects. China's investment rate has been steadily increasing, from 43–45 per cent in 2008 to 50 per cent by the end of 2009, a direct result of the stimulus package led by increase in public sector fixed investment. Concerns about overcapacity and investment efficiency are an ongoing topic for Chinese economists (Yu 2010). China's ICOR is rising instead of declining, from a relatively high ICOR of 4.1 in 1991–2003, to an estimated close to 6. By comparison Japan ICOR is about 3. There is also criticism that new infrastructural investment is skewed towards capital intensive prestige projects. Adding additional lanes for six-lane highways where traffic is still low is unlikely to do much for long-term growth or for that matter in reducing income inequality. Finally, there is a concern that the over-enthusiasm of local governments may actually worsen China's future fiscal position. The bulk of the local stimulus packages were underwritten by commercial loans guaranteed by local governments.

★★★

China is in many ways at crossroads. The process of trans-formation of Chinese society which started with Mao in the 1950s and 1960s and deepened under Deng's reforms over the last three decades is likely to continue as China plays catch-up with the developed world. In the process China is finding its rightful place in the global world. Increasingly its population of 1.3 billion, projected to rise to 1.5 billion by 2030 (Liu and Diamond 2005), is becoming a familiar part of the global econ-omy and society. One aspect of this rapid realignment of the 'face of the world' is the phenomenal growth in overseas Chinese tourism, estimated by UNWTO to reach 100 million annually by 2020. This and China's growing stakes in other parts of the world have meant that the Chinese are now visible as both tour-ists and investors not only in the developed world but equally in Africa, Asia, and Latin America. The year 2010 simply marks the unfinished journey of the Chinese.

The three development drivers—ownership, capacities, and policies—will continue to shape future development outcomes. How well they are aligned will define not only the specific development outcomes but also the ease with which they come about. As in earlier periods, this crossroads now requires new waves of reforms and the upgrading of institutions.

Rapid growth, rise in inequality, underinvestment in social services, all pose serious challenges to social cohesion (and social capital) and sustained growth in the future. Social capabilities require renewal as well, with reforms and higher levels of investment needed in health, education, and social protection. The intellectual requirements of a future society and economy are likely to be sharply different from the requirements of the past. To meet these objectives, fiscal revamping in particular may require priority attention to enable all Chinese citizens, in urban or rural areas, to have comparable access to quality social services. At the minimum this may warrant ensuring that local governments have sufficient fiscal support from the centre to meet their local mandates. The financial services sector itself, as many have argued, now needs to take the next step so that financial services can be adequately provided to an increasingly sophisticated population and capital markets are deepened to ensure that the savings generated get channeled to high return investment opportunities. Farmers in particular require stronger protection of their titles to land (their primary asset) and an enabling environment that allows for trade of such titles, within certain limits. The latter is important since what China does, given its scale, has large ramifications globally and for its own food security.

These points amply highlight the notion that as China takes the next steps in its modernization drive and develops the next stage of reforms, some features critical to the previous success may need to be revisited or simply done away with. For instance, as many Chinese economists have also argued, future growth requires reducing the existing impediments to the effective functioning of markets, such as the flow of labour to urban areas, and to make government more transparent and accountable to the citizens it is meant to serve. Policies are already moving in the right direction (*Xiaokang*, new socialist countryside, and so on), the challenge now is to refine them further and as before implement them effectively.

China as an economy and society is just too large and complex to manage easily, so strengthening 'rule of law' and 'evidence 'driven' policies have to become the norm. This is very much the intention behind the 'scientific approach to development' initiated by President Hu Jintao in 2002. Above all, there is now ample evidence in China and elsewhere to support the assertion that the old development strategy of 'polluting first and cleaning up later' was neither wise nor cost effective. Chinese development has to become more environmentally sustainable. Governmental structures in turn need to be revamped and upgraded to deal with these new challenges, as higher civic expectations require greater transparency and responsiveness from government.

In the coming years, the internal debate about how far China is from its stated goal of creating a 'socialist market economy' is likely to intensify. One leading exponent of this, the Chinese economist Chi Fulin, Director of CIRD (2010), highlights the many unfinished aspects of this task, one primary concern being the need to secure greater social equality. In his view, China's future now depends on a new round of comprehensive reforms which put the needs and aspirations of people first and foremost in all development initiatives (*China Daily* 2010). And, while opening up has brought considerable benefits to the Chinese people, equally, in his view it is inaccurate to describe China's development model as export-driven, given the limited direct contribution of 'net' exports to overall growth. Even then, this much is accepted, China's embrace of globalization has increased competition in her product markets, raised productivity, enhanced consumer welfare in China, and benefited consumers around the world.

Delivering on a sustainable Xiaokang vision is now the critical challenge for China. For this, the central government has to play a clearer, more robust role. Clarifying, for instance, what should be role of the state in the ensuring the provision of basic healthcare for all is likely to significantly determine the nature of health reforms. As the 11th Five Year Plan explicitly states, new challenges require new policies, which in turn require additional institutional reforms. There is now, for instance, a historic task of formulating and rolling out a universal, basic social security package. The enormity of this challenge cannot be over-emphasized since social security reform as a process has taken Western countries best part of a century to complete. In 2006, social insurance was accepted as a right of all Chinese.[9] Since then, social insurance reform is being fast tracked over a matter of years rather than decades to be extended to cover much of China's population.

In the past Chinese leaders embraced opening up and difficult transformative policies with a commendable mixture of pragmatism and courage, the same is now required to take on the next set of fateful challenges in China's drive to grow and modernize and become a more equal and caring society.

REFERENCES

Alon, T., G. Hale, and J. Santos. 2010. *What is China's Capital Seeking in a Global Environment*. FRBSF Economic Letter, 9.

Arora, V. 2009. 'The Global Financial Crisis and China's Situation—The Steps Ahead', *China Money Monthly*, 1: 16–23.

Asian Development Bank. 2007. *Key Indicators* 2007. Asian Development Bank.

———. 2010. *Asian Development Outlook 2010: Macroeconomic Management beyond the Crisis*. Available at http://www.adb.org/documents/books/ado/2010/default.asp, accessed on 4 July 2010.

Batson, A. 2010. 'China's Vanishing Fiscal Stimulus—China Real Time Report—WSJ'. Available at http://blogs.wsj.com/chinarealtime/2010/02/08/chinas-vanishing-fiscal-stimulus/tab/article/, accessed on 5 May 2010.

Bloom, D.E., D. Canning, and J. Sevilla. 2003. 'The Demographic Dividend: A New Perspective on the Economic Consequences of Population Change', Paper 8808, Rand Corporation, Santa Monica, CA.

Bloom, D.E. and J.G. Williamson. 1998. 'Demographic Transitions and Economic Miracles in Emerging Asia', *The World Bank Economic Review*, 12(3): 419–55.

Bottelier, P. and G. Fosler. 2007. 'Can China's Growth Trajectory Be Sustained?', Working Paper Series 6/07, The Conference Board.

---

[9] Announced by President Hu Jintao during the Sixth Plenum of the 16th CPC Central Committee in Beijing on 11 October 2006. See http://english.gov.cn/2006-10/11/content_410337.htm.

Brandt, L., T. Rawski, and X. Zhu. 2007. 'International Dimensions of China's Long Boom: Trends, Prospects and Implications', in W. Keller and T. Rawski (eds), *China's Rise and the Balance of Influence in Asia*, pp. 14–46. Pittsburgh: University of Pittsburgh Press.

Brown, L.R. 1995. *Who Will Feed China?: Wake-up Call for a Small Planet*. New York: W.W. Norton & Co.

Cai, F., A. Park, and Y. Zhao. 2008. 'The Chinese Labor Market in the Reform Era', in L. Brandt and T. Rawski (eds), *China's Great Economic Transformation*, pp. 167–214. Cambridge, Mass.: Cambridge University Press.

Chang, G.G. 2002. *The Coming Collapse of China*. New York: Random House Business.

China Daily. 2008. 'GDP Could Be 2.5 Times that of the US by 2030'. Available at http://www.chinadaily.com.cn/china/2008-05/03/content_6657813.htm, accessed on 2 June 2010.

————. 2009. 'China Sees Initial Results in Boosting Domestic Demand', 21 May.

————. 2010. 'Reforms Should Enhance Social Equality', 25 June.

Chinese Ministry of Education. 2009. *Statistical Bulletin on National Education Development 2008*. Available at http://www.fdi.gov.cn/pub/FDI_EN/Economy/Investment%20Environment/Macro-economic%20Indices/Human%20Resources/education%20conditions/default.htm, accessed on 1 July 2010.

Chinese Ministry of Foreign Affairs and the UN System in China. 2008. *China's Progress towards the Millennium Development Goals 2008 Report*, Available at http://www.un.org.cn/cms/p/resources/30/809/content.html.

Chinese Ministry of Health. 2008. 'Briefings on Health Development in China 2003–2007'. Chinese version available at http://www.moh.gov.cn/sofpro/cms/previewjspfile/mohbgt/cms_0000000000000000144_tpl.jsp?requestCode=27884&CategoryID=6690, accessed on 1 July 2010.

Chinese National Bureau of Statistics (NBS) Database. Available in Chinese at http://219.235.129.58/welcome.do, accessed on 5 July 2010.

Ding, Q., M.E. Akoorie, and K. Pavlovich. 2009. 'Going International: The Experience of Chinese Companies', *International Business Research*, 2(2): 148–52.

Elwell, C.K., Labonte, M., and W.M. Morrison. 2007. 'Is China a Threat to the US Economy?' CRS Report for Congress, Order Code RL 33604.

The Economic Observer Online. 2009. 'A Shift is Needed, But Not Overnight', 13 April.

Financial Times. 2010. 'The West is Wrong to Obsess about the Renminbi', 22 January.

Fogel, R.W. 2006. 'Why China is Likely to Achieve Its Growth Objectives', NBER Working Paper.

Garnaut, R., L. Song, and Y. Yao. 2006. 'Impact and Significance of State-owned Enterprise Restructuring in China', *The China Journal*, 55: 35–63.

Goldstein, M. and N.R. Lardy. 2009. *The Future of China's Exchange Rate Policy*, Policy Analyses in International Economics 87, Peterson Institute for International Economics.

Greenpeace and Oxfam. 2009. 'Climate Change and Poverty, China Case Study'. Available at http://www.greenpeace.org/usa/assets/binaries/poverty-and-climate-change, accessed on 17 March 2010.

He, J. and L. Kuijs. 2007. 'Rebalancing China's Economy—Modeling a Policy Package', World Bank China Research Paper 7.

He, J., S. Li, and S. Polaski. 2007. 'China's Economic Prospects, 2006–2020', Carnegie Paper 30, Carnegie Endowment, Washington DC.

Ho, M.S. and C.P. Nielsen. 2007. *Clearing the Air: The Health and Economic Damages of Air Pollution in China.* MIT Press.

Holz, C.A. 2005. 'China's Economic Growth 1978–2025: What We Know Today about China's Economic Growth Tomorrow', Paper provided by EconWPA in its series Development and Comp Systems with number 0507001.

———. 2008. 'China's Economic Growth 1978–2025: What We Know Today about China's Economic Growth Tomorrow', *World Development*, 36(10): 1665–91.

IMF International Financial Statistics. Available at http://www.imfstatistics.org/imf/, accessed on 2 June 2010.

Keidel, A. 1995. *China Regional Disparities.* Washington DC: World Bank.

———. 2008. *The Global Financial Crisis: Lessons for the United States and China.* Washington DC: Endowment for International Peace.

Krugman, P. 2010. 'China's Swan Song', *New York Times.* Available at http://krugman.blogs.nytimes.com/2010/03/11/chinas-swan-song/, accessed on 1 July 2010.

Landler, M. and K. Bradsher. 2005. 'VW to Build Hybrid Minivan with Chinese', *New York Times.* Available at http://query.nytimes.com/gst/fullpage.html?res=9C0DEFDD1331F93AA3575AC0A9639C8B63&sec=&spon=&pagewanted=all, accessed on 4 July 2010.

Lardy, N. 2007. 'China's Economy: Problems and Prospects', FPRI. Available at http://www.fpri.org/footnotes/124.200702.lardy.chinaseconomy.html, accessed on 3 July 2010.

Li, F. 2005. 'Youthful Mobility', *China Business Weekly*, 19–25 September.

Li, X. 2010. 'Reforms Should Enhance Social Equality', *China Daily*. Available at http://www.chinahttp://www.chinadaily.com.cn/bizchina/2010-06/25/content_10018815.htm, accessed on 5 July 2010.

Liu, J. and J. Diamond. 2005. 'China's Environment in a Globalizing World', *Nature*, 435(7046): 1179–86.

Lum, T. 2006. 'Social Unrest in China', Congressional Research Service (CRS) Reports and Issue Briefs, 19.

Maddison, A. 2007. *Chinese Economic Performance in the Long Run*. Paris: OECD Publishing.

Mundell, R. 2005. 'China Should Keep Currency Peg', *China Daily*, lecture organized by the Chinese University of Hong Kong, with speech published by the *China Daily*, (Agencies) Updated: 2005-06-03 20: 14.

———. 2009. 'The World Economy: Quo Vadis?', *Journal of Policy Modeling*, 31(4): 493–7.

Naughton, B. (2009). 'The Scramble to Maintain Growth', *China Leadership Monitor*, No. 27.

OECD (Organisation for Economic Co-operation and Development). 2009. *OECD Economic Outlook*, No. 86. Paris: OECD.

People's Daily. 2009. 'China's Urbanization Rate Expected to Reach 48 per cent in 2010', 22 December. Available at http://english.peopledaily.com.cn/90001/90778/90862/6848826.html.

Perkins, D.H. 2006. 'China's Recent Economic Performance and Future Prospects', *Asian Economic Policy Review*, 1(1): 15–40.

Prasad, E.S. 2007. 'Is the Chinese Growth Miracle Built to Last?', SSRN eLibrary. Available at http://papers.ssrn.com/sol3/papers.cfm?abstract_id=1012561, accessed on 3 July 2010.

Reuters. 2010. 'Rise in the Yuan Would Be a Disaster for Labor-intensive Chinese Exporters', 18 March.

Srinivasan, T.N. 2006. 'China, India and the World Economy', *Economic and Political Weekly*, 41(34): 3716–27.

Tseng, W. and H. Zebregs. 2002. 'FDI in China: Lessons for Other Countries', IMF Policy Discussion Paper 02/3, International Monetary Fund, Washington DC.

UN (United Nations). 2008. *The Millennium Development Goals Report 2008*. New York: United Nations Publications.

UNCTAD (United Nations Conference on Trade and Development). 2004. 'South–South Investment Flows: A Potential for Developing Country Governments to Tap for Supply Capacity Building', background paper prepared for the UNCTAD Secretariat, New York.

————. 2010. 'Global Monetary Chaos: Systemic Failures Need Bold Multilateral Responses', *UNCTAD Policy Briefs*, No. 12.

UNDP (United Nations Development Program) China. 2008. *China Human Development Report 2007/08*. Beijing: China Translation & Publishing Corporation.

————. 2010. *China Human Development Report 2009/2010*. Beijing: China Translation & Publishing Corporation.

UNESCAP (United Nations Economic and Social Commission for Asia and the Pacific). 2009.'Developing Coherent and Consistent Policies for Trade and Investment', Note by the Secretariat.

USDA (US Department of Agriculture). International Macroeconomic Data Set. Available at http://www.ers.usda.gov/Data/Macroeconomics/, accessed on 4 July 2010.

Wang, X., G. Fan, and P. Liu. 2007. 'Pattern and Sustainability of China's Economic Growth towards 2020', in *ACESA 2007 Conference: China's Conformity to the WTO: Progress and Challenges*.

Wolf, M. 2005. 'Why is China Growing So Slowly?', *Foreign Policy*, 146: 50–1.

World Bank. 2009. *From Poor Areas to Poor People: China's Evolving Poverty Reduction Agenda: An Assessment of Poverty and Inequality in China*. Available at http://web.worldbank.org/WBSITE/EXTERNAL/PROJECTS/0,,contentMDK:22131856~pagePK:41367~piPK:279616~theSitePK:40941,00.html, accessed on 4 July 2010.

World Bank Development Indicators. Available at http://data.worldbank.org/indicator, accessed on 4 July 2010.

World Health Organization. 2009. *World Health Statistics 2009*. Available at http://www.who.int/whosis/whostat/2009/en/index.html, accessed on 4 July 2010.

Xinhua News Agency. 2008. 'China Will Overtake U.S. in Year 2030 as World's Largest Economy'. Available at http://news.xinhuanet.com/fortune/2008-02/21/content_7639853.htm, accessed in June2010.

————. 2009.'China to Attach More Importance to Domestic Demand for Economic Growth: Premier', 10 September.

Yu, Y. 2010. 'China's Response to the Global Financial Crisis', East Asia Forum. Available at http://www.eastasiaforum.org/2010/01/24/chinas-response-to-the-global-financial-crisis/, accessed on 5 July 2010.

Zhou, Xiaochuan. 2009. 'Reform the International Monetary System', Speech by the Governor of the People's Bank of China, 23 March.

Index